GENDER BIAS IN SCHOLARSHIP
The Pervasive Prejudice

Edited by
Winnifred Tomm and Gordon Hamilton

This multi-disciplinary anthology is about hermeneutical issues pertaining to gender ideology in university scholarship. The authors provide, from their own discipline, an extensive examination of the issues raised in the Social Sciences and Humanities Research Council of Canada pamphlet, "On the Treatment of the Sexes in Research," by Margrit Eichler and Jeanne Lapointe (1985).

Gender bias is described and evaluated in the light of possible alternative perspectives which would alter the content and shape of research, including women as subjects of research and as researchers. The authors underscore the importance of acknowledging underlying gender imagery in the selection, interpretation, and communication of research data. They explore the notion of research as a social construction which is strongly aligned with the socially constructed notion of male and dissociated from the socially constructed notion of female. The focus is on reframing research ideology to include both female- and male-constructed imagery.

Contributors include Marlene Mackie (sociology), Carolyn Larsen (psychology), Estelle Dansereau (literary criticism), Gisele Thibault (education), Alice Mansell (art), Eliane Leslau Silverman (history), Yvonne Lefebvre (biochemistry), Petra von Morstein (philosophy), and Naomi Black (political science).

Winnifred Tomm and Gordon Hamilton held Post-Doctoral Fellowships at the Calgary Institute for the Humanities.

GENDER BIAS IN SCHOLARSHIP
The Pervasive Prejudice

Edited by
Winnifred Tomm and Gordon Hamilton

Essays by

Marlene Mackie
Carolyn C. Larsen
Estelle Dansereau
Gisele Thibault
Alice Mansell

Eliane Leslau Silverman
Yvonne Lefebvre
Petra von Morstein
Naomi Black

Published by Wilfrid Laurier University Press
for The Calgary Institute for the Humanities

Canadian Cataloguing in Publication Data

Main entry under title:

Gender bias in scholarship

Revised versions of papers presented at a conference held at the University of Calgary in November 1985.
Includes bibliographical references.
ISBN 0-88920-963-4

1. Sexism − Congresses. 2. Learning and scholarship − Congresses. I. Mackie, Marlene.
II. Tomm, Winnie, 1944- . III. Hamilton, Gordon, 1951- . IV. Calgary Institute for the Humanities.

HQ1154.G46 1988   305.4'2   C88-093443-3

Copyright © 1988
Wilfrid Laurier University Press
Waterloo, Ontario, Canada
N2L 3C5
88 89 90 91 4 3 2 1

No part of this book may be stored in a retrieval system, translated or reproduced in any form, by print, photoprint, microfilm, microfiche, or any other means, without written permission from the publisher.

TABLE OF CONTENTS

Preface vii

Acknowledgments ix

Dedication xi

Introduction xiii

SEXISM IN SOCIOLOGICAL RESEARCH
Marlene Mackie 1

THE TREATMENT OF THE SEXES
IN PSYCHOLOGICAL RESEARCH
Carolyn C. Larsen 25

REASSESSING INTERPRETIVE STRATEGIES
IN LITERARY CRITICISM
Estelle Dansereau 45

WOMEN AND EDUCATION: ON BEING FEMALE
IN MALE PLACES
Gisele Thibault 63

GENDER BIAS IN ART EDUCATION
Alice Mansell 99

RE-VISIONS OF THE PAST
Eliane Leslau Silverman 117

ON THE TREATMENT OF THE SEXES IN
SCIENTIFIC RESEARCH
Yvonne Lefebvre 131

EPISTEMOLOGY AND WOMEN IN PHILOSOPHY:
FEMINISM IS A HUMANISM
Petra von Morstein 147

WHERE ALL THE LADDERS START:
A FEMINIST PERSPECTIVE ON SOCIAL SCIENCE
Naomi Black 167

Subject Index 191

Name Index 195

PREFACE

The Calgary Institute for the Humanities was established at The University of Calgary in 1976 for the purpose of fostering advanced study and research in a broad range of subject areas. It supports work in the traditional humanities disciplines, such as languages and literatures, philosophy, history, etc., as well as the philosophical and historical aspects of the social sciences, sciences, arts, and professional studies.

The Institute's programs in support of advanced study attempt to provide scholars with time to carry out their work. In addition, the Institute sponsors formal and informal gatherings among people who share common interests, in order to promote intellectual dialogue and discussion. Recently, the Institute has moved to foster the application of humanistic knowledge to contemporary social problems.

The Calgary Institute for the Humanities was pleased to sponsor this initial enquiry into the important topic of gender bias in research. Credit is due to Winnifred Tomm for taking my suggestions and those of Marsha Hanen, and using them to organize a stimulating conference. For those who wish to study this issue further, the papers given at the conference are now published by the Institute.

Harold Coward,
Director,
The Calgary Institute
for the Humanities

ACKNOWLEDGMENTS

We are grateful to the Director of The Calgary Institute for the Humanities, Dr. Harold Coward, for his initiative in suggesting the conference on which this book is based and for his guidance throughout the editing process.

This book was completed during the editors' Postdoctoral Fellowships at The Calgary Institute for the Humanities, and we would like to express our appreciation for the Institute's generous support.

Mrs. Geraldine Dyer and Mrs. Beverley Gilavish provided especially helpful support in preparing this manuscript at the Institute. Their considerable patience and cheerfulness are deeply appreciated.

Thanks are also due to Dr. Marsha Hanen, Dean, Faculty of General Studies of The University of Calgary, for giving shape to the conference in the early planning stages. Her suggestions were invaluable, and her enthusiasm for the enterprise was inspirational.

The participation of Dr. Mike Ward, Vice-President Research, at the conference indicates an openness on the part of The University of Calgary to investigate the issue of gender bias in scholarship.

To Our Mothers

INTRODUCTION

Winnifred Tomm and Gordon Hamilton

A "Copernican Revolution" has been initiated in university scholarship. The centre of gravity is shifting away from an almost exclusively male perspective toward a more inclusive approach in which both male and female points of views are represented. Such a paradigm shift requires clear analysis of existing gender bias in university scholarship, its implications, and the possibilities for change. Gender bias extends from the exclusive or predominant use of males as the subjects of research to the employment of androcentric theoretical paradigms and methodologies. The lack of women scholars has also constituted a major source of gender bias in the university. The nine contributors to this anthology seek to provide information about gender bias in their respective academic disciplines, demonstrate the implications of such bias in current research, and suggest ways in which gender bias can be reduced or eliminated. These researchers integrate their experiences as women in the university and the larger society with critical analyses of their fields of intellectual enquiry. Practically every page manifests their overwhelming passion for accurate knowledge and their indignation at the prejudices they have experienced as women, particularly in the university.

This volume developed from a conference at The University of Calgary in November, 1985. A 1985 publication by M. Eichler and J. Lapointe, <u>On the Treatment of the Sexes in Research</u> (Ottawa: Social Sciences and Humanities Research Council of Canada), provided the impetus for the conference, which was sponsored by The Calgary Institute for the Humanities, the Faculty of General Studies, and The University of Calgary's Political Science Department. (Please see Acknowledgments regarding the several individuals to whom we are especially indebted.) Naomi Black of York University's Political Science Department acted as keynote speaker by presenting an overview of the historical context of this SSHRC report. The other researchers came from The University of Calgary. Extensive questions from the audience as well as passionate debate followed each presentation. Two aspects of this interchange are noteworthy. First, the audience's queries and criticisms at the conference helped the authors to revise their presentations for publication. The impact of this verbal interchange represents an example of the importance of contextual, interpersonal experience for feminists. Secondly, since both feminist and nonfeminist women and men attended and actively participated in this conference, we hope the readers of this volume will be equally diverse. Gender bias in university scholarship is neither an optional nor a peripheral area of concern. Every academic researcher or anyone who reads the findings of university research must recognize and strive to eliminate gender bias in all of its manifestations.

The meanings of the terms "gender" and "sex" need to be specified and contrasted. "Gender" refers to the socialized aspect of female or male nature and, accordingly, emphasizes social influences on the development of an individual of either sex. "Sex" refers to the biological nature of an individual. Sex differences are often mistakenly thought to be identical with gender differences so that arguments from biology are used to defend socialization practices which enforce sex-role stereotyping. Biological arguments are inappropriately used to support attitudes about what women or men can or cannot do simply because they are either females or males. Plato in the <u>Republic</u> (Book V, 454) demonstrated the inappropriateness of arguing that one's destiny is determined by one's biology. The biological aspect of a person's nature, for example, is not relevant to the issue of occupations. Quality of character is the determining factor. For Plato, quality of character is independent of sex. The fact that one individual is biologically fit to bear children while another is not does not affect the question of whose nature is best suited to be a philosopher king (in his terms). Equal social opportunity for individuals of both sexes is required for equal expression of individual character traits. Gender bias in the social domain results from concluding that destiny derives from biology and that sex-role stereotyping is justified. "Social domain" refers to the domain of all social activity, including university scholarship. Belief in objective neutrality in university scholarship is shaken when it is discovered that hidden assumptions regarding the importance of men and the insignificance of women have affected much of the scholarship conducted throughout academic history. Plato's insight was not very well heeded. Each of the following nine chapters discusses the importance of taking the gender factor into account in scholarship--recognizing the unfounded assumptions about biologically determined character traits as well as the different patterns of socialization which result from those unfounded assumptions.

This anthology begins with the foundational question "Does anyone care that there is gender bias in sociological scholarship?" The authors show why gender bias matters to those affected by it and why it should matter to those interested in good scholarship and balance in education.

The omission of females in scholarship--including teachers, researchers, subjects of research, literary figures, definers of knowledge, art and literary critics, political subjects--reflects the exclusion of women from historical significance. In this volume, Marlene Mackie claims that, since 1969, feminist-oriented sociologists have called attention to the fact that while women have always been part of society, their activities have been either largely ignored or inaccurately described by men. To accept the "science of society" as "male science of male society" would be to accept gender bias in sociological research. In psychological scholarship, gender bias has been used as "a weapon for keeping woman in her place," according to Carolyn Larsen. She confirms that faulty research methodologies in psychology, which assume the superiority of maleness and measure female qualities by male standards, translate into fallacious theories about female nature. In all the disciplines, one finds evidence of the underlying assumption that society is rightfully described from the perspective of those who have the authority to speak on behalf of those who have not had a legitimate voice of their own. Deviance has been associated with those who have rejected the authoritative spokesmen of society. Exclusion of women from seats of authority has been accomplished by rewarding women for compliance with the hierarchical gender-relation paradigm and by systematically rejecting those who refused to comply. The institutionalized invisibility of women has provided the context for prior unqueried gender bias in research.

The exclusion of women from positions of authority in the social domain has a rationale derived from the assumption that women do not have the intellectual capacity for authority and therefore cannot be trusted to exercise it over others. The negative impact of the assumption that women do not have the same degree of personal authority as men was enhanced by the further assumption that their strength lies in their ability to support men of authority. These two assumptions provide the fundamental rationale for prohibiting women from full participation in public endeavour and for the associated idealization of the feminine qualities which serve to support dominant-subordinate gender relations, defined by those whose voice is imbued with authority. As Naomi Black affirms, the greatest form of insubordination is the rejection of male authority. This is true for all classes and races; accordingly, hierarchical relations between the sexes cuts across all other forms of oppression and is at the bottom of human rights issues. Academic feminists aim to expose and eliminate gender bias in scholarship and thereby contribute toward the redefinition of gender relations. Such a redefinition, based on egalitarian assumptions regarding human potential and purpose, is required in order to bring women into the realm of significance in scholarship.

Gender bias is reflected in scholarship through refusal to examine areas of endeavour which do not conform to the interests defined by the ruling ideology. Ideology is about doctrines, myths, and symbols which are intended to depict the ideals of any given society. A bias is enshrined in the ruling ideology when the ideals are stipulated predominantly from the perspective of one gender. The establishment of gender bias in favour of the male voice of authority has led to general acceptance of male categorizations of history, education, art, philosophy, literature, social and psychological phenomena. Women's place in that schema has been secondary to men's; consequently, scholarship by women and about women's activities and interests has been considered relatively trivial compared with the work of men as defined by men. Gisele Thibault shows that the educational system serves as a socialization process which maintains dominant ideologies and that feminist approaches critique the educational paradigm shaped by those ideologies. In art education, students have been oriented towards analyzing art according to discrete, differentiated parameters so that it can be described in categorical, impersonal propositions without recourse to affective, nondiscursive meaning. Alice Mansell urges that art education allow for alternatives other than the "scientific" one in the classroom. In the discipline of history, Eliane Silverman claims that "individuation, separation, territoriality, and conflict" have been the dominant components of the ideology governing scholarship. The public realm has been the subject of history, a subject influenced by the topic of one nation or people conquering another and the "progress" achieved through scientific and military power. Women have been virtually invisible in the periodization of history established on the accomplishments of men in the world of action outside the home. Activity inside the home, including gender relation patterns, was considered separate and irrelevant to the activities of history. According to Naomi Black, social movements have been sharply distinguished from political movements. The distinction has been associated with the trivialization of social movements, the area of participation of those concerned with human rights issues, many of whom are women. Political rather than social movements have traditionally been the accepted subjects of political science research. The definition of political science has been governed by the same biased interests as those which have defined the discipline of history and which are compatible with the restricted descriptions of the other disciplines described in the following chapters. Each author examines the ways in which gender ideology determines the hermeneutics of academic scholarship.

Hermeneutics involves the interpretation and justification of data, whether it is textual or empirical. Interpretation of data is shaped largely by the presuppositions that the researcher or teacher brings to the analysis and discussion. Petra von Morstein shows how the philosophical presuppositions concerning knowledge have led to a distorted account of the basis of knowledge. Analytic philosophy emphasizes knowledge independently of subjective felt experience; its aim is to know objectively and dispassionately. Thus, philosophical texts have been interpreted in light of their contribution to knowledge from the perspective of knowing objectively. However, interpretations of the same texts which include both the subjective and objective aspects of knowledge are often considered unphilosophical. The assumption that knowledge consists only in procedural, analytic knowledge and not in subjective, nondiscursive knowledge underlies much of the hermeneutical bias found in scholarship. This unbalanced theory of knowledge influences research in all areas and sharply reduces interest in much of what is of concern to women. Indeed, the argument here is that all persons have knowledge only when it is grounded in subjective experience and that this experience is given meaning through description. One requires a voice that is publicly validated if one's experiences are to be taken into account; often one person cannot speak for another. In view of the different socialization of boys and girls, for example, it is unlikely that one gender can invariably speak for the other. It is important, therefore, that the gender factor be taken into account in theories of knowledge (i.e., epistemology). That is not to say that epistemology is determined by gender, but rather that epistemology is often empirically affected by gender. Ideally, knowledge may transcend gender, but the social realities impinge heavily on different points of view, on the ways in which one knows the things that one knows. Because gender is a social construct, one can infer that socially constructed knowledge necessarily includes the gender factor.

The orientation of this anthology is towards exposing hidden assumptions regarding the differential between the significance of men and women in society. The scholarship described in the following pages indicates that the greater value attached to male existence and activity stems from the inveterate belief in the superiority of rationality and in the association of rationality with maleness. Taking the male as the normative expression of humanity has meant that women are considered inferior in areas where they appear to differ from men. Because such differences have been tied to inferiority, women have been reluctant to discuss the ways in which they differ from men. Many women continue to feel comforted when told they think like a man or are "one of the boys." There are a growing number of women, however, who have no desire to deny their female qualities in order to be accepted by the ruling group. Nor do these women wish to abdicate their power of personal authority by conforming to the dominant-subordinate gender relation pattern. The tension between affirmation of the self as woman and the limited opportunity for social expression of women's personal authority has created the context in which feminist-oriented scholars attempt to reduce gender bias and thereby decrease the tension.

The authors in this text systematically critique the "ruling ideas" inherent in scholarship in all academic disciplines. Sociological and psychological analyses, for example, have often distorted women's experiences by describing them through alien media. Estelle Dansereau points out that female figures in literature and women's "unconsecrated" genres have been presented to readers through the lenses of those who have largely accepted the view of women as interesting but inconsequential individuals in the evolutionary process. Scholarship in education is tied to the view that the educational system legitimizes and preserves the status quo. In addition, the multidisciplinary character of education implies that the same kind of gender bias found in other disciplines will qualify education scholarship. The ruling ideas in art have had the effect of invalidating work that cannot be adequately described in terms of particular "isms" (e.g., cubism, constructivism, abstract minimalism). Again the emphasis is on rationality at the expense of emotive expression, which can reflect more completely a prereflective experience. In the discipline of history, women's contributions have generally not been part of the idea of history as defined by those who have adopted a differential value scale regarding men and women's realities. When she critiques scientific scholarship, Yvonne Lefebvre shows that the long-established views about the normative character of males and the deviant nature of females shape the choice of subjects for research and are engrained in the training processes of scientists. The universality of the male standard is assumed, and objectivity entails systematic exclusion of female deviance. Petra von Morstein, the author of the chapter on philosophy, claims that feminism is a humanism, but only if humanism actually refers to both males and females. She suggests that we can take the gender factor out of humanism only after it has been acknowledged. This anthology is an extended effort to acknowledge the importance of the gender factor in scholarship. The importance of recognizing the interrelation between the kitchen and the study is that, in doing so, we connect the activities of daily life with the abstract principles which give those activities direction.

The authors of this anthology show that the bias which has governed each discipline is grounded in prejudice against anything which cannot be analysed concisely by quantitative or theoretical models. Such models often oversimplify the presentation of data in order to make it consistent and coherent. By pointing out the specific areas in which gender bias distorts representation of phenomena studied, these authors indicate the need for transforming academic scholarship. They go beyond indicating areas of gender bias to formulate new approaches to research and teaching. In suggesting new approaches to scholarship, the authors are not suggesting separate methodologies for the study of men and women; rather they are urging more comprehensive and inclusive approaches to the study and teaching of all academic topics, taking the gender factor into account when it is relevant.

Feminists are working to overcome gender bias and are bringing about fundamental changes--not only in university research but also in the nature of social interaction. Feminist reactions to gender bias in academic scholarship are permeating much of society outside the university. Each author illustrates, in her own way, how gender bias in research reflects our society's biases. Conversely, changes in research methodologies, theories, and conclusions affect society's biases, as will the presence--in large numbers--of women academics. There is a mutually informing relationship between the dominant attitudes of society and the presuppositions which govern university scholarship. Such a reciprocal relationship between societal attitudes and all our activities means that we must care about the gender bias in all academic fields of inquiry.

The contributors to this anthology have made it clear that gender bias must be acknowledged and eliminated by including women in all academic work. Women must be included as the subjects of study as well as scholars who determine the subjects to be studied and the approaches to be used. Feminism is a humanism, and feminists will have achieved their goals when society, including contemporary scholarship, is free from the pervasive prejudice of gender bias.

SEXISM IN SOCIOLOGICAL RESEARCH

Marlene Mackie

> There once lived an Emperor with a serious sartorial obsession. For reasons that need not concern us, he acquired a new suit fashioned from invisible material and paraded about the streets stark naked. The townsmen encouraged the Emperor's performance. "What a splendid design! What glorious colors!" "But the Emperor has nothing on at all!" cried several brave women. Some of the onlookers suddenly realized they were viewing not the Emperor's magnificent new suit, but his private parts. However, their dissident voices were drowned out by loud groans and hoots of laughter. The people with the deviant perspective (mostly women) stood confused on the margins of the assembly. Should they slip inconspicuously into the crowd? To this day, the Emperor prances about naked whenever he likes. The dissidents discuss their objections among themselves. Whenever they try to share their views with the townspeople, the latter say, "There, there, my dears," to avoid hurting their feelings.[1]

In 1969, North American sociology discovered females.[2] In retrospect, it seems odd that it was the "revival of organized feminism" (Oakley 1974: 1), not their own theories, which alerted these professional students of society to the fact that the world contains women as well as men. The feminist movement had an impact on many women sociologists (along with their sisters in other disciplines) analogous to the cry, "The Emperor is naked!" in the original version of the Hans Christian Andersen fable. Blinders were suddenly removed. "Like the onlookers in the Emperor's parade, we can see and plainly speak about things that have always been there, but that formerly were unacknowledged" (Millman and Kanter 1975: vii).

The women's movement provoked a fundamental realization: the sociology that had previously been accepted as the science of society was really the male science of male society (Bernard 1973: 777). Feminist sociologists (of both sexes, but primarily female) spent the first half of the decade of the 1970s diagnosing and documenting this claim. Soon, it became obvious that the linchpin of sexism in sociology is its methodology. Faulty methodology is tied to fallacious theory and empirical generalizations. Under the creative guidance of Smith (1974; 1975) and Daniels (1975), feminists derived from the sociology of knowledge an appreciation of the politics of social science enquiry. In the words of Berger and Luckmann (1966: 109), "he who has the bigger stick has the better chance of imposing his definitions of reality." For many, the manifest implication of these insights was a radical transformation of sociology, a complete reorientation of the discipline's paradigms.

More than a decade has passed since the debunking phase of feminist sociology. What results have accrued? An enormous amount of remedial research has been accomplished. A variety of gender-relations courses are now taught. Books, articles, and graduate theses have been written. Special series of journals and sections of conferences are devoted to women's experiences.[3] However, progress appears to be restricted, for the most part, to the internal development of gender studies. The main body of sociological theory remains untouched. Research goes on much as it always has.

This paper discusses first, feminists' early methodological critique of sociology. Next, it outlines the sociology of knowledge perspective on sexism in scholarship. It concludes with the urgent question of the relationship between feminist and "male-stream" (O'Brien 1979: 100) sociologies.

Feminist Critique of Methodology

"The selective eye of sociology...has been blind to women for decades" (Epstein 1981: 149). The charge that sociology is androcentric and hence incomplete and distorted, rests upon four interrelated, general arguments (Ward and Grant 1985): the invisibility of females; the exclusion of women through choice of research topics; the use of masculine research style; and maleness as the norm.

The Invisibility of Females

Feminists of the early 1970s (e.g., Acker 1973; Daniels 1975; Oakley 1974) criticized sociology for its underrepresentation of women as subjects of research. Often, male-only research was implicitly or explicitly generalized to persons of both sexes (e.g., that people respond to leaders generally as they respond to male leadership). Sometimes, female behaviour was assumed to be the reverse of male behaviour. The traits of ambitiousness and competitiveness, for example, were often associated with masculinity and dissociated from femininity. The syntax of sexism, in other words, the fact that females are ignored in "man-made" languages (Spender 1985), contributed to women's invisibility in scholarship.

Work, long a central area of sociological study, provides a good illustration of what the discipline looked like before the discovery of women. Until recently, books often bore titles such as <u>Man and His Work</u> (Ritzer 1972) and concentrated on masculine occupations and work problems. For example, analyses of work organizations overlooked clerks and secretaries. If women's work was mentioned at all, it tended to be confined to special sections, in one case coyly labelled "Having a Career of Her Own" (Anderson 1964: 141). Until 1978 (Blishen and Carroll), the most widely used index for measuring socio-economic status in Canada (Blishen 1967; Blishen and McRoberts 1976) completely omitted female occupations. Relatively little was known about secretaries, teachers, nurses, waitresses, or beauticians. Housework, an activity engaged in by nearly all adult women, was not even regarded as real work.

Since the advent of the women's movement, considerable research has responded to the omissions or underrepresentation of women as subjects (Ward and Grant 1985). "Sex-difference" studies became a thriving enterprise in sociology, replicating or extending earlier research conducted on male-only samples. However, much of this work simply reports female-male differences, without reflecting on their causes. For example, a study such as Herzog (1982), which simply reports that female high school students have lower occupational aspirations than their male counterparts, does not consider gender as social structure (Ward and Grant 1985: 145). Instead, gender, like sex, seems to be an immutable attribute of the individual.

Exclusion of Women Through Choice of Research Topics

Male sociologists have tended to focus their research on settings and institutions where males predominate, such as the occupational, political, and legal systems. For example, urban sociology overlooked the behaviour of mothers and children in parks, women in beauty parlours, or widows in coffee shops (Lofland 1975). Labelling the suburb as the "bedroom community" because its men leave during the day conveyed the message that what its women and children do is unimportant (Richardson 1981). Bart (1971: 735) wrote: "who really gives a damn about reading studies...about women, their dilemmas, their problems, their attempts at solutions?" For the most part, women's social behaviour became topics for research when it touched on men's lives, for example, their sexuality and maternity in the sociology of the family.

This concentration on public domain and rational, masculine preoccupations ignored informal, domestic, and affective behaviour. Until the women's movement, topics such as the following went unstudied: pregnancy, childbirth, and motherhood (Bernard 1981; Chodorow 1978; Oakley 1980); emotions (Hochschild 1975; 1979; 1983); women's aging (Abu-Laban 1980; 1981); women's domestic labour (Oakley 1974; Luxton 1980); rape (Brownmiller 1975); wife battering (Dobash and Dobash 1979); women's medicine (Scully 1980); widowhood (Lopata 1979); women's roles in cultural production (Tuchman 1975; Sydie 1980); gender and language (Spender 1985); obesity (Millman 1980). This listing is but a sample of the new topics that have been explored. Obviously, the prefeminist male view had been a "myopic view," which by omitting the concerns of over half the world, led to "skewed insights into human behavior" (Epstein 1981: 149).

Use of Masculine Research Style

The identification of a "machismo element" in sociological research (Bernard 1973), a preferred masculine research mode which distorted women's experiences, located sexism in the methodological foundations of the discipline. Bernard (1973), following the ideas of psychologist Carlson (1971; 1972), argued that a major sex difference is associated with preferred research mode, with the "agentic" method being more congenial to male sociologists and the "communal" method being more congenial to female sociologists. "Agency tends to see variables, communion to see human beings" (Bernard 1973: 784). Agentic research is specified as preference for "hard" data, quantitative methods, laboratory experiments, social indicators, isolation and control of variables, and statistical tests of significance. Communal research, on the other hand, involves "soft" data, qualitative methods, verstehen knowledge, case studies, observation of social behaviour in situ, and no attempt to control variables or even to talk in terms of variables.

Bernard explains why the agentic mode reflects <u>machismo</u>:

> The scientist using this approach creates his own controlled reality. He can manipulate it. He is master. He has power. He can add or subtract or combine variables. He can play with a simulated reality like an Olympian god. He can remain at a distance, safely invisible behind his shield, uninvolved. The communal approach is much humbler. It disavows control, for control spoils the results. Its value rests precisely on the absence of controls (1973: 785).

As Gould (1980: 465) points out, "the search for new and the restoration of old methods suited to the study of women has proceeded vigourously since...[Bernard] identified the 'machismo factor' in sociological research." Many women prefer qualitative methods, which allow them to "take the role of the other," to see the world through the eyes of the people being studied. Understanding the experiences of women--treated as subjects, not as objects to be manipulated--takes priority over translating data into statistics. A positivistic view of sociology, that is, one that stresses its similarities with the physical sciences, is not embraced. A sense of history and of cooperation with practitioners in other disciplines is considered to be especially important. Finally, the researcher's own experiences and biography play a prominent role in the research process. The desires for improvement in the status of women and for personal growth supplement simple intellectual curiosity as motivations for research (Vaughter 1976: 146).

Maleness as the Norm

As indicated by the above charges, prior to the women's movement, males "held 'normative power': the right to define what was appropriate, legitimate, important" (Ward and Grant 1985: 143). Definition of research problems, data gathering, interpretation, and publication of findings were all male-dominated. According to Smith (1974: 7), "how sociology is thought--its methods, conceptual schemes and theories--has been based on and built up within, the male social universe." Until recently, women sociologists were trained by males and functioned in a masculine system where only masculine thought-patterns held legitimacy. To succeed in this male-dominated realm, women have had to adopt masculine ideas as their own. In Vickers' (1982: 29) words, "like Queen Elizabeth in Arab lands, I became an honourary male, and certainly my mind worked from within the male-stream thought I had learned."

Men were right, not because of their arguments or their explanations, but because of their gender (Spender 1981b: 4). Men have been the traditional gatekeepers of academia (Smith 1975), reviewers of graduate thesis prospectuses, appraisers of proposals for research funding, editors of journals and books. Publishing is critical. As Spender (1981a: 188) notes, "in a very fundamental sense, research which is not in print does not exist."

Especially in previous years, maleness as the norm meant the exclusion of female academics from colleagueship. Bernard (1964: 303) coined the term "stag effect" to describe "the easy social contacts possible for men but not women at meetings of learned societies and elsewhere." Theodore (1971: 30) commented upon women's exclusion from the peer relations "where professional decisions are made, knowledge shared, and favors exchanged in terms of clients, consultantships, grants, and research collaborations." Sociologists of science have demonstrated the importance of informal "networks" (Mullins 1973), "social circles," and "invisible colleges" (Crane 1972) in the development and diffusion of knowledge. In addition, "collegial recognition and esteem are the prime rewards for scientific achievement" (Zuckerman 1977: 62). As well, colleagues are a source of professional socialization and professional identity, of friendship and support. Preliberation women sociologists were often lonely people (Simon et al., 1967: 236).[4] Equally important, sociology was deprived of the feminine intellectual perspective.

The Sociology of Knowledge Perspective on Sexism in Research[5]

The sociology of knowledge is a branch of sociology concerned with the "social location of ideas" (Berger 1963: 110), the "relation between thought and society" (Coser 1968: 428). Utilization of this perspective to discuss the concerns mentioned above facilitated feminist sociologists' understanding of the history and probable future of the "gender factor" in scholarship. Two tenets of the sociology of knowledge are relevant here: the existential conditioning of thought and the ruling ideas proposition.

The Existential Conditioning of Thought

Existential conditioning affects all thought so that, to varying degrees, it is bound to locations within the social structure (Coser 1968: 430). In Marx's (1913: 11-12) words, "it is not the consciousness of men that determines their existence, but on the contrary their social existence determines their consciousness." This tenet's expression in the context of gender may be labelled "the two worlds metaphor." Smith (1974), for example, speaks of the "world of men" and the "world of women" and argues that different locations in the social structure are associated with particularized boundaries of experience and thought patterns. Similarly, Bernard (1981: 3) claims that "most human beings live in single-sex worlds, women in a female world and men in a male world [which differ] both subjectively and objectively."[6]

Differences in productive, reproductive, and sexual activities contribute to gender differences in consciousness. Different work activities in the home and the labour force lead to men and women having distinctive consciousnesses (Armstrong and Armstrong 1984: 188). Moreover, Stanley and Wise (1983: 146) claim that "women do experience reality differently, just by having 'different' bodies, 'different' physical experiences, to name no others" (emphasis in original).

The two worlds metaphor is an heuristic device. However, it is one which makes truth claims. For instance, is it true that female-male differences in thought override class, age, ethnic, and regional social locations? These are empirical questions. However, in addition to sexual and reproductive capabilities, Canadian women share with all others a vulnerability to sexual objectification and rape. Most of these women face sex segregation and low pay at work, and housework and the domestic power of men in the home.

Only recently have women scholars "undertaken serious research specifically on the female world with the attitude that it is worthy of consideration in and of itself" (Bernard 1981: 14). Since agentic methodology cannot capture adequately the communal methodology. The sociology of knowledge's ruling ideas proposition explains why female sociologists' efforts to do so have been hampered.

The Ruling-Ideas Proposition

Not only are ideas socially located, but some ideas are more influential than others. Marx and Engels (1947: 39) wrote: "The ideas of the ruling class are in every epoch the ruling ideas." Powerful people control the production and distribution of ideas, and they do so to buttress their own interests. When subordinate groups accept as valid and authoritative the ideology of the dominant group, they are engaging in false consciousness. False consciousness is "thought that is alienated from the real social being of the thinker" (Berger and Luckmann 1966: 6).

So far as gender is concerned, female and male intellectual worlds are unequal in status. If mental production is the privilege of the "ruling class," and men dominate women, then the authoritative perspective, the ideas that matter, obviously originate with men. In Smith's (1974: 7) words, "the world as it is constituted by men stands in authority over that of women." Similarly, Bernard (1981: 11) says that "the male world is not only segregative and exclusionary vis-à-vis the female world but is even, in varying degrees, positively hostile to it." Moreover, women are excluded from the "social circles" of people whose experiences count, whose interpretations of these experiences have integrity. "Men attend to and treat as significant what men say and have said" (Smith 1979: 137). Although males have only a partial view of total "reality," they are in a position to insist that their views are the real views and the only views (Spender 1985: 1-2). Women have traditionally been "...'overlooked', 'muted', 'invisible': mere black holes in someone else's universe" (Ardener 1975: 25).

Four complex and interactive processes have been responsible for women's "long silence" (Rowbotham 1973: 30). Women have been "voluntarily" silent in mixed company. Convinced that they are both less important than men and have little which is worthwhile to say, women have let men do most of the talking. Like good servants and good children, they have been "there," seen but not heard (Lofland 1975: 145).

A second process which has contributed to women's silence involves the edging out and taking over of their ideas by the dominant sex (Tuchman and Fortin 1984). Women's intellectual accomplishments have been expropriated by men. For example, women's traditional wisdom regarding herbs, healing, and childbirth was superseded by the "scientific" expertise of the male medical profession (Ehrenreich and English 1978).

A third process responsible for women's silence and invisibility may be labelled the "losing" of ideas. The ideas referred to are those which disturb the equanimity of the ruling sex. According to Spender (1981b: 10), men "have dismissed and 'lost' those views which are not consistent with their own." Foreign or irritating ideas disappear when they are unpublished or when they fail to please the critics, who have traditionally been men (Lanser and Beck 1979). Such ideas are not cited, quoted, anthologized, or taught.

The final cause of women's long silence lies in the fact that women have become alienated from their own experience, and hence, mute. Females raised in the shadow of the dominant male ideology think about themselves and the world, to some extent at least, in male terms; consequently, they lack the ability to express themselves in their own idiom. In Smith's (1975: 357) words, "for it is men who produce for women...the means to think and image." In part, women are mute because males have had the "power to name" (Stimpson 1979).

To succeed in male-dominated realms such as academia, women have had to adopt masculine ideas as their own. Relatively few and lowly in status (Tancred-Sherriff, 1985: 109), women sociologists "are those whose work and style of work and conduct have met the approval of judges who are largely men" (Smith, 1975: 361). The ruling-ideas proposition refers to the power of the dominant class to distribute as well as produce ideas. As noted above, men have been the gatekeepers in academia, as elsewhere. Until 1969, false consciousness prevailed.

The Impact of the Women's Movement

The women's movement brought female sociologists the realization that, until then, research had reported men's voices almost exclusively. The machismo factor (Bernard 1973) had alienated them from the research process. Inevitably, they themselves had used men's eyes to look out on the world (Rowbotham 1973: 40). They came to realize that the sociological theories designed to guide research and to explain social behaviour were grounded in male perception and experience; they therefore omit the feminine perspective. Since theory has often served to justify a sexist status quo, sociology's founding fathers were called "sexists to a man" (Schwendinger and Schwendinger 1971). As Epstein (1981: 160) points out, sociology's failure to deal meaningfully with more than half the members of society "throws a harsh light on the theoretical models that have shaped the profession for the past quarter-century." Through the women's movement, women have thrown off their false consciousness and have become a gender-for-themselves. They have attempted to retrieve the experiences they had nearly lost in the "male non-experience of them" (Rowbotham 1973: 37).

According to Eichler (1984), a "Copernican revolution in scholarship" will be needed for sociology really to take gender into account. In sociology, "we have envisioned our social universe as if men were in the centre and everything and everybody--women, other men, children, social institutions, etc.--revolved around men" (Eichler 1984: 35). A recentred sociology, a sociology for rather than of women (Smith 1975: 367), demands a radical shift in thinking. Above all, the sociology of knowledge instructs us in the politics of knowledge. Power is the key to the future of gender studies in sociology.

Current Relationship between Feminist and Mainstream Sociologies

The diagnostic and programmatic phase of feminist sociology has been essentially complete for a decade. An astonishing amount of empirical work has been done both to launch new topics of research and to correct biases in established areas, such as stratification, deviance, and organizations.[7] What impact have these insights had upon the methodological and theoretical paradigms of mainstream sociology? Do masculine ideas continue to override feminine insights? Or has the feminine world inside and outside academia achieved due recognition?

Research Style

An exploratory study (Mackie 1985) asked, "is the 'communal' approach to research more characteristic of female sociologists and the 'agentic' approach more characteristic of male sociologists?" In other words, was Bernard (1973) correct when she hypothesized differences in the styles of the genders? If so, has women's use of the communal research mode become more pronounced over time? If sociology has become less androcentric in recent years, such changes should be accompanied by some acceptance of the communal research mode. Research articles in five sociology journals of general interest (American Journal of Sociology, American Sociological Review, Pacific Sociological Review/Sociological Perspectives, Social Forces, Sociological Quarterly) and sociologists' publications in two interdisciplinary journals of women's studies (Signs, International Journal of Women's Studies) were coded as being within agentic or communal. Agentic articles are those which yield "hard" data: variables, hypothesis testing, indices, attitudinal scales, statistics, tests of significance, experiments, large scale surveys, and so on. Communal articles involve "soft" data: historical information observation, detailed intimate knowledge from informal interviews, ethnomethodology, etc.

With regard to the research mode employed, the analysis found that a gender difference does indeed exist in research orientations. When the five general interest journals between 1967 and 1981 were combined, male-authored articles containing data were 89.7 percent agentic, compared with 71.2 percent of the female- authored articles. Some 45 percent of women sociologists' articles versus 14.3 percent of men sociologists' articles in the two journals of women's studies (from the time of their inception until 1981) were communal. It is extremely unlikely that these differences are a product of chance.[8]

Gould (1980: 467) argues that "feminist sociologists often find themselves torn between wanting to do a sociology of/for women that is challenging and critical, and wanting their work to be seen as legitimate by those who control the discipline." Evidently, the greater proportion of female sociologists' communal articles in the women's studies journals (versus the general sociology journals) indicated what female sociologists would prefer to do, as opposed to what they feel they must do to please editorial gatekeepers.

When trends in women's use of the communal mode were examined, an increase was registered between 1967 and 1973 (from 0 to 48 percent), and a decrease between 1973 and 1981 (from 48 to 20.8 percent). This pattern suggests the continuing power of male-ruling ideas and co-optation of women into the male-dominated discipline. This exploratory study concluded that feminists' "rebellious constructions of the mind" (Berger 1963: 133) have not revolutionized mainstream sociology's methodology.

Theoretical Paradigms

Ten years ago, feminist sociologists, informed by the sociology of knowledge, called for a radical revision of sociological theory. For example, Smith (1975: 367) argued that academic women "are confronted virtually with the problem of re-inventing the world of knowledge, of thought, of symbols, and images." A "Copernican revolution in scholarship" (Eichler 1984) cannot countenance androcentric theoretical paradigms. Careful assessments (Gould 1980; Tancred-Sherriff 1985; Stacey and Thorne 1985; Ward and Grant 1985) conclude that these hoped-for conceptual transformations have not occurred. Sociologist Tancred-Sherriff (1985: 106) speaks of the denigration of women-created knowledge. Stacey and Thorne (1985: 302) say, "feminist sociology...seems to have been both co-opted and ghettoized, while the discipline as a whole and its dominant paradigms have proceeded relatively unchanged." Moreover, Stacey and Thorne (1985) argue that feminists in sociology have been less successful in reconstructing their discipline than have their counterparts in history, anthropology, or literary criticism.

What has happened to feminists' optimistic expectations? The explanation involves three factors: the nature of sociology as a discipline, women's status in the discipline, and limitations in feminists' theoretical thought.

First, several aspects of the nature of sociology as a discipline have influenced its receptivity to feminist ideas. Sociology is a pluralistic discipline. Instead of orthodoxy, many competing theories coexist. Therefore, feminist rebellion did not challenge, threaten, or demand response from advocates of a unitary, prevailing theory. Instead, women's thought became encapsulated in the special area of gender-relations and was thus ignored. Women sociologists are left alone, with courses, textbooks, and conferences of their very own. Many male sociologists likely view women's studies as esoteric or downright silly. However, most men are careful not to say so in public. Moreover, the size and fragmentation of sociology mean that feminist theorists need to wage battles on many fronts: "The conceptual transformation we might hope for would have to be multiple and diverse" (Stacey and Thorne 1985: 306). The positivistic (versus verstehen) ruling methodology in sociology also contributed towards co-optation of the feminist challenge. Gender became a well-funded, trendy variable for mainstream research. By viewing gender as a property of individuals, rather than a principle of social organization (Stacey and Thorne 1985: 307), this sex-difference research undermined the feminist critique, and completely misunderstood feminists' theoretical point.

A second basic reason why sociology resists feminist transformation is, of course, women's status in the discipline. Because women generally lack power and prestige, "the results of their labours are denigrated through mechanisms of privatization, ridicule and the male-defined aura of insignificance" (Tancred-Sherriff, 1985: 116). Women are on the periphery of central specialty areas in sociology, and play leading roles only in specialties that some deem marginal to the discipline. Moreover, female sociologists are relatively few in number, especially as senior professors, department heads, deans, and editors of mainstream journals. Consequently, they lack "clout" in "what comes to count as scientific knowledge" (Collins 1983: 267). To some extent, "reality" is a function of the sheer number of voices in the chorus crying that it is so (Festinger et al. 1956: 28).

Finally, certain limitations in feminist thought also account for its failure to crack the theoretical foundations of the discipline. For one thing, the iconoclastic thrust of this thought has "worked better to criticize than to reconstruct most bodies of theoretical knowledge" (Stacey and Thorne 1985: 312). As well as content, the raw feelings expressed by feminist theorists, the open acknowledgment of values and power may discomfit many male theorists. In addition, feminist theory has been charged with "falsely universalizing the category of 'women'" (Stacey and Thorne 1985: 311) and downplaying other categories, such as social class, race, and ethnicity. Even the attention given to gender is considered a matter of debate. It is paradoxical that feminists have emphasized the importance of gender in order to end the unequal treatment of women in society and to motivate the social scientific study of gender. Sexists also notice gender, but they employ these distinctions to bolster traditional gender arrangements. Indeed, one sociologist, Matthews, has argued that "gender is not a good index to understanding the social world" (1982: 29) and further that gender may often be "irrelevant information masquerading as an index to a structural feature of the social situation" (1982: 33). Frequently, what seem to be gender differences are actually power and status differences correlated with gender (Kahn and Jean 1983: 663). Essentially, then, male-stream sociology proceeds untouched by the feminist critique of the way enquiry is carried out and social reality understood.

The Future

What happens now? Should feminist sociologists give up trying to influence the discipline and concentrate on communicating with one another? Should they settle for the creativity associated with working on the margins of the discipline? Certainly, it seems a waste of the best theoretical minds to continue the critique of mainstream sociology. Accordingly, it would seem that priority should be given to getting on with the work of interest to women (Gould 1980: 460).

We now need to transform these "sparks for the sociological imagination" into energy that is directed at substantive problems. According to Vickers (1982: 40-41),

> Few feminists...are willing to waste time and effort over the receptivity of traditional disciplines to their discoveries and insights. Far more important is the transmissibility to the community of feminist scholars and researchers, which is taking on the character of a meta-discipline, and to the movement.

It would be most unfortunate if feminist sociologists were to settle for a meta-discipline or ghetto. Sociology needs the feminists. The criticisms reviewed above make this clear. A "dual perspective" (or appreciation of the "two worlds") advocated by Eichler and Lapointe (1985) can only come to be if feminists keep negotiations open. However, feminists also need sociology and the cachets of social science and the academy. The fact that they are feminist sociologists is critical. Mere propagandists lack credibility in the marketplace of ideas. As Tancred-Sherriff (1985: 116) notes, "there is little point in creating if one's creation is relegated to insignificance."

But how can the "insignificant" work of the "insignificant" gender come to be taken seriously? If there is any solution at all to this dilemma, it lies in the politics of knowledge (Spender 1981). First of all, the politics of knowledge implies scrutiny of the impact of our politics on our research, that is, the examination of the interaction between ideological and social scientific thought. Although neither mainstream nor feminist social science is value-free, it is important not to confuse our facts with our values, or expect our studies to substantiate our own ideologies (Mackie 1977). Safeguards lie in the logic of the scientific method. Genderless aspects of that method, such as skepticism for received truths and replication of findings, override both masculine and feminine biases. Ideological influences are mitigated, though not eradicated, by the "accumulation of different perspectives on the subject matter" (Berger and Luckmann 1966: 10). So far as sociologists are concerned, male and female worlds should not continue in their separate orbits. Neither should male hegemony and female muteness prevail. Ideally, desirable aspects of both perspectives should be salvaged in a perspective to which both sexes contribute and which both sexes can respect. Female and male sociologists share the social location of work, including the scientific ethos. Their separate sexual, reproductive, and work elsewhere should contribute to their sensitivity, as sociologists, to the experiences of their own sex. In sum, feminists' hope for the future lies in industry and excellence, in doing the calibre of sociological work that simply cannot be ignored, not in grumbling on the sidelines (Mackie 1977). Bracketing together politics and knowledge in this context implies close attention to the elementary steps by which power in academia is accomplished. This means attending to the number of feminists in sociology, their placement as department heads, journal editors, research-grant reviewers, and graduate thesis committees. In short, hard work, good work, and politically astute work should bring about a day when women's complaints about the Emperor's nakedness are heeded.

Endnotes

1. Millman and Kanter (1975) first used the story of the Emperor's New Clothes as an allegory to describe the sociology of gender relations. However, the version at the beginning of this paper was written by the author.

2. At the 1969 meeting of the American Sociological Association, a women's caucus met to protest discrimination against female sociologists in the profession, discrimination against women in society at large, and the sexist bias in research. Similar concerns were expressed by women in the other social sciences in both Canada and the United States, though the Canadian reaction came somewhat later. In 1971, the Canadian Sociology and Anthropology Association passed a resolution opposing discrimination on the grounds of sex, age, or marital status and encouraging the recruitment of women. In the same year, Robson and Lapointe published a comparison of Canadian academic men and women's salaries and fringe benefits for the Royal Commission on the Status of Women. This report, as well as a series of studies of women's status in particular Canadian universities, was analysed by Hitchman (1974). The first issue of the Canadian Newsletter of Research on Women was published in May 1972 under the editorship of Margrit Eichler and Marylee Stephenson. (The newsletter is now titled Resources for Feminist Research.) The first Canadian academic books on women (Andersen 1972; Henshel [Ambert] 1973; Stephenson 1973) also appeared in the early 1970s. The formation of an association of women in sociology and anthropolgy was announced in 1974. Before the revival of the feminist movement, the significance of such pioneering work as Bernard (1964), Hacker (1951), and Komarovsky (1946) was simply not appreciated (Mackie 1983: 11-13).

3. Carrigan et al. (1985: 557), who counted articles in the Sociological Abstracts, graph between zero and ten research articles on women between 1963 and 1969, and over 450 in 1978.

4. Mackie (1985) employed such publications as journal articles to indicate women sociologists' status in the discipline. The pattern of single authors and joint authorship of articles tells us something about women's inclusion in the circles of collegiality in mainstream sociology. Percentages of joint-authored articles in fourteen sociology journals shows that women's collaboration with colleagues of both sexes increased significantly in the period 1973-1981 over the period 1967-1973. The amount of collaboration of both sexes is now nearly identical.

5. This section is based, in part, on Mackie, Constructing Women and Men: Gender Socialization in Canadian Society, Holt, Rinehart and Winston (forthcoming).

6. Gilligan (1982) analyses two "voices" or modes of thought about morality which she labels feminine and masculine.

7. Nevertheless, according to the empirical analyses of Ward and Grant (1985), articles treating only one gender continue to appear in print.

8. For general interest journals, chi-square was significant at the .005 level, one-tailed test. For the women's-studies journals, chi-square was significant at the .025 level, one-tailed test.

References

Abu-Laban, Sharon.
1980 Social Supports in Older Age: The Need for New Research Directions. Essence 4: 195-210.

1981 Women and Aging: A Futurist Perspective. Psychology of Women Quarterly 6: 85-98.

Acker, Joan
1973 Women and Social Stratification: A Case of Intellectual Sexism. American Journal of Sociology 78: 936-45.

Andersen, Margaret (ed.)
1972 Mother Was Not a Person. Montreal: Black Rose.

Anderson, Nels
1964 Dimensions of Work: The Sociology of a Work Culture. New York: David McKay.

Ardener, Edwin
1975 The "Problem" Revisited. Pp. 19-27 in Perceiving Women, ed. Shirley Ardener. London: Malaby.

Armstrong, Pat, and Armstrong, Hugh
1984 The Double Ghetto: Canadian Women and Their Segregated Work. Rev. ed. Toronto: McClelland and Stewart.

Bart, Pauline B.
1971 Sexism and Social Science: From the Gilded Cage to the Iron Cage, or, the Perils of Pauline. Journal of Marriage and the Family 33: 734-45.

Berger, Peter L.
1963 Invitation to Sociology: A Humanistic Perspective. Garden City, NY: Doubleday Anchor.

Berger, Peter L., and Luckmann, Thomas
1966 The Social Construction of Reality. Garden City, NY: Doubleday Anchor.

Bernard, Jessie
1964 Academic Women. Cleveland, OH: Meridian.

1973 My Four Revolutions: An Autobiographical History of the ASA. American Journal of Sociology 78: 773-91.

1981 The Female World. New York: Free Press.

Blishen, Bernard R.
1967 A Socio-economic Index for Occupations in Canada. Canadian Review of Sociology and Anthropology 4: 41-53.

Blishen, Bernard R., and Carroll, William K.
  1978   Sex Differences in a Socio-economic Index for Occupations in Canada. *Canadian Review of Sociology and Anthropology* 15: 352-71.

Blishen, Bernard R., and McRoberts, Hugh A.
  1976   A Revised Socio-economic Index for Occupations in Canada. *Canadian Review of Sociology and Anthropology* 13: 71-9.

Brownmiller, Susan
  1975   *Against Our Will: Men, Women and Rape.* New York: Simon and Schuster.

Carlson, Rae
  1971   Sex Differences in Ego Functioning: Exploratory Studies of Agency and Communion. *Journal of Consulting and Clinical Psychology* 37: 267-77.

  1972   Understanding Woman: Implications for Personality Theory and Research. *Journal of Social Issues* 28: 17-32.

Carrigan, Tim; Connell, Bob; and Lee, John
  1985   Toward a New Sociology of Masculinity. *Theory and Society* 14: 551-604.

Chodorow, Nancy
  1978   *The Reproduction of Mothering.* Berkeley, CA: University of California.

Collins, H.M.
  1983   The Sociology of Scientific Knowledge: Studies of Contemporary Science. *Annual Review of Sociology* 9: 265-85.

Coser, Lewis A.
  1968   Sociology of Knowledge. Pp. 428-35 in *International Encyclopedia of the Social Sciences*, ed. David L. Sills. New York: Macmillan.

Crane, Diana
  1972   *Invisible Colleges: Diffusion of Knowledge in Scientific Communities.* Chicago: University of Chicago.

Daniels, Arlene K.
  1975   Feminist Perspectives in Sociological Research. Pp. 340-80 in *Another Voice: Feminist Perspectives on Social Life and Social Science*, ed. Marcia Millman and Rosabeth Moss Kanter. Garden City, NY: Doubleday Anchor.

Dobash, R. Emerson, and Dobash, Russell
  1979   *Violence against Wives: A Case against the Patriarchy.* New York: Free Press.

Ehrenreich, Babara, and English, Diedre
  1978   *For Her Own Good: 150 Years of the Experts' Advice to Women.* Garden City, NY: Doubleday Anchor.

Eichler, Margrit
   1984 Sexism in Research and Its Policy Implications. Pp. 17-39 in *Taking Sex into Account: The Policy Consequences of Sexist Research*, ed. Jill McCalla Vickers. Ottawa: Carleton University.

Epstein, Cynthia F.
   1981 Women in Sociological Analysis: New Scholarship versus Old Paradigms. Pp. 149-62 in *A Feminist Perspective in the Academy*, ed. Elizabeth Langland and Walter Gove. Chicago: University of Chicago.

Festinger, Leon; Riecken, Henry W.; and Schachter, Stanley
   1956 *When Prophecy Fails*. New York: Harper and Row.

Gilligan, Carol
   1982 *In a Different Voice*. Cambridge, MA: Harvard University.

Gould, Meredith
   1980 Review Essay: The New Sociology. *Signs* 5: 459-67.

Hacker, Helen M.
   1951 Women as a Minority Group. *Social Forces* 30: 60-9.

Henshel, Anne-Marie (Ambert)
   1973 *Sex Structure*. Don Mills, ON: Longman.

Herzog, A.
   1982 High School Seniors: Occupational Plans and Values: Trends in Sex Differences. *Sociology of Education* 55: 1-12.

Hitchman, Gladys S.
   1974 A Report on the Reports: The Status of Women in Canadian Universities. *Canadian Sociology and Anthropology Association Bulletin* 35: 11-13.

Hochschild, Arlie R.
   1975 The Sociology of Feeling and Emotion: Selected Possibilities. Pp. 280-307 in *Another Voice: Feminist Perspectives on Social Life and Social Science*, ed. Marcia Millman and Rosabeth Moss Kanter. Garden City, NY: Doubleday Anchor.

   1979 Emotion Work, Feeling Rules, and Social Structure. *American Journal of Sociology* 85: 551-75.

   1983 *The Managed Heart: Commercialization of Human Feeling*. Berkeley, CA: University of California.

Kahn, Arnold S., and Jean, Paula J.
   1983 Integration and Elimination or Separation and Redefinition: The Future of the Psychology of Women. *Signs* 8: 659-71.

Komarovsky, Mirra
   1946 Cultural Contradictions and Sex Roles. *American Journal of Sociology* 52: 184-9.

Lanser, Susan S., and Beck, Evelyn T.
    1979   Are There No Great Women Critics?: And What Difference Does It Make? Pp. 79-91 in The Prism of Sex: Essays in the Sociology of Knowledge, ed. Julia A. Sherman and Evelyn T. Beck. Madison, WI: University of Wisconsin.

Lofland, Lyn H.
    1975   The "Thereness" of Women: A Selective Review of Urban Sociology. Pp. 144-70 in Another Voice: Feminist Perspectives on Social Life and Social Science, ed. Marcia Millman and Rosabeth Moss Kanter. Garden City, NY: Doubleday Anchor.

Lopata, Helena Z.
    1979   Women as Widows: Support Systems. New York: Elseview North-Holland.

Luxton, Meg
    1980   More Than a Labour of Love: Three Generations of Women's Work in the Home. Toronto: Women's Press.

Mackie, Marlene
    1977   On Congenial Truths: A Perspective on Women's Studies. Canadian Review of Sociology and Anthropology 14: 117-28.

    1983   Exploring Gender Relations: A Canadian Perspective. Toronto: Butterworths.

    1985   Female Sociologists' Productivity, Collegial Relations, and Research Style Examined through Journal Publications. Sociology and Social Research 69: 184-209.

Marx, Karl
    1913   A Contribution to the Critique of Political Economy. tr. N.I. Stone. Chicago: Kerr.

Marx, Karl, and Engels, Friedrich
    1947   The German Ideology, ed. R. Pascal. New York: International.

Matthews, Sarah H.
    1982   Rethinking Sociology through a Feminist Perspective. The American Sociologist 17: 29-35.

Millman, Marcia
    1980   Such a Pretty Face: Being Fat in America. New York: Berkley.

Millman, Marcia, and Kanter, Rosabeth Moss (eds.)
    1975   Another Voice: Feminist Perspectives on Social Life and Socal Science. Garden City, NY: Doubleday Anchor.

Mullins, Nicholas C.
    1973   Theories and Theory Groups in Contemporary American Sociology. New York: Harper and Row.

Oakley, Ann
    1974   The Sociology of Housework. London: Martin Robertson.

    1980   Women Confined: Towards a Sociology of Childbirth. London: Martin Robertson.

O'Brien, Mary
    1979   Reproducing Marxist Man. Pp. 99-116 in The Sexism of Social and Political Theory, ed. L. Clark and L. Lange. Toronto: University of Toronto.

Richardson, Laurel W.
    1981   The Dynamics of Sex and Gender. 2nd ed. Boston: Houghton Mifflin.

Ritzer, George
    1972   Man and His Work: Conflict and Change. New York: Appleton-Century-Crofts.

Robson, R.A.H., and Lapointe, M.
    1971   A Comparison of Men's and Women's Salaries and Employment Fringe Benefits in the Academic Profession. Royal Commission on the Status of Women in Canada, Substudy 1. Ottawa: Queen's Printer.

Rowbotham, Sheila
    1973   Women's Consciousness, Man's World. Markham, ON: Penguin.

Schwendinger, Julia, and Schwendinger, Herman
    1971   Sociology's Founding Fathers: Sexist to a Man. Journal of Marriage and the Family 33: 783-99.

Scully, Diana
    1980   Men Who Control Women's Health. Boston: Houghton Mifflin.

Simon, Rita James; Clark, Shirley Merritt; and Galway, Kathleen
    1967   The Women Ph.D.: A Recent Profile. Social Problems 15: 221-36.

Smith, Dorothy E.
    1974   Women's Perspective as a Radical Critique of Sociology. Sociological Inquiry 44: 7-13.

    1975   An Analysis of Ideological Structures and How Women Are Excluded: Considerations for Academic Women. Canadian Review of Sociology and Anthropology 12: 353-69.

    1979   A Sociology for Women. Pp. 135-87 in The Prism of Sex: Essays in the Sociology of Knowledge, ed. Julia A. Sherman and Evelyn T. Beck. Madison, WI: University of Wisconsin.

Spender, Dale
    1981a   The Gatekeepers: A Feminist Critique of Academic Publishing. Pp. 186-202 in Doing Feminist Research, ed. Helen Roberts. London: Routledge and Kegan Paul.

    1981b   Men's Studies Modified: The Impact of Feminism on the Academic Disciplines. Oxford: Pergamon.

    1985   *Man Made Language.* 2nd ed. London: Routledge and Kegan Paul.

Stacey, Judith, and Thorne, Barrie
    1985   The Missing Feminist Revolution in Sociology. *Social Problems* 32: 301-16.

Stanley, Liz, and Wise, Sue
    1983   *Breaking Out: Feminist Consciousness and Feminist Research.* London: Routledge and Kegan Paul.

Stephenson, Marylee (ed.)
    1973   *Women in Canada.* Toronto: Free Press.

Stimpson, Catharine R.
    1979   The Power to Name: Some Reflections on the Avant-garde. Pp. 55-77 in *The Prism of Sex: Essays in the Sociology of Knowledge,* ed. Julia A. Sherman and Evelyn T. Beck. Madison, WI: University of Wisconsin.

Sydie, Rosalind
    1980   Women Painters in Britain: 1768-1848. *Atlantis* 5: 144-75.

Tancred-Sherriff, Peta
    1985   Women's Experience, Women's Knowledge and the Power of Knowledge: An Illustration and an Elaboration. *Atlantis* 10: 106-17.

Theodore, Athena
    1971   The Professional Women: Trends and Prospects. Pp. 1-35 in *The Professional Women,* ed. Athena Theodore. Cambridge, MA: Schenkman.

Tuchman, Gaye
    1975   Women and the Creation of Culture. Pp. 171-202 in *Another Voice: Feminist Perspectives on Social Life and Social Science,* ed. Marcia Millman and Rosabeth Moss Kanter. Garden City, NY: Doubleday Anchor.

Tuchman, Gaye, and Fortin, Nina E.
    1984   Fame and Misfortune: Edging Women out of the Great Literary Tradition. *American Journal of Sociology* 90:72-96.

Vaughter, Reesa M.
    1976   Psychology: Review Essay. *Signs* 2: 120-46.

Vickers, Jill McCalla
    1982   Memoirs of an Ontological Exile: The Methodological Rebellions of Feminist Research. Pp. 27-46 in *Feminism in Canada: From Pressure to Politics,* ed. Angela R. Miles and Geraldine Finn. Montreal: Black Rose.

Ward, Kathryn B., and Grant, Linda
    1985   The Feminist Critique and a Decade of Published Research in Sociology Journals. *The Sociology Quarterly* 26: 139-57.

Zuckerman, Harriet
    1977   *Scientific Elite: Nobel Laureates in the United States.* New York: Free Press.

THE TREATMENT OF THE SEXES IN PSYCHOLOGICAL RESEARCH[1]

Carolyn C. Larsen

Introduction

Psychology, until recently, has neglected and misrepresented women. This neglect has pervaded all areas of this discipline: theory development, research, publication, position within professional organizations, access to educational programs, and entry to and advancement in employment. As in most other disciplines, and indeed society in general, there has been an awakening within psychology to issues and concerns of women and some significant efforts towards change. Even the most ardent feminists (Frieze et al. 1978, Stark-Adamec and Kimball 1984) admit that there has been no conscious maliciousness in the perpetuation of stereotyping which was largely responsible for this neglect. Psychologists have been as much victims of a nonconscious ideology about women as anyone, unaware of many of the beliefs and stereotypes which result in the failure to imagine any alternatives to the status quo. Psychology viewed women (and many psychologists still view women) in the stereotypical ways common to most of our society. Martha Mednick (1978: 80) states that

> psychology has been a weapon for keeping woman in her place: it has perpetuated the myth of women as a victim of her biology....Psychology has also depicted women as incompetent, incapable of abstract thinking, passive, inferior--in short, deservedly powerless victims. None of the areas of psychology has escaped this discouraging assessment.

Psychology was no more introspective about its role in perpetuating stereotypes about women than any other discipline. It is a paradox that psychology, the study of how and why people act as they do, has been unable, until very recently, to disengage itself enough to achieve some perspective on this neglect and misrepresentation. Granted, some writers throughout the history of psychology have raised these issues, but their views were not heard by many until the issues become a significant wave of concern, and until critiques and research findings could no longer be easily ignored. Psychology is now reflecting upon and leading the correction of this state of affairs. This progress is evident in Sandra Pyke's survey (oral communication)[2] of the efforts by the Learned Societies in Canada to deal with sex and gender bias in their disciplines. Her survey demonstrated that psychology, as a discipline, has addressed these issues, implemented action in many areas, and made significantly greater progress to remedy the problem than any other discipline in Canada.

It took a scathing article by Naomi Weisstein (1971), "Psychology Constructs the Female, or the Fantasy Life of the Male Psychologist," to provide the jolt that psychology needed to begin to respond responsibly to women's issues. In this article Weisstein (1971: 70) states, "psychology has nothing to say about what women are really like, what they need and what they want, essentially because psychology does not know." She goes on to say (1971: 71),

> The first reason for psychology's failure to understand what people are and how they act is that psychology has looked for inner traits when it should have been looking for social context; the second reason for psychology's failure is that theoreticians of personality have generally been clinicians and psychiatrists, and they have never considered it necessary to have evidence in support of their theories.

Weisstein was referring to the lack of attention to social influences, as well as to the invisibility of women, in much of psychological scholarship, although much speculation has been heaped on women and used as if it were true.

Sherif (1979: 119) concluded more recently,

> of course, the most devastating power plays through psychological theorizing ignore both the social environment and behaviour as much as possible by focusing exclusively upon the internal psychological world--on so-called psychodynamics. If one were to design a theory to keep women in an inferior position and at lowered worth, none is more suitable than locating the causes of women's behavior and problems inside the woman.

A great deal of work emerged in the early 1970s that heightened the significant wave of concern about women's place in psychology. The following examples serve to illustrate this rising wave. Judith Bardwick (1971) and Julia Sherman (1971) published the first two texts on the psychology of women. The work of Matina Horner (1972), with her concept of the "fear of success," challenged

McClelland's theory of achievement (1953). Sandra Bem (1974) developed the concept of androgyny, a balance of feminine and masculine intellectual and personal qualities, in addition, she developed a program of research to study and measure this concept. A landmark study by Broverman et al. (1970) revealed that clinicians have different criteria for describing the mental health of men and women. Both male and female clinicians were shown to describe healthy men and women in terms of their sex-role stereotypes. Clinicians described healthy men and healthy adults as alike and as fitting the male sex-role stereotype, but women were described differently from healthy adults.

Topics relevant to women were beginning to be discussed and researched in the 1970s: family violence, incest, the female reproductive cycle, depression, sexuality, agoraphobia, lesbianism, sexual harassment, eating disorders. By the mid-1970s, review articles on women psychologists and the psychology of women began to appear (e.g., Astin 1972; Greenglass 1973a, 1973b). And for the first time there was a chapter in the Annual Review of Psychology about women (Mednick and Weissman 1975).

Vaughter (1975: 20) defined the new psychology of women according to four basic characteristics: (1) the psychology of women is concerned with constructing a psychology relevant to women as well as men; (2) it studies women as well as men; (3) it employs a methodology that is appropriate to, meaningful for, and congruent with both women and men's lives; (4) it asks questions of interest to women as well as to men. "In brief, the goal of the psychology of women is the development of a non-sexist science, a psychology of human behavior" (Vaughter 1975: 120).

The goals of this paper are to describe sex and gender bias in psychological scholarship and the efforts that have been made to counteract this bias. Some historical information has been presented in this introductory section to provide a context for that examination. The next section describes some sources of bias in psychological theory and research. This is followed by an account of developments in Canada and the United States that demonstrate how professional psychology organizations provided reforms for the treatment of the sexes in many areas of the discipline. Particular emphasis is given to the efforts of the Canadian Psychological Association and Canadian women psychologists to influence research, practice, education, and the professional associations. Guidelines for researchers regarding treatment of the sexes in research are summarized. Last, some suggestions are offered for continued efforts to reduce sex and gender bias.

Sources of Sex and Gender Bias in Psychological Theory and Research

What are the ways in which sex and gender bias occur in psychological theory and research? Many of the answers to this question are similar to those outlined in the booklet <u>On the Treatment of the Sexes in Research</u> by Margrit Eichler and Jean Lapointe (1985), which was the impetus for this paper and this volume. I shall analyse seven sources of sex and gender bias in psychological research and theory: building psychological theories on data obtained exclusively from males; using male behaviour as the norm; employing only male subjects in experiments; the lack of knowledge about sex roles; testing for sex differences; viewing masculine and feminine as dichotomies; the high value given to men's roles and the underevaluation to women's roles in Western culture.

Psychological theories built on data from only male subjects have been a serious source of bias. The area of achievement motivation is a prime example of a theory developed primarily with reference to men (Frieze et al. 1978: 21) state that this may have occurred due to a nonconscious assumption that it was not important to study women because "they obviously" are not interested in achievement. Also, they suggest that earlier data collected on achievement in women was likely dropped when it did not fit with the findings of McClelland and his colleagues (1953) about male-achievement motivation.

Secondly, sex and gender bias results from the use of male behaviour as the norm for describing and understanding human behaviour. Often cited is the work of Kohlberg (1969) on the development of moralization of judgment. Kohlberg's theory stipulates that six stages of moral development must be passed through in sequence and that no stage is skipped. Kohlberg developed his theory from research on males (1969). His theory has been challenged by the work of Carol Gilligan (1979, 1982), which shows a different moral development for women. Whereas Kohlberg sees an ethic of justice in males, Gilligan presents an ethic of care and responsibility in women. Women's life-long concern with relationships often appears as a weakness rather than as a strength in theories developed from and about males. Because autonomy and achievement are usually seen as indications of maturity, women are viewed as underdeveloped compared to men. Thus, Gilligan's work has been central in challenging an existing theory and in valuing women's experience as different from but as valid as that of men.

Another new theoretical direction in understanding women's development, one which meshes very well with that of Gilligan, is the concept "self-in-relation." Jean Baker Miller (1976) was an early proponent of self-in-relation, which is now being developed further by A.G. Kaplan and Janet Surrey (1984) in their work at the Stone Center at Wellesley College. They find that women's self-esteem emerges from a relational self rather than the autonomous self proposed by male personality theorists (e.g., Erikson 1964). Kaplan and Surrey suggest that child-raising patterns that encourage development of their relational self may result in women's greater ability to feel and express emotions, an ability which has often been seen as a liability. Walker (1984: 15) states,

> It is possible that women experience emotions in a different way than do men, which can allow for women to be more intense and perhaps even seem to become lost or enmeshed in their feelings without losing their sense of self (as is suggested in earlier literature). Many women diagnosed as borderline [psychotic] may actually be functioning in a normal way for a woman, even though their behavior may make male-identified therapists anxious. The diagnostic labelling of women's emotional experience into categories proposed by the male-dominated psychiatric structure has been challenged by Kaplan (1983) in an article in <u>American Psychologist</u>.

Personality theories extensively criticized for their androcentric approach are those of Erikson (1950, 1964) and Freud (1950). Also, until recently, theories of career development were based on the typical cycle men go through in their lives. Women were often disregarded because their experience did not fit the male pattern, rather than considered as having career patterns of their own.

A third source of bias is the use of only male subjects in experiments. This bias has resulted from most experimenters being male and studying topics of interest to men. It also reflects the fact that many experiments use university students, who at one time were mostly men. However, the exclusive use of males continued long after women were available as subjects. Prescott (1978) found that researchers gave many reasons for restricting their samples to one sex. These reasons were categorized as follows: "scientific" reasons, which included reducing the variation in the data, limiting the hypotheses to men, or reducing experimental complexity; "practical" reasons, which resulted from time constraints, limited financial resources, the availability of only one sex, or the claim that sample size would be cumbersome if both sexes were included; and "extra scientific" reasons that the inclusion of both sexes might yield confusing results, that it would be "safer" to include only one sex, or that the investigators understood the phenomena only in relation to one sex. Prescott also noted that five reasons were offered for not including men in experiments but twenty-six reasons were given for not including women (as cited in Stark-Adamec and Kimball 1984: 27).

A fourth source of bias stems from the lack of knowledge about sex roles and how they influence behaviour. Sex-role differences can affect, sometimes in unknown ways, the outcomes of experiments (Deaux 1984; Lott 1985). The context of the experiment and the tasks presented can be unwittingly biased so that each sex will respond differently. For example, how tasks are described to subjects, the competitiveness of the situation, the sex of the experimenter, the sex composition of the research group, the differential familiarity of materials to males and females, and the expectations of the experimenter can all bias the results of an experiment.

A fifth type of bias is related to the testing for sex differences. "The term 'sex differences' suggests that differences between the sexes are more frequent, more interesting or more important than similarities between the sexes" (McHugh et al. 1981: 20). Another problem is that when sex differences of significance are found, these may be interpreted to mean that all women have character traits that are different from those of all men. More commonly, there are overlapping distributions in characteristics or behaviours of men and women. Another concern with sex differences is the interpretation that such differences are due either to innate differences between men and women's natures or entirely to the socialization process. Thus, McHugh et al. (1981: 21) have cautioned that "researchers should avoid implying that the sexes represent non-overlapping distributions or that their responses fall on opposite ends of the single dimension."

The issue of testing for sex differences is related to a sixth source of bias: masculinity and femininity are viewed as dichotomies rather than as overlapping distributions of characteristics. Psychological research shows that men and women are more alike than they are different but, partly because of the artifact of publishing only significant (i.e., unusual) results, sex differences have engendered more interest. Where nonsignificant (i.e., usual) results are available or presented, they are often not reported in the literature.

A seventh bias relates to the value system prevalent in Western culture, in particular, the high value placed on the role of men in society. One effect of this patriarchal system is that women's issues have not been valued and thus not investigated. Bias against investigating women's issues has resulted in a double standard in the funding of research (Stark-Adamec 1981), as well as in the dissemination of research findings. Much information about women is published in women's journals and thus is still not part of mainstream psychology. Another effect of the patriarchal system is collegial pressures placed on theorists to conform to views about men's dominant position in society. This pressure is illustrated in a controversial example from Freud's own research (Masson 1984). Walker (1984: 9) states that Jeffrey Masson, a former Projects Director of the Sigmund Freud Archives,

> presents compelling evidence that Freud's original theory that all neuroses comes from adult males forceful sexual seduction of young female children was changed because he could not bear the pressure of ostracism by his colleagues and their invalidation of this theory by pretending they did not hear what he said.

Walker indicates that Freud changed his theory to see it as the unconscious wish fulfillment of what was later labelled children's sexual fantasies. Walker (1984: 9) goes on to characterize this situation as

> a good example of protecting collegial maleness at the expense of women. Today, of course, we are reevaluating Freud's original seduction theory as more accurate than the substituted fantasy theory in light of the large numbers of women still seeking therapy for the same kinds of damages that occurred a century earlier when society would not tolerate acknowledgement of them.

Towards the Reduction of Sex- and Gender-Biased Research in Psychology

The increasing development of interest in the psychology of women, the paucity of information about women, and the awareness of the underrepresentation of women within the profession resulted in efforts, mostly by women, to redress psychology's neglect and misrepresentation. These efforts occurred on a number of fronts within and outside of professional organizations. Only changes that have been initiated by formal organizations will be examined here. In North America, the American Psychological Association (APA) and the Canadian Psychological Association (CPA) responded to pressures from within and without their organizations to assess and redress the status of women.

In Canada, during the early 1970s the annual convention program committees of the CPA were unresponsive to submissions of topics related to the psychology of women, (Pyke [oral communication]; Stark-Adamec 1981). The same researchers point out that such topics were also not represented in the CPA's three journals. A symposium dealing with women's issues in psychology was held independent of but parallel to the 1972 CPA annual convention. Since this maverick beginning, there have been many developments to amend the status of women in Canadian psychology and to give the study of the psychology of women an equitable role within the profession. The CPA Section on Women and Psychology (SWAP), formed in 1975, has provided women psychologists with a network to develop unity and power to push for change within the CPA.

The CPA took a comprehensive approach to women's concerns in 1975 by setting up the Task Force on the Status of Women in Canadian Psychology. This Task Force produced ninety recommendations (Wand 1977) to remedy problems in four areas which had been identified in the report: the status of women within the discipline of psychology; the education and training of women in psychology; sex bias in psychological research; and psychological services for women. The Committee on the Status of Women was established and has been active in implementing these recommendations. While only one of these four problem areas is directly related to research, all the areas are relevant to nonsexist research, as will be noted.

In the United States, the Association for Women in Psychology (AWP) was founded in 1970; it pressured the APA from the outside to include more women in governing the organization. Division 35 of the APA, The Psychology of Women, was founded in 1973 and began publication of the Psychology of Women Quarterly in 1976. This and other journals, such as Sex Roles, which appeared in 1975, provided a needed forum for the growing research about the psychology of women. The APA established a Committee on Women in Psychology in 1978 and later a Women's Programs Office to promote the status of women in psychology.

One of the first issues to be addressed by the APA was the use of sexist language in the communication of research and in educational materials. In 1977, the APA published <u>Guidelines for Non-Sexist Language in APA Journals</u>, which was endorsed the same year by the CPA Executive. These guidelines are now part of the <u>Publication Manual of the American Psychological Association</u> (3rd ed., 1983) and are accepted practice in all journal publications. However, it was not until 1982 that the APA established a policy which requires authors who submit manuscripts to use nonsexist language. Since these publication guidelines are used by other disciplines, their influence has spread beyond psychology.

Another major issue considered by the APA was bias in psychotherapy. The Task Force on Sex Bias and Sex Role Stereotyping in Psychotherapeutic Practice published thirteen "Guidelines for Therapy and Counselling of Women" (1978). Four categories of behaviours which occur in therapy with women were identified: (1) fostering traditional sex roles; (2) bias in expectations and evaluation of women; (3) sexist use of psychoanalytic concepts; and (4) responding to women as sex objects, including the seduction of female clients. A similar set of guidelines was developed by the APA Counselling Psychology Division. Thirteen "Principles Concerning the Counselling and Therapy of Women" focused on the specialized skills, attitudes, and knowledge required by therapists to be effective in working with women (1979). The CPA also adopted "Guidelines for Therapy and Counselling with Women," which has been developed by a Calgary-based subcommittee of the CPA Status of Women Committee (1980). While these guidelines address issues which arise in counselling and therapy, they are similar to some issues raised about nonsexist research. Research on women will develop the knowledge base needed to provide effective, ethical, psychological treatment. Conversely, therapy needs to be freer of bias in order for researchers to conduct meaningful research.

Developments in other areas of psychology have significant implications for the reduction of bias in psychological scholarship, as was emphasized by the CPA Status of Women recommendations (Wand 1977). The status of women within the discipline of psychology is relevant because women have been underrepresented in decision-making positions. This situation is being corrected. Women are now equitably represented on the CPA Board of Executives and increasingly as editors and on the editorial boards of journals.

Improving women's representation in these key positions was the first priority of the CPA Status of Women Committee. Recommendations regarding the education, training, and hiring of women are also considered critical to the development of nonsexist research. In order for women's interests and perspectives to be represented within the profession, women need to have equal opportunity to access advanced education and to be treated equally with men in all areas of consideration in employment. The importance of female role models in encouraging graduate students and junior faculty is well recognized. Similarly, it is a policy of CPA that there should be equitable treatment in the education of graduate students regardless of sex, marital, or parental status. This policy extends to the recruitment of graduate students as well as to their acceptance and recommendation for various types of funding. Women are now well represented in masters programs in psychology in Canada though they are still not participating in equal numbers to men in doctoral programs (Kalin and Grant 1981). The representation of women in all areas and levels of psychology is important because of the implications for the future development of a psychology that represents both sexes.

Guidelines for the Conduct of Nonsexist Research

A number of efforts to address concerns about sexism in psychological research preceded the development of formal guidelines (Mednick 1978; Sherif 1979; Weyant 1979). For example, a seminar entitled "Directions in Research: Women's Studies in the Social Sciences and the Humanities" was held at The University of Calgary in 1977. A special section of the Psychology of Women Quarterly on feminist research presented several articles (Grady 1981; Parlee 1981; Unger 1981; Wallston, 1981) exploring various research problems. The theme at the annual conference of the Canadian Research Institute for the Advancement of Women in 1982 was "Sexism in Research and its Policy Implications." The proceedings of this conference were published in Taking Sex into Account: The Policy Consequences of Sexist Research (Vickers 1984).

Both the APA and CPA adopted guidelines for conducting nonsexist research. "Guidelines for Non-Sexist Research" were developed by a Task Force of the APA, Division 35, chaired by Maureen McHugh, Randi Koeske, and Irene Frieze (1981). An article, "Science Free of Sexism: A Psychologist's Guide to the Conduct of

Non-Sexist Research," by Cannie Stark-Adamec and Meredith Kimball (1984) presents the approved and endorsed position of the Canadian Psychological Association. These two documents represent formal attempts by these organizations to put in place policy and practice that will assist in creating research that is fair to both sexes. McHugh et al. (1981: 1) make the following statements in their introduction:

> The starting assumption for these guidelines is our belief that many research projects in psychology should attempt to meet established methodological and ethical standards, while avoiding sexism, racism and other forms of bias....Bias operates whenever untested values and assumptions underly research hypotheses, procedures, analysis or interpretations. Sexism characterizes psychology to the extent that <u>unexamined assumptions about the sexes or untested distinctions based on sex</u> enter into the hypotheses, rationales, norms of adjustment, or coverage of topics in the field. It is when such untested values and assumptions are implicit and unexamined that they undermine the research process. By making them explicit, examining them by means of accepted scientific standards, and exposing them to public scientific debate, such "biases" become hypotheses and theories which are part of science, not outside it.

These authors explore sexism in research and depict its consequences by identifying seven areas, each of which corresponds to a section of the guidelines. A number of recommendations follow the discussion of each area to guide researchers raising questions about bias in their work. The seven areas are: excessive confidence in traditional research methods; the conceptualization and labeling variables; use of precise conceptual models and explanatory systems; choice of research topics and participants; the influence of contextual factors on the behaviours of research participants; examination of sexrelated differences; and special problems with animal research. While these areas are interrelated and reflect general concerns about scientific methods, the focus in these guidelines is specifically on sexism. The authors acknowledge that they did not deal with other issues relevant to the development of nonsexist psychology, sexism in language, and sex bias in psychological testing.

The CPA's position covers many of the same issues as the APA version, although they are presented in quite a different manner. The authors of the CPA's position make the point that "while research is essential if change in the status and quality of life of women is to be achieved, no amount of research will benefit women if the research itself is sex biased or sexist" (Stark-Adamec and Kimball

1984: 24). The following assumptions also underlie the CPA position: (a) a lack of awareness of the issues and factors involved is primarily responsible for sexist biases in research; (b) the persistence of sex bias in psychological research is largely unintentional sexism; (c) research so influenced is unscientific; and (d) given the implications of such research for women in particular--in terms of equal opportunity, quality of life, and psychological health--the support, conduct, and publication of sex biased research are unethical. Stark-Adamec and Kimball (1984: 24) go on to state,

> Sexist research includes not only the misrepresentation of sex differences in existing research but also the exclusion of women in issues relevant to women's psychology from the body of current psychological research. Therefore, in this paper two aspects of creating a non-sexist psychology are addressed. First, guidelines and suggestions are provided that will help to ensure that the work that is done in existing areas of psychology such as sex differences, will be free of sexist bias. Second, throughout the paper it is also emphasized that more work involving women and women's issues needs to be done so that psychology as a discipline, not just individual studies, can become non-sexist. Furthermore, although the focus of this paper is on non-sexist research, the principles and guidelines discussed apply equally well to any minority group in our society.

They proceed by defining sexist research "as based on the premise that men, and the behavior patterns characteristic of males, are superior to and more representative of the human experience than are women or behavior patterns characteristic of females" (1984: 24).

Stark-Adamec and Kimball chose to look at each stage of the research process, describing problems of bias that could be encountered at each stage. They consider the following stages: review of background literature, formulation of the research question, research design, sample selection, dependent variables, statistical analysis, reporting of results, and interpretation of findings. They present a checklist of specific questions that can be used to evaluate individual studies at each of these stages of the research process (see below).

Stark-Adamec and Kimball's approach to dealing with sex bias in research can be illustrated with reference to some issues related to sample selection in research. As previously noted, much psychological research has been carried out on samples of white, middle-class, male, university students. The problem of bias results when generalizations are made to other groups in society, including women, from these restricted samples. A similar sampling bias is illustrated when generalizations are made to women in general from data gathered on samples of female patients. For example, recent studies of menopausal patients have been generalized to menopausal women (Goodman 1980), and information gathered on women suffering from premenstrual syndrome has been generalized to all women (Dalton, oral communication).[3]

The appropriateness of the sample in the comparability of control or contrast groups is another important consideration. It is critical to consider what character traits are significantly related to a hypothesis. Age may be a very important factor in certain developmental studies but may not be relevant for comparisons of certain life-span activities where different age groups might appropriately be compared. For example, men may achieve peak-career orientation around age thirty, whereas women achieve this peak closer to age forty. So it could be appropriate to compare different ages of men and women regarding career orientation. Knowledge about differences in male and female life-span development is needed to in choosing appropriate control or contrast groups.

Furthermore, Stark-Adamec and Kimball (1984: 27) are concerned about the appropriateness of some uses of nonhuman species in the study of certain human behaviours. Questions about the applicability or accuracy of generalizations based on these nonhuman samplings to more complex, human behaviours need to be addressed.

The following is a checklist of questions, with particular reference to sampling, which researchers, authors, reviewers of research proposals, editors, and readers should raise to assess sex bias:

1. Is the species studied appropriate to the question being asked?

2. Are the samples large enough and representative enough (age, education, occupation, sex, gender, life-cycle stage, patient, nonpatient status etc.) that some generalizability will be possible? If the samples are restricted in size and representativeness, is there any indication of an awareness of the limitations thus imposed?

3. If both sexes are included, are the samples comparable on the relevant dimensions? Does the investigator evidence an awareness of the multiplicity of variables which would result in noncomparability of female and male samples?

4. If both sexes are not included:

   a) Do all references to the participants throughout the document (i.e., title, abstract, text) indicate that only one sex was studied? The reader should be clear at any point, from glancing at the title to reading the full article, that only one sex was sampled.

b) Does the Introduction or Method section include a justification or adequate rationale for having studied one sex only? (Stark-Adamec and Kimball 1984: 31)

Conclusions

This paper has described the growing awareness in psychology of sex and gender biases and the steps taken to reduce them. Although Stark-Adamec (personal communication)[4] reports a positive response to the CPA Guidelines from researchers, educators, and students, it is too soon to assess the impact of these guidelines and of other changes made within the discipline. However, two major efforts need to be continued or increased to maintain the current momentum.

First, steps need to be taken to monitor systematically sex and gender biases in scholarship and to evaluate the effectiveness of all the changes put in place to contribute to an equitable treatment of the sexes. Responsibility for this evaluation rests largely with the formal organizations that have initiated these measures. Each psychologist also shares this responsibility to monitor her or his own work for biases.

Secondly, research efforts need to continue vigourously to examine girls' and women's experiences, with theories of human development continuing to incorporate new research findings. Psychologists must increase communication on an interdisciplinary basis to acquire a comprehensive understanding of women's development. They also need to communicate with the public about what is being learned about women's experiences, and how, when their experiences are different from men's, they can be normal in their own right. The reduction and, hopefully, eventual elimination of sex and gender bias in psychological scholarship has significant consequences for education, provision of services, and development of policies.

Endnotes

1. I wish to thank Donald E. Larsen for his invaluable editorial assistance and Nancy Norman for her patient retyping during the development of this paper.

2. Pyke's survey was presented at the Symposium entitled, "Women and Psychology in the '80s," at the annual conference of the Psychological Association of Alberta, October 1984, in Calgary, Alberta.

3. Dalton presented her research in a paper "Violence in the Premenstrual Syndrome," delivered at the meeting of the International Society for Research on Aggression in Norton, MA, U.S.A. in August, 1981.

4. Stark-Adamec 1986, personal correspondence.

References

American Psychological Association (APA)
- 1975 Task Force on Sex Bias and Sex-Role Stereotyping in Psychotherapeutic Practice. American Psychologist 30: 1169-75.

- 1977 Guidelines for Non-Sexist Language in APA Journals: Publication Manual Change Sheet 2. American Psychologist 32: 487-94.

    Principles Concerning the Counselling and Therapy of Women, Counselling Psychologist 8: 21.

- 1981 Guidelines for Nonsexist Research. Division 35 Task Force Report, M.C. McHugh, R.D. Koeske, and I.H. Frieze Cochairs. Available from the American Psychological Association, 1200 Seventeenth St. N.W., Washington, D.C., U.S.A. 20036

- 1983 Publication Manual of the American Psychological Association. 3rd ed. Available from the American Psychological Association, 1200 Seventeenth St. N.W., Washington, D.C., U.S.A. 20036.

Astin, H.S.
- 1972 Employment and Career Status of Women Psychologists. American Psychologist 27: 371-81.

Bardwick, J.M.
- 1971 On the Psychology of Women. Springfield, IL: Charles C. Thomas.

Bem, S.L.
- 1974 The Measurement of Psychological Androgyny. Journal of Consulting and Clinical Psychology 42: 155-62.

Broverman, I.K.; Broverman, D.M.; Clarkson, F.E.; Rosenkrantz, P.S.; and Vogel, S.R.
- 1970 Sex Role Stereotypes and Clinical Judgments of Mental Health. Journal of Consulting and Clinical Psychology 34: 1-7.

Canadian Psychological Association
- 1980a Canadian Psychological Association Guidelines for Therapy and Counselling with Women. Ottawa: Canadian Psychological Association.

- 1980b Guidelines for Therapy and Counselling of Women. Canadian Psychologist 21: 185-86.

Deaux, K.
    1984   From Individual Differences to Social Categories: Analysis of a Decade's Research on Gender. American Psychologist 39: 105-16.

Eichler, M., and Lapointe, J.
    1985   On the Treatment of the Sexes in Research. Ottawa: Social Sciences and Humanities Research Council of Canada.

Erikson, E.H.
    1950   Childhood and Society. New York: Norton.

    1964   Inner and Outer Space: Relections on Womanhood. Daedalus 93: 582-606.

Freud, S.
    1950   Some Psychological Consequences of the Anatomical Distinction between the Sexes. Pp. 241-60 in Collected Papers, vol. 19, ed. James Strachey. London: Hogarth.

Frieze, I.H.; Parsons, J.E.; Johnson, P.; Ruble, D.N.; and Zellman, G.
    1978   Women and Sex Roles: A Social Psychological Perspective. New York: Norton.

Gilligan, C.
    1979   Women's Place in Man's Life Cycle. Harvard Educational Review 49: 431-46.

    1982   In a Different Voice: Psychological Theory and Women's Development. Cambridge, MA: Harvard University.

Goodman, M.
    1980   Towards a Biology of Menopause. Signs 5: 739-53.

Grady, K.E.
    1981   Sex Bias in Research Design. Psychology of Women Quarterly 5: 628-36.

Greenglass, E.
    1973   Women: A New Psychological View. Ontario Psychologist 5: 7-15.

    1973b   The Psychology of Women: Or the High Cost of Achievement. Pp. 108-18 in Women in Canada, ed. M. Stephenson. Toronto: New Press.

Horner, M.S.
    1972   Toward an Understanding of Achievement-Related Conflicts in Women. Journal of Social Issues 28: 157-75.

Kalin, R., and Grant, B.A.
    1981   Sex Differences in Employment Experiences of 1976 Canadian Graduates in Psychology. Canadian Psychology 22: 238-46.

Kaplan, A.G., and Surrey, J.L.
    1984   The Relational Self in Women: Developmental Theory and Public Policy. Pp. 79-94 in *Women and Mental Health Policy*, ed. L.E. Walker. Beverly Hills, CA: Sage.

Kohlberg, L.
    1969   Stage and Sequence: The Cognitive-Developmental Approach to Socialization. Pp. 347-480 in *Handbook of Socialization Theory and Research*, ed. D.A. Goslin. Chicago: Rand McNally.

Lott, B.
    1985   The Potential Enrichment of Social/Personality Psychology through Feminist Research and Vice Versa. *American Psychologist* 40: 155-64.

Malmo, C.
    1984   Sexism in Psychological Research. Pp. 116-32 in *Taking Sex into Account: The Policy Consequences of Sexist Research*, ed. J.M. Vickers. Ottawa: Carleton University.

Masson, J.
    1984   Freud and the Seduction Theory. *The Atlantic Monthly* February: 23-60.

Mednick, M.T.S.
    1978   Psychology of Women: Issues and Trends. *Annals of the New York Academy of Sciences* 309: 77-92.

Mednick, M.T.S., and Weissman, H.J.
    1975   The Psychology of Women: Selected Topics. *Annual Review of Psychology* 26: 1-18.

McClelland, D.C.; Atkinson, J.W.; Clark, R.A.; and Lowell, E.L.
    1953   *The Achievement Motive*. New York: Appleton-Century-Crofts.

Miller, J.B.
    1976   *Toward a Psychology of Women*. Boston: Beacon.

Parlee, M.B.
    1981   Appropriate Control Groups in Feminist Research. *Psychology of Women Quarterly* 5: 637-44.

Prescott, S.
    1978   Why Researchers Don't Study Women: The Response of 62 Researchers. *Sex Roles* 4: 899-905.

Pyke, S.W., and Stark-Adamec, C.
    1981   Canadian Feminism and Psychology: The First Decade. *Canadian Psychology* 22: 38-54.

Sherif, C.W.
    1979   Bias in Psychology. Pp. 93-133 in *The Prism of Sex: Essays in the Sociology of Knowledge*, ed. J.A. Sherman and E.T. Beck. Madison, WI: University of Wisconsin.

Sherman, J.A.
  1971 On the Psychology of Women. Springfield, IL: Charles C. Thomas.

Stark-Adamec, C.
  1981 Is There a Double Standard in Mental Health Research Funding as Well as a Double Standard in Mental Health? The Ontario Psychologist 13: 5-16.

Stark-Adamec, C., and Kimball, M.
  1984 Science Free of Sexism: A Psychologist's Guide to the Conduct of Non-Sexist Research. Canadian Psychology 25: 23-34.

Unger, R.K.
  1981 Sex as a Social Reality: Field and Laboratory Research. Psychology of Women Quarterly 5: 645-53.

Vaughter, R.H.
  1975 Review Essay: Psychology. Signs 2: 120-46.

Vickers, J.M. (ed.)
  1984 Taking Sex into Account: The Policy Consequences of Sexist Research. Ottawa: Carleton University.

Walker, L.E. (ed.)
  1984 Women and Mental Health Policy. Beverly Hills, CA: Sage.

Wallston, B.
  1981 What Are the Questions in Psychology of Women? Psychology of Women Quarterly 5: 597-617.

Wand, B. (ed.)
  1977 Report of the Task Force on the Status of Women in Canadian Psychology. Canadian Psychological Review 18.

Weisstein, N.
  1971 Psychology Constructs the Female, or the Fantasy Life of the Male Psychologist. Pp. 68-83 Roles Women Play: Readings toward Women's Liberation, ed. M.H. Garskof. Belmont, CA: Brooks/Cole.

Weyant, R.G.
  1979 The Relationship between Psychology and Women. International Journal of Women's Studies 2: 358-85.

REASSESSING INTERPRETIVE STRATEGIES IN LITERARY CRITICISM

Estelle Dansereau

Western literature, at least in the official form represented by European literature, is essentially man-made and dominated by masculine concerns. It is not surprising, then, that literary criticism has also been generated from an essentially androcentric perspective, a perspective which, when it does not exclude works by women, does reduce their value. Ellmann (1968: 158) observes that in the nineteenth century, when women began to publish in more significant numbers both as novelists and essayists, criticism came to view and represent masculine and feminine writing as parts of a dichotomy, each imbued with its own characteristics related to biologically and socially-determined roles. The dominance of the masculine mode was reinforced by its association with reason, knowledge, intellect, and creativity; in contrast, the subsidiary position of the feminine mode was confirmed by its association with intuition, sentiment, reproduction, and deviance. Anglo-American feminist critics, among them Ellmann (1968), Showalter (1971), Cornillon (1972), and Kolodny (1975), have documented and exposed countless instances of sex-linked interpretations of literary works based on negative notions of femininity. Women's writing has been dismissed as too feminine or sexless (Woolf 1972: 43-112); women have been denigrated for writing like men, for writing about women's experiences, or writing in a lower, that is, "unconsecrated" genre.[1] Particularly in those instances where women's writing has been trivialized by critics, where judgments are based on sexist preconceptions, feminist literary criticism has been and continues to be instrumental in calling for a reexamination of sexism.

Why have women been relegated to the periphery of literature by critics and history? Their absence and their silence have been determined by historical and social circumstances: the powerfully effective deterrents of lack of education, lack of leisure, and poverty kept and often still keep women from engaging in literary production.[2] In some instances, however, as in the cases of Colette and George Sand, financial exigency was an important factor in bringing them to challenge the myth of authorship as an exclusively male activity. But feminist critics have exposed much more subtle and powerful determinants that continue to operate to this day; these determinants are psychological, ideological, and aesthetic (Mora 1982: 9). How can women aspire to authorship when their society has conspired to convince them of the triviality of their experience and has promulgated myths about ridiculous, abnormal, neurotic women writers (Showalter 1971: 850)?[3] By being deprived of the means to create ideas and images, women came to represent the Other in literary activity and, correspondingly, the negative side of a whole series of readily accepted oppositions: man/woman, writing/reading, production/consumption, subject/object, active/passive. With the recognition of the legitimacy of feminine perspectives and experiences, women writers will be encouraged, through readings and criticism, to assume more control and influence over the processes of both production and consumption.

Critics especially have contributed towards silencing women by failing to recognize that they generally criticize with sex-biased literary standards. Literary misogyny, says Josephine Donovan (1975: 34), has almost become a literary convention, but feminist criticism is finally challenging its basis. If androcentric assumptions about literature are also at the centre of the discipline, then the entire Western literary tradition must be challenged (Donovan 1975: 74). Sexism has been imposed on literary production over the centuries by critics who contributed to defining literary value, literariness, and the conventions of writing. It has not yet been determined to what extent literary style, rhetoric, narrative patterns, and structure, for example, are related to ideology, but literary history illustrates that it was almost exclusively men writers who established the premises on which literary excellence rests. I am not dismissing the important contributions women novelists such as Mme de Lafayette (1958), Jane Austen (1813), and Charlotte Brontë (1847), to name only three, made to the development of the novel, nor am I ignoring that they did so to a large extent because they were excluded from the masculine writing community of their times. These rare cases notwithstanding, the literary traditions and conventions women have inherited are essentially man-made (Moi 1985: 8); hence the evaluation and establishment of the great works would seem to have been based on principles other than scholarly objectivity, that is, on principles which defined greatness according to a masculine orientation.

It has been suggested that the inaudibility and invisibility of women in the literary ranks is due to discrimination, not necessarily against women per se, but against literary genres preferred by women. The genres pertaining to what was considered private writing--diaries, letters, treatises by women, and novels[4]--were deemed fit only for private consumption by women readers. Estelle C. Jelinek (1980: 11-17) finds that even in the acceptance of autobiography a subtle bias was at work. Successful masculine autobiographies were goal-oriented, coherent, and concerned with the subject's professional life and his relationship with the times; in contrast, women's autobiographies tended to favor their domestic lives, often the limit of their experience. They also tended to be fragmentary and disconnected or, in other words, lacking in coherence--that so desirable unifying trait of all texts. A writer unable to conform to the literary and verbal forms established mainly by men risked being, and often was, dismissed as trivial, undisciplined, and inferior to the lofty task, literally, at hand. Western literary criticism has traditionally maintained that its criteria for selection apply universally to all texts and has thus ensured the central importance of masculine production and standards.[5] However, if no discourse, as we now commonly contend, is entirely free of ideology, then surely "all structures and techniques, including language itself, are impregnated with the values and thought-patterns of the community to which they belong" (Durham 1985: 85).

The factors which contribute to gender bias also ensure cultural and class dominance over the literary canon. In the discipline of comparative literature, the central object of study, the established literary canon, includes almost exclusively works in the mainstream written by upper- and middle-class European men.[6] When I was a graduate student braving the dreaded candidacy examinations, I proposed a list of readings entitled World Literature by women in order to counterbalance the imposed list of World Literature. The choices from which this latter list was to be derived failed to include even one woman writer, for it was meant to represent--and the pun is intended--the masterpieces of the Western literary tradition. There seemed to me to be some contradiction between the idea of being a certified comparatist and knowing little more than the names of

Sappho, Marie de France, Sor Juana Inés de la Cruz, Jane Austen, or Virginia Woolf. Symbolically, the year was 1975 (International Women's Year). This situation would seem to confirm Josephine Donovan's contention that the "dominant patriarchal attitudes and customs of our culture [have been] reified in the institutions of literature and literary criticism" (1975: 74). Having worked subsequently in what the discipline calls "marginal" literatures--in my case the literatures of the Americas--I can only observe that changes in the consecrated canon take place very slowly, much more slowly than in each of the national literatures. And yet, for women critics every reminder of exclusion is a productive act. For the time being, the "universal" literary criteria, derived through the centuries, have yielded an androcentric and Eurocentric body of works on which the entire discipline is based.

Masculine ideology is the "unmarked form" (Spender 1985: 20) which insidiously--because it fails to declare its biases--creates, selects, consecrates, and disseminates for broader readership the product of authorial activity.[7] In North American universities, although for the past fifteen years the majority of graduate students in the language and literature departments have been women, the majority of professors participating in critical activity and shaping the critics of the future have been men. However, some inroads have been made since American feminists, in particular, have been redefining the canon not only through their feminist criticism but also in their classrooms where they can begin to counteract a prevalent and pernicious gender-biased literary standard. Although the results of feminist criticism and post-structuralist literary theory are manifesting themselves in important journals like PMLA, Critical Inquiry, New Literary History, Diacritics, and Tel Quel, change is not yet obvious in comparative literature publications themselves. Women writers have not only been rendered invisible and inaudible, but criticism has been permitted to operate within a narrow framework which, while making claims to objectivity and impartiality, promotes and exalts the works of one sex over those of the other.

Paradoxically, the nature of literature and its raw material, namely language, would seem not only to permit but to require flexibility in criticism. Given that meaning is not made explicit in a literary text but that multiple possibilities are inscribed in it which render it subject to varied readings, critics consciously or unconsciously interpret the text from a gender bias which may seem perfectly justified to them. By seeing the act of reading in this way, we can understand how the critic as creator of meaning may also become the creator of myths about masculine and feminine nature, based covertly on cultural misconceptions. Thus, a myth deduced from the text, but not necessarily expressed in it, may be deliberately inscribed in a later text and so give truth to the lie.

There have been, in the past twenty years, countless studies of the stereotypes of women presented in literary works, images of women too often based on certain standards of femininity defined essentially by men according to women's biologically and socially determined roles.[8] Aside from the danger that this kind of representation may be used to impose certain standards of behaviour on all women, it presents particular problems for the woman critic who may be asked implicitly to read like a man, to suppress her anger at distortions and exaggerations embedded in a work she would otherwise admire (Showalter 1971; Cornillon 1972: 338). Kate Millett, for example, was lambasted by critics of both sexes (Jehlen 1981)[9] for admitting in Sexual Politics (1971: 12) that, in spite of Lawrence's sexist portrayal of women, she still found much to admire in his novels. Literary critics generally do not use texts as mirrors which reflect society, but feminist critics recognize that gender can be inscribed in texts; thus, when women's experience is brought to a reading, different values and criteria may yield different readings. For example, from a woman reader's perspective, if a heroine is presented as an obstacle to a hero's freedom--an obstacle to a resolution of his dilemma--the woman reader may well attach different values and characteristics to these two figures and to the work as a whole. The consequences could be interesting if we were to examine the portrayal of heroism. While being presented as a universal quality to be admired and cultivated, heroism in texts is too often limited to the male protagonist's experience while belittling women (Coquillat 1982: 23-34; Lipking 1983a: 79).[10] Gender bias, while conspiring to trivialize women's experience and women's texts, may also account for the fact that certain aspects of men's texts are not sufficiently explored. Simone de Beauvoir (1949) brought a new perspective to the works of Montherlant, Lawrence, Claudel, Breton, and Stendhal while she confronted the problem of women as consumers of literature produced by men.

Anglo-American feminist critics have channeled some of their efforts into unearthing lost or ignored texts by women. Through this historically important research activity, several reasons for the suppression of women's writing are coming to the fore: women wrote in minor genres (e.g., Mme de Sévigné's letters [1927]); they wrote novels; and they included "insignificant" subjects in their works (e.g., nurturing activity, sentiment, self-actualization). By labelling one gender's experiences and texts more valuable, of more consequence than the other's, primarily male critics promulgated a double standard. The arbitrariness of this standard is revealed in some well-documented cases where a work originally thought to have been written by a man was later known to have been authored by a woman. Upon learning the feminine identity of the author of Wuthering Heights, critics of the period preferred to concentrate on the many and myriad details of Emily Brontë's life, whereas the novel's "masculine" author previously had been chastised for the crude and shocking language and emotions depicted. Little wonder then that Mary Ann Evans subsumed her feminine identity under a masculine one, George Eliot, and thus counteracted efforts to silence her (Showalter 1972: 456-8). The double standard may also have been the origin of the cruel and biting observations made by critics of Claire Martin's autobiography, Dans un gant de fer (1965), in which she portrayed a husband who beat his wife and terrorized his children mercilessly.

As long as women stayed silent, they would remain outside the historical process; but as they began to use their feminine voice, they became the Other. At the centre of traditional humanism, suggests Carolyn Durham, rises the image of the masculine self which "...from Descartes, Hegel and Lacan, focuses on individuation through opposition to and domination of an other" (1985: 87). The dualistic world view, embedded in the very foundation of intellectual thought, reflects patriarchal ideology, relegates women to the periphery, and grants men the guardianship of language conventions and aesthetic values.[11] It becomes thus a matter of course to dismiss women's writing for not observing or using the accepted rules of discourse, imagery, and structure. Unfortunately, both men and women critics who have been trained in a critical practice based on inherently sexist preoccupations may be ill-equipped to read without bias works by women and to identify their unique organizing patterns (Durham 1985: 83). A case in point is the criticism generated by Eudora Welty's The Golden Apples (1947) which insisted on the femininity of the work but was blind to the "covert ideology of gender."

Patricia Yaeger cites this example to illustrate critics' perceptions of feminine style: "The most startling quality of Eudora Welty's art is her style: shimmering, hovering, elusive, fanciful, fastening on little things" (1984: 971).

Starting with the acknowledgment that gender inevitably "informs and complicates both the writing and reading of texts" (Abel 1982: 1), feminist enquiry has devised several critical methods which are leading to the reduction of gender bias in literary research. As a woman and a critic, I am encouraged by the quality and quantity of studies of all kinds which disclose not only the presence but also the importance of gender in literature. Although the generation of such an abundance of material stems from a feminist perspective, this in no way implies uniformity of approach or method,[12] or even consensus on how literary texts signify.

Pioneering feminist critics (e.g., Millett 1971; Cornillon 1972; Appignanesi 1973) identified, through close textual readings and critiques of biased studies, patterns of the stereotyping of women in works written mainly by men. This kind of criticism continues to be valuable in unearthing and exposing a tradition of literary misogyny, and in explaining women's marginal place in literature on the basis of social rather than biological determinants. Concurrent with this activity, there continues to be a need for the identification of positive images of women[13] and for the rediscovery and reexamination of texts written by women in order to bring about their full enfranchisement. Once the strategy of silencing women is exposed,[14] the figure of the writer can become not exclusively masculine nor androgenous, but gender specific. Criticism has much to contribute to the study of the distinctiveness and dynamics of women's writing and of women as participants in a literary community. The results of such research will not only significantly modify the accepted canon but profoundly question the legitimacy of such a closed canon of literature.

Now that the contributions of women writers are in the process of being recovered, some formulations of feminine literary history can begin, based on the results of those individual enquiries. Eventually literary critics will be equipped to examine particular historical periods which produced works by women and eras which did not. Such comparisons may reveal where the biases are in literary conventions. Why, for example, does Symbolism (<u>Modernismo</u> in Latin America) include so few women writers? The critic must ask if it is because, as Cora Kaplan claims: "the language most emphatically denied to women is the most concentrated form of symbolic language--poetry,"[15] or because that movement's idealization of transcendence and syntactic abstraction had little relevance to feminine preoccupations. The map I see traced for critics working on this issue is a highly complex one. The subject would require comparatists to examine the post-symbolist production of texts by women poets, many of them from the Americas (e.g., Anne Hébert 1942; Rina Lasnier 1972; Delmira Agustini 1962; Gabriela Mistral 1954; and others), in terms of the goals and aspirations of Symbolism.[16]

Future studies would also have to consider the possibility of self-censure, of the re-vision of masculine convention by women writers. This practice, as some critics have shown us, permits subversion within conformity (Yaeger 1984: 955-73). Where the role and place of women writers are rendered invisible or where authorial anonymity is desirable, there are myriad ways of manipulating language in order to camouflage a level of meaning, or to achieve self-effacement while inscribing one's identity in the text.[17] Perhaps because women's works were seen as based primarily on women's experience, only recently have critics begun to explore hidden levels, patterns or techniques designed to subvert patriarchal authority. Via the concepts and insights generated by Bakhtin (1981) and poststructuralism,[18] Patricia Yaeger uncovers the covert rhetorical and ideological strategies of Eudora Welty's The Golden Apples. Based on the perspective that language is open to intention and change, Yaeger extends this theory into the realm of gender (1984: 957). Sandra Gilbert and Susan Gubar (1973) reveal Jane Austen's use of multiple discourse. François Rigolot (in press) examines Louise Labé's deliberate misuse of grammatical constructions which had become a convention in Renaissance love-poetry (see also Yaeger 1984). These critics suggest a profitable avenue for research where "resisting readers,"[19] readers who reject a learned reading of a text, seek to go beyond the academic, interpretive strategies normally associated with the genre and the period. By questioning concepts and notions which belong to an androcentric criticism--these may be historical, rhetorical, archetypal, formalist, etc.--feminist critics are not only reappropriating lost, devalued, or misread worksm but are presenting these women writers as "powerful figures that elicit texts crafted to appropriate or mute their difference" (Abel 1982: 2). Rather than leading to silence, self-censure can be seen by critics as a covert and creative way to expose the oppressive circumstances of the text's production.

The sophisticated and extremely fruitful readings these kinds of approaches are generating inform us not about the limits feminist criticism has reached but rather about the unplumbed depths still to be explored. I do not want to suggest, however, that there are to be found in texts certain identifiable absolutes awaiting a "resisting reader." Feminist criticism has tended to ally itself with the latest literary theories or readings, especially post-structuralism, which offer the fluidity and openness necessary[20] not only to avoid gender bias but also to distance the critic from learned methods of reading. Language is considered fluid; meaning is constantly deferred, never stable. Furthermore,

> the power of the post-structuralist reading...lies in its relentless questioning of texts. In one respect it can afford to pursue its analysis much further than conventional methods can, since it does not consider itself obliged to offer a defense of value or coherence of the works it questions (Lipking 1983b: 26).

According to Robey, a New Critical approach, on the other hand, which treats the literary work independently of its author and its historical context, gives preference to form, universality, coherence, and meaning (1982: 65-83), all concepts derived from an androcentric criticism.[21] Moreover, post-structuralist or deconstructionist approaches[22] have, for the concern of gender bias, the advantage of disclosing the complicities and biases of their practice. Such freedom, a stretching of the boundaries, is necessary in order to define women's specificity in writing, since language--the medium of expression--is itself a product of culture and hence a conveyor of biases.[23]

French feminist critics are providing us with a model of subversive criticism whose concerns and strategies go beyond those described so far. Where Anglo-American feminist critics are generally revisionists seeking to recover women in literature as both subject and object, some French critics, informed by philosophical and psychoanalytic discourse (Marks and Courtivron 1980), opt for dialectical reasoning and reject the masculine/feminine opposition on which traditional feminist criticism operates (Moi 1985: 13). Their perspective has the added advantage of doing away with the concept of Other in favour of difference and pluralism, of rejecting totally the concept of the One, the universal of patriarchy. Whereas most critics still operate from the premise that men and women share the same linguistic code but not the same cultural codes, French feminist critics such as Garcia reject all possibility of sameness in either sphere and opt for subverting language through women's writing and readings: "Dans l'univers clos des signes, où la femme se trouve enfermée par tout un système de dénotations, elle se fraie un passage, une ouverture en trouvant son écriture d'une multitude de connotations" (1981: 8).[24] They thus produce a totally new feminine discourse.[25] It would seem to me that the feminist primary texts being produced today require a totally new kind of reading, which holds promise for the future of feminist criticism, but which does not help us to read texts linked historically to sexism.[26]

These are without doubt exciting developments in bringing forward resolutions for eradicating sexism from critical inquiry. As I have indicated in this paper, the task is a complex one because language itself is a conveyor of ideology and, inevitably, gender bias becomes contextualized through it. Critical practices which seek to undermine conventional literary structures and conventions, as well as discourse itself, allow the critic to expose the mechanisms by which traditional modes of thought have been transmitted. Even more significant and promising for the discipline as a whole is the rapprochement effected between feminist criticism, post-structuralism, and reader-oriented approaches. This rapprochement means that one of feminist criticism's central concerns, the role of gender in texts and criticism, is moving into the mainstream of critical discourse. Once feminist criticism is no longer perceived to function from separate ideology, the polarization of masculine and feminist works may disappear. If all critics recognize that no interpretive strategy is without bias, no discourse or text free of its cultural context, then we can begin to "develop critical modes in which the concepts that are products of male authority are inscribed within a larger textual system" (Culler 1982: 61).

Endnotes

1. Many feminist critics have dealt extensively with these questions, and the discrimination which occurred historically has been the basis for much literary reevaluation (Showalter 1972: 452-79; Donovan 1975; Gilbert and Gubar 1979; and Russ 1984).

2. It is not accidental that early feminists and writers argued that there was a correlation between society's perception of women as inferior and their lack of education (to name only three: Christine de Pisan [ca. 1405], Sor Juana Inés de la Cruz [1691], and Mary Wollstonecraft [1792]). Much has been made by feminist critics of Elizabeth Barrett Browning's privileged access to the best education and the luxury of time to pursue knowledge and writing (Moers 1977: 5-10).

3. In spite of the positive example she sets in her writings, and in her public and private lives, Gertrude Stein has rarely been portrayed as the confident, innovative myth-breaker she was (Jelinek 1980: 149-62). Cf. also Carolyn Burke's article, "Gertrude Stein, the Cone Sisters, and the Puzzle of Female Friendship" (1982: 221-42).

4. In the eighteenth and nineteenth centuries, women were considered to be the main consumers of novels and, therefore, the genre became associated with women (Moers 1977).

5. In _Profession 85_, the publication of the Modern Language Association of America which best reflects the most recent critical trends in North America, Jeffrey M. Peck foresees a shift in comparative literature to textuality, a change which will be better suited to the examination of gender-specific factors: "The revolution in literary theory has recaptured history and with it the reader: texts and their interpretations by specific readers are seen as conditioned by cultural, social, political economic and gender-specific factors" (1985: 51).

6. As long as Eurocentrism remains the main arbiter of literary excellence in the discipline, works by women or by any group considered to be marginal have little hope of achieving recognition in any significant way. Lawrence Lipking states the problem rather succinctly:
   > The boundaries of male-created, male-elaborated theories may be stretched to accommodate the challenges of women, but no amount of stretching will put women at the center....and no established literary theory has yet been devised that builds from the ground up on women's own experience of literature, on women's own ways of thinking (1983a: 63).

7. Hélène Cixous makes the important claim in "The Laugh of the Medusa" that women's writing has been "marked" writing:
   > ...until now, far more extensively and repressively than is ever suspected or admitted, writing has been run by a libidinal and cultural--hence political, typically masculine--

economy; that this is a locus where the repression of women has been perpetuated, over and over, more or less consciously, and in a manner that's frightening since it's often hidden or adorned with the mystifying charms of fiction; that this locus has grossly exaggerated all the signs of sexual opposition (and not sexual difference), where woman has never <u>her</u> turn to speak--this being all the more serious and unpardonable in that writing is precisely <u>the very possibility of change</u>, the space that can serve as a springboard for <u>subversive</u> thought, the precursory movement of a transformation of social and cultural structures (as cited by Marks 1980: 249).

8. Mary Ellmann's <u>Thinking About Women</u> (1968) is still among the best and most enjoyable to read. Toril Moi analyses Ellmann's book as a "deconstructive project" (1985: 31-41).

9. The broader issue is discussed by Toril Moi in her chapter, "Two Feminist Classics" (1985: 21-41).

10. Judith Little, in her article "Heroism in <u>To the Lighthouse</u>," shows how Mrs. Ramsey qualifies as "hero" in <u>Virginia Woolf</u>'s novel (see Cornillon 1972: 237-50).

11. Catherine Belsey outlines excellent critical and reading strategies to detect unstated but embedded ideological assumptions in texts (1980).

12. Feminist criticism incorporates such different approaches as formalist, archetypal, historical, generic, structuralist, Marxist, psychoanalytic, and post-structuralist.

13. I prefer not to discuss here, mainly because the stance seems to me counterproductive, the strategy of equating equality with similarity. Given women's history, this would not only distort the reality of their situation but would simply reinforce the belief that the feminine mode is deviant, and the masculine normative. Furthermore, such an activity would serve to undermine the achievement of women writers who cultivated their difference and channeled it into creative activity.

14. The case of Sor Juana Inés de la Cruz--the Mexican seventeenth-century baroque poet who, after publishing an important body of work, was silenced by the Roman Catholic Church--has been the subject of just such a study by Octavio Paz (1982).

15. Quoted from Dale Spender (1985: 192-3). Cf. Cora Kaplan (1976).

16. In the International Comparative Literature Association's monumental <u>mise à jour</u> of Symbolism, this issue is not addressed in any significant way (Balakian 1982).

17. Claudine Herrmann (1976) testifies eloquently and spiritedly to women's practice of subverting literary convention. In English, cf. Joan DeJean, "Lafayette's Ellipses: The Privileges of Anonymity" (1984).

18. Post-structuralism is based on the perspective that language is open to intention and change. Yaeger extends this theory to deal with questions of gender (1984: 957).

19. In his chapter, "Reading as a Woman," Jonathan Culler (1982) gives credit to Judith Fetterley (1978) for this term.

20. Herbert Lindenberger (1984) foresees the effect on literary history of the anti-authoritarian critical theories, especially the feminist critical perspective, and anticipates that these will divert the study of literature away from the traditional empirical and hierarchical bases from which much gender bias originates.

21. New Criticism's emphasis is on form over content; it insists on timelessness and universality, and it rejects all social referents (Donovan 1975: 10; Jefferson 1982).

22. These approaches are predicated on the elusive and ambiguous nature of language fundamental to Jacques Derrida's theory. Ann Jefferson explains it in this way: "A deconstructive reading tries to bring out the logic of the text's language as opposed to the logic of its author's claims. It will tease out the text's implied presuppositions and point out the (inevitable) contradictions in them" (Jefferson 1982: 110).

23. This point, the basis essentially of post-Saussurian theory, is made by Catherine Belsey in Critical Practice:
    ...Language is not transparent, not merely the medium in which autonomous individuals transmit messages to each other about an independently constituted world of things. On the contrary, it is language which offers the possibility of constructing a world of individuals and things, and of differentiating between them (1980: 4).

24. "In the closed universe of signs, within which women find themselves imprisoned by a whole system of denotations, they create an opening by making holes in their writing through the use of a multitude of connotations" (my translation).

25. See especially Julia Kristeva (1974) for ways in which women's writing subverts temporality, syntax, and structure.

26. Annette Kolodny has been attempting to identify a feminine style in texts, one which will show that
    what women have so far expressed in literature is what they have been able to express, as a result of the complex interplay between innate biological determinants, personal and individual talents and opportunities, and the larger effects of socialization which, in some cases, may govern the limits of expression or even of perception and experience itself (1975: 76).

References

A. Primary Texts

Agustini, Delmira
 1962 Poesias completas, ed. Alberto Zum Felde. Buenos Aries: Losada.

Colette, [Sidonie Gabrielle]
 1966 Earthly Paradise: Colette's Autobiography Drawn from the Writings of Her Lifetime, tr. Herma Briffault, Derek Coltman et al., and ed. Robert Phelps. New York: Farrar, Strauss, and Giroux.

 1984 Oeuvres, ed. Claude Pichois. 4 vols. Paris: Gallimard.

Cruz, Juana Inés de la
 1976 Respuesta de la poetisa a la muy ilustre Sor Filotea de la Cruz. Pp. 769-808 in Obras selectas, ed. Georgina Sabát de Rivers. Barcelona: Noguer.

Eliot, George (Evans, Mary Ann)
 1872 Middlemarch.

Hébert, Anne
 1942 Les songes en équilibre. Montréal: L'Arbre.

Lafayette, Madame de (Pioche de la Vergne, Marie-Madeleine)
 1958 La Princesse de Clèves. Paris: Gallimard.

Lasnier, Rina
 1972 Poèmes I and II. Montréal: Fidès.

Martin, Claire
 1965 Dans un gant de fer. Montréal: Cercle du Livre de France.

Mistral, Gabriela (Godoy Alcayaga, Lucila)
 1954 Desolación. Vol. 2. Chile: del Pacifico.

 1971 Selected Poems of Gabriela Mistral, tr. and ed. Doris Dana. Baltimore: Johns Hopkins.

Pisan, Christine de
 1982 The Book of the City of the Ladies, tr. Earl Jeffrey Richards. New York: Persea.

Sand, George (Dupin, Aurore)
 1970 Oeuvres autobiographiques, ed. Georges Lubin. Paris: Gallimard.

Sévigné, Madame de (Rabutin-Chantal, Marie de)
 1927 The Letters of Madame de Sévigné, ed. Françoise-Mallet-Joris. Paris: Le Club des Classiques.

Stein, Gertrude
　　1923　The Autobiography of Alice B. Toklas.

Welty, Eudora
　　1947　The Golden Apples. New York: Harcourt.

Wollstonecraft, Mary
　　1974　A Vindication of the Rights of Women, ed. Carol H. Poston. New York: Norton.

Woolf, Virginia
　　1969　To the Lighthouse. Harmondsworth, UK: Penguin.

B. Criticism

Abel, Elizabeth (ed.)
　　1982　Writing and Sexual Difference. Chicago: University of Chicago.

Appignanesi, Lisa
　　1973　Femininity and the Creative Imagination: A Study of Henry James, Robert Musil, and Marcel Proust. London: Vision.

Bakhtin, M.M.
　　1981　The Dialogic Imagination: Four Essays, tr. Caryl Emerson and Michael Holquist, and ed. Michael Holquist. Austin, TX: University of Texas.

Balakian, Anna (ed.)
　　1982　The Symbolist Movement in the Literatures of European Languages. Budapest: Académiai/Kiadó.

Beauvoir, Simone de
　　1949　Le deuxième sexe. Paris: Gallimard.

Belsey, Catherine
　　1980　Critical Practice. London and New York: Methuen.

Burke, Carolyn
　　1982　Gertrude Stein, the Cone Sisters, and The Puzzle of Female Friendship. Pp. 221-42 in Writing and Sexual Difference, ed. E. Abel. Chicago: University of Chicago.

Cixous, Hélène; Gagnon, Madeleine; and Leclerc, Annie
　　1977　La venue à l'écriture. Paris: Union Générale d'Edition.

Coquillat, Michelle
　　1982　La poétique du mâle. Paris: Gallimard.

Cornillon, Susan Koppelman (ed.)
　　1972　Images of Women in Fiction: Feminist Perspectives. Bowling Green, OH: Bowling Green University Popular.

Culler, Jonathan
　　1982　On Deconstruction: Theory and Criticism after Structuralism. Ithaca, NY: Cornell University.

DeJean, Joan
　　1984　Lafayette's Ellipses: The Privileges of Anonymity. PMLA 99: 884-902.

Donovan, Josephine (ed.)
　　1975　Feminist Literary Criticism: Explorations in Theory. Lexington, KY: University of Kentucky.

Durham, Carolyn A.
　　1985　Feminism and Formalism: Dialectical Structures in Marie Cardinal's Une vie pour deux. Tulsa Studies in Women's Literature 4: 83-99.

Ellmann, Mary
　　1968　Thinking about Women. New York: Harcourt Brace Jovanovich.

Fetterley, Judith
　　1978　The Resisting Reader: A Feminist Approach to American Fiction. Bloomington, IN: Indiana University.

Garcia, Irma
　　1981　Promenade femmilière: recherche sur l'écriture féminine. Paris: des femmes.

Gilbert, Sandra M., and Gubar, Susan
　　1979　The Madwoman in the Attic: The Woman Writer and the Nineteenth-Century Literary Imagination. New Haven, CN: Yale University.

Herrmann, Claudine
　　1976　Les voleuses de langue. Paris: des femmes.

Jefferson, Ann
　　1982　Structuralism and Post-structuralism. Pp. 84-112 in Modern Literary Theory: A Comparative Introduction, ed. A. Jefferson and D. Robey. London: Batsford Academic and Educational.

Jehlen, Myra
　　1981　Archimedes and the Paradox of Feminist Criticism. Signs 6: 575-601.

Jelinek, Estelle C. (ed.)
　　1980　Women's Autobiography: Essays in Criticism. Bloomington, IN: Indiana University.

Kaplan, Cora
　　1976　Language and Gender. Pp. 21-37 in Papers on Patriarchy. London: Women's Publishing Collective.

Kolodny, Annette
　　1975　Some Notes on Defining a "Feminist Literary Criticism." Critical Inquiry 2: 75-92.

Kristeva, Julia
　　1974　La révolution du language poétique. Paris: Seuil.

Lindenberger, Herbert
 1984 Toward a New History in Literary Study. Pp. 16-23 in *Profession 84*. New York: Modern Language Association of America.

Lipking, Lawrence
 1983a Aristotle's Sister: A Poetics of Abandonment. *Critical Inquiry*: 10: 61-81.

 1983b The Practice of Theory. Pp. 21-28 in *Profession 83*. New York: Modern Language Association of America.

Marks, Elaine, and Courtivron, Isabelle de (eds.)
 1980 *New French Feminisms: An Anthology*. Amherst, MA: University of Massachusetts.

McCallum, Pamela
 1985 New Feminist Readings: Women as *Ecriture* or Women as Other. *Canadian Journal of Political and Social Theory* 9: 127-32.

Millett, Kate
 1971 *Sexual Politics*. New York: Avon.

Moers, Ellen
 1977 *Literary Women*. Garden City, NY: Anchor/Doubleday.

Moi, Toril
 1985 *Sexual/Textual Politics: Feminist Literary Theory*. London and New York: Methuen.

Mora, Gabriela, and Van Hooft, Karen S. (eds.)
 1982 *Theory and Practice of Feminist Literary Criticism*. Ypsilanti, MI: Bilingual/Bilingüe.

Ohmann, Carol
 1971 Emily Brontë in the Hands of Male Critics. *College English* 32: 906-13.

Paz, Octavio
 1982 *Sor Juana Inés de la Cruz o la trampa de la fe*. Barcelona: Seix Barral.

Peck, Jeffrey M.
 1985 Advanced Literary Study as Cultural Study: A Redefinition of the Discipline. Pp. 49-54 in *Professions 85*. New York: Modern Language Association of America.

Rigolot, François
 In press Gender vs Sex Difference in Louise Labé's Grammar of Love. In *Rewriting the Renaissance: The Discourse of Sexual Difference in Early Modern Europe*, ed. Margaret Ferguson, Maureen Quilligan, and Nancy Vickers. Chicago: University of Chicago.

Robey, David
 1982 Anglo-American New Criticism. Pp. 65-83 in *Modern Literary Theory: A Comparative Introduction*, ed. A. Jefferson and D. Robey. London: Batsford Academic and Educational.

Russ, Joanna
   1984   How to Suppress Women's Writing. London: Women's Press.

Showalter, Elaine
   1971   Women and the Literary Curriculum. College English. 32: 791-805.

   1972   Women Writers and The Double Standard. Pp. 452-79 in Women in Sexist Society: Studies in Power and Powerlessness, ed. Vivian Gornick and Barbara K. Moran. New York: New American Library.

Spender, Dale
   1985   Man Made Language. 2nd ed. London: Routledge and Kegan Paul.

Woolf, Virginia
   1972   A Room of One's Own. Harmondsworth, UK: Penguin.

Yaeger, Patricia
   1984   "Because a Fire Was in My Head": Eudora Welty and the Dialogic Imagination. PMLA 99: 955-73.

WOMEN AND EDUCATION: ON BEING FEMALE IN MALE PLACES

Gisele Thibault

> Whether it be educational theory or practice which is analyzed it can generally be claimed that it is a product of male experience and remains firmly in male control. Patriarchy is the educational paradigm (Spender 1981a: 157).

I shall be as explicit as I dare in this chapter in supporting Dale Spender's observation that "patriarchy is the educational paradigm." The problem, as Spender herself notes (1981a: 157), is not in proving that education is fraught with gender bias, but rather in giving expository order to the precise locations of that bias. Education, unlike some other disciplines, is difficult to pinpoint exactly, leaving the writer of a review with a task of giving determinate shape to an almost amorphous mass.

One of the reasons for this difficulty is that education, as an autonomous academic discipline, encompasses an eclectic range of interests. Education, especially during the last last two decades, has become an umbrella discipline which covers a whole set of subfields and specialties. It amalgamates such diverse fields as educational psychology, history of education, educational policy and administration, art education (see the following chapter), etc. Consequently, education, as a discipline, stands in a uniquely precarious position among the branches of scholarship. Any attempt to chart the precise limits of its parameters is bound to be presumptuous.

Even a comprehensive account of the feminist challenge to education would require more space than is available here. As Florence Howe has suggested, "most of us live in two worlds: our discipline and Women's Studies" (1984: 176). For feminists, working in education has meant living in these two worlds: in the many, tangled branches of our discipline and in women's studies. Nonetheless, living in these two worlds has proven advantageous to feminists. For example, it has given feminists a broader, interdisciplinary perspective of education's theories and methodologies. The interdisciplinary nature of the discipline has, in turn, been compatible with a feminist philosophy that "rejects disciplinarity itself as a fragmentation of social experience, a male mode of analysis that cannot describe the whole of female--or human--existence" (Boxer 1982: 261). Feminists within education have argued, increasingly successfully, that the issue of women's subordination in educational scholarship transcends the boundaries of this field. The shared concern about the neglect or misrepresentation of gender links the work of feminists in the many different areas of education.

The structures of the discipline, however, militate against feminists' collective efforts to exchange ideas and theories. Between the wide range of subject areas, boundaries exist which prevent the practice of interdisciplinarity. Feminists often feel frustrated at working in the same discipline as their colleagues while being precluded from collaborating with them because they lack a means of communication across various fields As a result, feminist scholarship is frequently scattered in the numerous publications of the diverse subspecialties. Thus any review of feminist analyses of education must necessarily cross the boundaries of these several areas and cannot claim to present itself as the feminist critique.

With these caveats in mind, I shall address the issue of gender bias in educational research by focusing on three major topics below: subject matter; educational theory; and research methodology.

Gender Bias in Educational Subject Matter

The Omission of Women

Women have systematically been omitted in the subject matter, theory, and research of education. The male has been regarded as the prototype of humanity; the female--if considered at all--has been viewed only in relationship to him. The "male-as-prototype pattern" is particularly problematic in the way it has frequently excluded women altogether. For example, until recently the accepted fields of education (e.g., sociology of education, history of education, schooling and learning theory) have been defined from a perspective in which the male is the norm, whereas women have been defined empirically and have been theoretically omitted or misrepresented (e.g., Arnot 1981; Clarricoates 1978; Spender 1981a). The problem is not only that women have been relatively ignored, but that gender has not been adequately addressed as a social fact. As in other disciplines, feminists in education (e.g., Roberts 1976; O'Brien 1984) argue that before we can abolish gender as an oppressive "cultural reality," education must be forced to take it into account and analyse it as an aspect of the social domain. Roberts (1976) and Spender (1980; 1981a; 1982) claim that the omission of women manifests distortions in empirical data which lead to nonrepresentative theories. Some of these distortions are particularly clear in educational subject matter.

The Absence of Women in Educational Subject Matter

When we look closely at the "themes of relevance" in education, it becomes apparent just how ubiquitous the problem of women's absence is. For instance, Acker's survey of British sociology of education (as cited by Spender) indicated that the study of women has been minimal: "While 58% of the articles purported to be studying both sexes, 37% had all male samples and only 5% all female samples" (Spender 1981a: 161). Other feminist researchers have demonstrated that traditional educational research has focused almost exclusively on male activities (e.g., Arnot 1981; Astin and Bayer 1973; David 1978; Deem 1980; 1981; Eichler 1977; Gaskell 1977; 1981; Janeway 1971; O'Brien 1984).

Feminists in educational psychology, like their counterparts in sociology of education, have shown that a male perspective prevails. Topics such as personality, motivation, anxiety, interpersonal interaction, learning theory, social roles, intelligence, and achievement have been conceptualized in male forms and, consequently, have had little relevance to women's experiences (e.g., Malmo 1983; Frazier and Sadker 1973; Vaughter 1976).

In the history of education, feminists have also demonstrated how traditional accounts of the historical development of educational systems have continued to overlook women (Prentice and Houston 1975; Pierson and Prentice 1982). The persistent preoccupation with males' relation to those systems is contiguous with the history of education. In their article, Pierson and Prentice suggest, however, that "it is the feminist perspective that has exposed the preoccupation with men in, and the general absence of women from, most official, published and academically respectable history" (1982: 109).

Studies of contemporary schooling that deal with questions of policy, processes, teacher/student interaction, and curriculum design are conspicuously devoid of any mention of gender (Clarricoates 1978; Deem 1980). Serious gaps can also be found in research on teacher training, the teaching profession, higher education, sports and science education, educational policy and administration, as well as the school/labour force connection (see, for example, Brodribb 1983; Ayim 1983; Shack 1975; Ferguson 1982; Thibault and Laidlaw 1984; Thibault in press; MacDonald 1980; Bunch and Pollack 1983; Perun 1982; Diller and Houston, oral communication;[1] Clarricoates 1978; and Lefebvre in this volume).

Women are also absent in the subject matter of each of these areas of education: sociology of education, educational psychology, history of education, and contemporary schooling. Characteristically, the research conducted in education's numerous subfields has been conservative, using "structural-functionalist" methodologies to support, rather than to question, existing educational ideologies. This has been the case until well into the 1960s, though much less so since then. Educational practices were seen in these studies as essentially performing necessary, benevolent functions in society. The studies were designed to discourage criticisms of schools. Generally, they were resistant to any work which cast a skeptical eye at educational systems. From this perspective, it is understandable why feminist ideas would be immediately dismissed, if not because of their feminism, at least because of their critical nature. And it is equally clear why feminist ideas would have a difficult time germinating in such a theoretical climate. The strict adherence to conservative frameworks, nevertheless, gave way in the 1960s to a predominance of iconoclastic research, most of which was carried out in sociology of education. The educational research of this period served as an academic chronicle of the social context. Within this context, a number of educationalists emerged with incisive criticisms of the educational enterprise (e.g., Friedenberg 1965; 1970; Holt 1964; Illich 1970). Many of these now classic writings heavily influenced the direction of subsequent educational research, particularly in the sociology of education. And many of these analyses were to lay the groundwork for later feminist challenges to education. But even the classic, critical works which were, and are, highly critical of educational systems and of mainstream educational research have paradoxically excluded any mention of gender.

Even humanists and civil libertarians have been preoccupied not with gender in education, but with order in the schools. In North American sociology of education, by way of illustration, critical scholars have contended that order is the most important characteristic schools share (e.g., Erikson 1963; Friedenberg 1970; Holt 1964; Illich 1970; Silberman 1970; Hickerson 1966). The means of socialization used by schools, they purported, are neither innocuous nor banal. Rather, as Silberman pointed out (1970: 62), schools discourage students from developing the capacity to learn by and for themselves (something John Holt favours [1964]). Schools are also structured in ways which make students dependent on teachers and other "authority personnel." At the same time, teachers have the use of the "hidden curriculum" (the process of transmission of implicit norms, values, and beliefs through the written curriculum's underlying structure) and the "overt curriculum" (the articulated, written agenda of schooling) to achieve their desired effect. In Friedenberg's elliptical, socio-psychological study of adolescent character (1970), he brilliantly attacks the school not only as "a sorting station for academic aptitude, but a moniter for conduct and personality as well" (Riesman 1970: 13).

The insights of Friedenberg and others (e.g., Illich 1970; Young 1971) were instrumental in exposing myths about the supposed social and political neutrality of schools. They were equally effective in displaying how educational knowledge is a "social invention, reflecting conscious or unconscious cultural choices that (accord) with the values and beliefs of dominant groups" (Whitty 1985: 8).

In later research, analyses of "cultural deprivation" and "the disadvantaged child" were seen in a radically changed light, as were issues of the educational status of language differences (Bernstein 1977; 1982). The issue of language is the focus of Basil Bernstein's work on cultural codes (1977) and of the work of Bourdieu and Passeron (1977), for example. Willinsky (1984) follows in this critical tradition, although he is exceptional in his inclusion of gender. With regard to language, the earlier critique of Silberman, Holt, and Friedenberg, for instance, also prompted the exposure of linguistic prejudice (Giroux 1983) and cultural imperialism (Apple 1982) in mainstream research and provoked a proliferation of differing viewpoints in the debate about the equality of educational opportunity. Finally, while theorists in the "new sociology of education" criticized the humanists for not going far enough in their critiques of the school, it is clear that the writings of the humanists/libertarians made an immeasurable impact on the direction and focus of sociological and psychological research in education, and they continue to affect the discipline as a whole.

From a feminist perspective, the humanists fell short of their intended explication of education. Their explications did not discuss the processes through which gender is ordered, controlled, and maintained in educational practice. Riesman (1970) uncovered a significant gender bias in Friedenberg's work (1970): The Vanishing Adolescent was consciously more concerned with boys' experience of alienation than with girls'. Friedenberg's work was the rule in sociology of education, not the exception. In all cases, issues of school practice, teacher/student interaction, differential treatments, and analyses of the "hidden curriculum" were conceptualized exclusively in terms of their impact on males. The means by which teacher/student interchange and differential treatments operate in relation to the sexes have been left to feminists to analyse. Similarly, the fact that the "hidden curriculum" actually intends and accomplishes very distinct things along gender-divided levels, has been made academically known primarily because of feminist efforts in this area (e.g., Clarricoates 1978; Blackstone 1976). Finally, the fact that the "overt curriculum" is blatantly ideological in its philosophical and practical execution of gender reproduction is now recognized because of feminists' insistence on including gender in educational research (e.g., Arnot 1981; MacDonald 1980; Gaskell 1983; Thibault and Laidlaw 1984).

Young (1971) effectively altered the course of the study of school curricula within sociology of education. Whereas previous humanistic analyses had emphasized the dehumanizing aspects of schooling and the alienation pupils experienced in educational institutions, Young and those who became part of the "new sociology of education" asserted that we must treat "what we know" as problematic. Further claims were made that education was class biased, socially constructed, and culturally controlled by dominant groups. Like the humanists, radical scholars in the "new sociology of education" (e.g., Apple 1983; Young 1971; Giroux 1983; Bernstein 1977; Bourdieu and Passeron 1977) deliberated over the role of social and political forces in the school curriculum. Also like the humanists, they described the curriculum as an ideological practice (which was, in fact, the centre of their studies) and made no mention of gender in their research. Certainly as Spender (1980; 1981a; 1982) and others have repeatedly made clear, curricular knowledge is a social and cultural artifact. However, feminist perspectives have altered how one views such knowledge. Feminism also points to new directions in the teaching of knowledge. Nonetheless, Spender (1982: 3) is ultimately pessimistic: "If sexism were to be removed from the curriculum there would be virtually nothing left to teach because our society knows so little that isn't sexist." The reason for this, Spender continues, is that "the interests of men are pursued; knowledge is produced about men's interests and fed into the whole society, while the questions that may interest women too frequently 'evaporate' when men are in control." From this standpoint, it is apparent that both the radical sociologists and the humanists' critiques of education are consistent with and shaped by their male interests. These shortcomings aside, their critiques themselves are part of the same process that legitimates and conceals ideological dimensions of educational research. It also seems clear (and ironic) that male critical theorists could use their own theories to illuminate their own roles in perpetuating a particular kind of knowledge that speaks to humanity through the lens of a male perspective.

Once education's topics were demonstrated to be male defined, feminists challenged what they saw as untenable in those topics by doing research that made women the centre of focus. In the early stages of this scholarship, adding women to traditional paradigms was seen as a necessary corrective to the problem and a point of entry to the discipline. Ironically, the difficulties feminists faced in using the "add women and stir method"[2] made it possible for feminists to assert that the underlying frameworks to which women have been attached are, in themselves, problematic. This "add women and stir method" also allowed feminists to see the depth of the antagonism between women's experience and the way that experience is presupposed in research models. Feminists found that the antagonism exists more deeply at the level of educational theory and method--not only with respect to the choice of paradigms and concepts, but more fundamentally at the level of ideology.[3] This discovery in turn led feminists to recast gender bias as something larger than those instances where women are simply not seen in subject matter.

The role of educational research in perpetuating ideological constructs of gender is less visible, and therefore harder to display concretely, than its role in sustaining women's invisibility. In the next section some general considerations are given to the ideological function of educational research in constructing and maintaining cultural models of femininity.

Gender Bias in Educational Theory

The Privatization of Women

The ideological model of femininity can be depicted with unusual precision and confidence. Throughout history, women have been defined by their association with the domestic sphere: as wives, mothers, housekeepers (Oakley 1972; 1974; 1977; 1981; Laurin-Frenette 1982). These roles have been constructed according to cultural definitions of femininity which change in form depending on the historical context. The ideology which underpins these definitions has consistently prescribed to women a "whole range of physical and psychological qualities, skills and dispositions which are associated with the performance of tasks and the exercise of women's domestic functions, taking into account the relationships of exploitation and domination they involve" (Laurin-Frenette 1982: 27). This ideology of femininity is juxtaposed to the modern division between the private and public spheres, therein "circumscribing women into the domestic realm, or, insofar as they are drawn into the public domain, relegating them to menial and low-status positions" (Pierson and Prentice 1982: 106).

The major institutions of our society have overwhelmingly supported this circumscription of women's activities. Educational research has participated in this circumscription in both practices and theory. Theorists' concentration on "public," "formal," and "authoritative" educational practices and structures, on the one hand, and their relative inattention to the "private," "informal," and "nonauthoritative" educational structures, on the other, have reinforced this ideology of femininity. The concentration on what is ideologically considered the "male realm," has not only led educational research to exclude women (as we saw in the preceding section), but also reinforced ideological constructs of femininity (and necessarily the private/public dichotomy) even when it has included women.

An examination of educational literature (see below) reveals that educational research has relied on traditional categories for analysing social life, including such classical distinctions as those erected between public and private life, as well as political and personal experience. Since this research has formed an information circle with educational practice, the privatization of women--or their relegation to the private sphere--has influenced for the ways in which women are treated in educational institutions.

Women's privatization in educational practice can be clearly seen throughout the history of nineteenth-century North America. The extension of higher education to women was a double-sided concession on the part of reformers and educators. On the one hand, it expressed a genuine need to provide necessary changes in the society. On the other hand, it manifested the desire by institutions to manage and control the social order, effectively including women's "proper sphere." Many opponents of education for women argued that women "were biologically inferior to men--they were weak, frail, incapable of strenuous mental and physical exertion" (Gordon et al. 1971: 36). It was thought that too much study--like employment outside of the domestic sphere--would fatigue women (because they had smaller brains; see Lefebvre in the present volume) and ruin their reproductive organs (Rosenberg 1982: Gordon et al. 1971; Fee 1976; Gillett 1981). The paradox of such a notion is evident in the manner that working class women were seen: "Women who worked as domestics, factory workers and farm hands were often accused of immoral behavior, thought to be a result of their working conditions and environment causing a disordered biology" (Kealey 1974: 8). Advocates of women's education argued that because women were "better" and "more pure" than men, education itself would improve whenever "good" and "ladylike" women were allowed to participate (Prentice 1977). Thus sexist stereotypes were used as the basis for arguments both in favor of and against higher education for women. Once women were admitted to some institutions, academic provisions for them consisted of curricula designed from the Victorian ideal of segregated respectability (Light and Prentice 1980: 204).

The debate about women's higher education in Canada also raged on in the nineteenth century. An article written in The Educational Review in 1887, entitled "Educational Advantages for Girls in the Maritime Provinces," extolled the impressive and progressive record of a Maritime university:

> Dalhousie College, in Halifax, has for five years admitted ladies on exactly the same footing as male students, and of the five ladies who have been graduated there every one came off with honours, three winning the degree of B.A., one that of B.Sc., and one that of B.L. But besides that there have been one hundred ladies who have taken special

courses not leading to degrees (as cited by Prentice and Houston 1975: 259).

Even though women were admitted into Canadian universities later than they were in the United States, the Canadian concession to women was no less double-edged or free of ideology. In a Canadian document from 1867 (again reproduced in Prentice and Houston 1975), the tendency of increasing numbers of universities in the United States towards coeducation was greeted with mixed feelings:

> We may content ourselves, however, for the present, with the Arts course. Happily, our young dominion is not yet ripe for throwing open the bench, and the Bar...to the gentler sex, however well our fair Portias might become the Doctor's gown, or even the Episcopal silks and lawn (Prentice and Houston 1975: 256).

Within the university context, the ideology implied by the word "domestic" was extended into the kinds of course curricula offered to women (e.g., domestic science, childhood education), who were relegated to so-called "feminine" fields. The definition of an "academic" as a male left women marginalized. This marginalization was accomplished, in part, by means of university entrance requirements to certain fields. Requirements were such that women could not possibly fulfill them with the types of preceding school preparation given to them. Because women generally did not have the appropriate prerequisites, they could not apply for university education in many fields (Rosenberg 1982).

The rise of professionalism also served to support the ideology of femininity. One of the most obvious examples of this phenomenon is the teaching profession, where historically women have comprised a substantial percentage of the teacher population. As Prentice (1977) points out, the incorporation of women into the teaching profession in the early to late nineteenth century in Canada, represented a seemingly altruistic, liberal-spirited, and benevolent reform on the part of educators. When scrutinized carefully, however, this seemingly progressive rationale for wanting women teachers was neither free of ideology nor exorcised from patriarchal formulations about women's "true" nature. In the case of elementary school teaching, for instance, women's involvement was seen as an extension of, not a separation from, their domestic functions of wife, mother, nurse, babysitter, or nurturer. Women's roles in teaching were viewed as natural extensions of their "biological capacity for maternal nurturance." Hence, it was rationalized that women were the natural choice of the sexes to work with very young children.

The ideology in this thinking is revealed poignantly when one considers contemporary education. The fact that women remain the majority of elementary school teachers (though this trend shifts as the economy fluctuates), but constitute a minority of university professors (even in education) indicates how the ideology continues to the present.

Another way in which the ideology works is evidenced by two levels of educational research. First, traditional, historical studies ignore the role of the private/public ideology in the evolution of education. Secondly, researchers in the other fields of education continue to use certain methodologies--ostensibly to examine both men and women-- from the male-as-norm perspective. Thus they have perpetuated the repressive categories of public and private associated with ideological notions of gender. For example, in educational psychology, Lawrence Kohlberg's developmental, moral-stage theory (1966), epitomized this kind of biased methodology, which employs categorizations that strengthen ideological definitions of "women" (see Gilligan 1982 and Larsen in this volume). Kohlberg adopted the sine qua non approach to educational theory in his categorization of people, behaviours, events, and in his employment of a bipolar notion of gender roles. Kohlberg also described "instrumental" and "expressive" roles as belonging to two, qualitatively separate "stages" (1966: 73). One role is represented in the public world of instrumental principles of morality, embodied in stage-four reasoning, into which males typically fall; the other role is manifested in the personal world of affect, emotion, and approval embodied in stage-three reasoning, into which females typically fall. Kohlberg viewed gender as involving polarized clusters of attributes, masculine and feminine. He believed that what he described exists in the real world and, more important, that it is essential and desirable. At the heart of this, one finds the public/private dichotomy and, necessarily, an acceptance of the ideology of femininity. The bipolar model thus embodies the power divisions of sexist society. It is this model that feminists reject (see, for example, Gilligan 1982; Stanley and Wise 1983; and Silverman in this volume).

Kohlberg's model is redolent of the various stage theories one finds in educational research. These approaches formulate research along the line of sex differences and tend to conceptualize gender in dichotomous opposites--e.g., subject/object, nature/culture, male/female. Such research again takes as the norm the androcentric view of the world in which the experience of women is seen as the deviant, the Other, the exception. As feminists have stated, simply adding women to these models does not change the underpinning masculine biases which rely on ideological constructions of gender. Rather, what is needed are methods and theories that go beyond these traditional paradigms, methods, and theories, ones that offer strategies for change through the research process itself, as well as through the results. Feminist scholars are currently concerned with the very basis of gender bias in education: the male hegemony over educational theory. It is to this issue that we now turn.

Education Theory and Women

> The dependence of women on theories whose primary aim is other than the liberation of women has limited women's ability to seek an end to their own oppression. The time has come for a theory which is unique to women's experiences(Hughes 1982: 16).

The most fundamental and perhaps the most powerful criticism made of education is that it omits the experience of women in its conceptualization and therefore in its research (see Stanley and Wise 1983). The "ideology of gender" embedded within educational paradigms also leads to research that construes social reality in sexually dichotomous and patriarchal forms. In other words, woman has been defined as "not-a-man." Consequently, the androcentric perspective in education has rendered women not only unknown, but virtually unknowable. Feminists, since the 1970s (Mies 1983; Du Bois 1983; Stanley and Wise 1983), have emphasized that this has to do with both the substance of theories and the processes of research. In short, the androcentric perspective has determined what is worthy of study and what is not, how it is studied, and how it is known.

A perusal of some of the dominant theoretical frameworks in education indicates that women have not been seen as worthy of study. Weisstein (1971) asserted that psychology has little to tell us about women, because quite simply, psychology does not know. Analogously, education has had little to say about women because it, until very recently, did not know and did not care to know. I will go one step further, as Weisstein did (1971), and suggest that what education has known about women has been largely ideological.

We have not isolated the education of women as a subject of study, or, at least, we have no coherent theory about women in education. It is only through feminist scholarship that we are beginning to learn and understand women's relationship to the discipline and the practice. Through feminist scholarship we have learned that theoretical paradigms in education have marginalized women: either their presence is minimal, or they are totally absent (Arnot 1981; Howe 1984; Spender 1981a). Their exclusion in educational theories has been no less pernicious than their omission in subject matter. Even when women are studied, the modes of study have remained sexist, with the accompanying prescriptions, myths, and stereotypes about who and what women should be (Du Bois 1983). The male perspective, once again, is axiomatic and unquestioned. The point to be developed here is that "women have not been part of, and may even [contradict] predominant theoretical accounts of human life" (Keohane et al. 1982: vii). I will illustrate this point with reference to some of the more widely used theories in educational psychology and the sociology of education. In order to give the discussion some disciplinary coherence, I will rely on O'Brien's (1984) outline of educational theories. She argued that these theories can be classified under conservative, liberal, and socialist frameworks (1984: 7). Leaving aside the conservative model, brief examples of the theories which involve liberal and socialist ideals will be discussed. The conservative model has, fundamentally, been antithetical to feminism and has largely been ignored by feminists because of its covert misogyny. For this reason, it will not be dealt with here. Finally, it is _not_ my intention to comment on liberal or socialist philosophy, but to concentrate on the gender bias of these theories.

Liberal Theories of Education

Liberal theories in education derive especially from the liberal tradition of John Stuart Mill (see Jagger 1983). This tradition supposes that education has the greatest potential for social good in society. The liberal tradition, "first posited education as an active instrument for the development of human potential and the affirmation of individual freedom and political rights" (O'Brien 1984: 9). John Dewey captured the essence of traditional liberal theory when he wrote: "I believe that education is the fundamental method of social progress and reform" (1966: 45). This ideal of progress and reform through education forms one of the bedrock beliefs in our culture.

"Liberal states have propagated the notion of individual rights to free, universal education, while ensuring that curricula are attuned to liberal policies and 'acceptable' forms of knowledge" (O'Brien 1984: 9). However, universal, free education generally referred in the past to the rights of working- and middle-class males to acquire an education. Currently, equal opportunity to acquire an education has not precluded the development of gender-differentiated curricula, the ideological perpetuation of women's devalued status, and a gender-divided labor force (Spender 1982; MacDonald 1980). It is clear that free, universal education has been a positive and important development. Nonetheless, gender discrimination gained momentum throughout this evolution (Spender 1980; 1981b; 1982; 1983).

The famous debate over equal opportunity in education, which gained academic impetus and intellectual notoriety from the Coleman Report (Coleman et al. 1966), is a concrete expression of liberal thinking. The debate examined the issue of social class and racial discrimination in educational institutions. Prompted by political and economic imperatives, the Coleman report set out to discover why particular groups in the society performed poorly in schools. It hoped that the school could be elevated to its previous stature as an institution of "social progress" and "opportunity." Though the debate occupied a central place in the writings of educational theorists (Karabel and Halsey 1977), and in education's literature, it did not deal with gender and it was not seen to have any relevance to women. Subsequent research in the liberal tradition of "equality of opportunity" also turned a deaf ear to issues of gender bias. From this standpoint, it seems that the educational "equality of opportunity" debate had as its referrents only males of different social and racial backgrounds. This appearance led feminist researchers (e.g., Arnot 1981; Clarricoates 1978; Deem 1980; Gaskell 1981) to reject much of the theoretical and methodological underpinnings of the liberal tradition, even though strands of the model have proved useful in explaining particular aspects of women's relation to education. One such strand is manifested in psychological theories of education.

Liberal Psychology in Education

Liberal philosophy is central to theories of development and behaviour in educational psychology. Theories of learning, pedagogical practice, motivation, school hierarchy, cognitive growth, achievement, school performance, and I.Q. measurements assume that learning is an individual event, which takes place largely in isolation from the social structures of the society. These theories posit, furthermore, that learning can be quantitatively (i.e., "objectively") measured as a function of external stimulation of individual potential. Cognitive and Developmental-Stage Theories (e.g., Kohlberg 1966; Piaget 1968; Erikson 1963; and Freud 1959) see an individual as active in making choices and not simply internalizing stimuli from the environment. The limitations of these approaches, however, are visible in the methodologies on which such researchers rely in their analyses of the sex-differentiated experiences of boys and girls in schools. The methodological problems stem from the underlying liberal-based notion that socialization is essentially a positive process. More fundamentally still, their methods assume a bipolar model of gender roles which perpetuates ideological notions of femininity. Freud's analysis of sexuality suggests that the development of "normal" femininity results in an inferior morality in women because they lack a penis (1959). Kohlberg's theory (1966), in a parallel vein, places women at a lower level of moral reasoning than men because of women's "natural" propensity to be "expressive." Erikson (1963) carefully characterizes women as passive, dependent, and emotional; his gender-divided paradigm of psycho-social growth implies that these features are biological givens. In Piaget's analysis of cognitive growth (1968: 16), biological components of mental structures are environmentally determined. Piaget's arbitrary categories of intellectual development, however, depend on the independence of biology from environmental influences. Environment cannot shape what is not given to a child genetically. Nonetheless, in his scheme much of what girls are able to do (differently than boys) is biologically programmed. There is, then, an inevitable polarization of males and females in all of these models. Despite their insistence on the influence of the environment, these theories postulate a pre-formed and almost autonomous unfolding of the individual.

Wood (1977) critiqued these psychological theories as being one-sided, ethnocentric, and androcentric. Their focus on the individual, as opposed to the group, is grounded in the desire to predict and control individual behaviour. Wood emphasizes that the individual is not seen as actively changing the processes which impinge on him or her. These models of educational psychology are not concerned with the ways in which individuals understand their own experiences. Most important, these theoretical models put forward a normative view of society and its agents of socialization. As Wood argues, this normative view reinforces prevailing notions of masculinity and femininity.

Although the developmental and behaviourist paradigms have been identified as problematic, some feminists have seen in them possible explanations for gender bias in educational practice. By way of illustration, feminist psychologists who utilize behaviourist and social-learning theories have noted the processes which inculcate socially defined sex roles and the effect these processes have had on women (Weitzman 1975). In particular, a great deal of work has been done in school socialization. Embracing social learning theories, feminists have pointed out that the educational system has generally reinforced sex-role stereotypes (e.g., Federbush 1972; Sario, Nagy-Jacklin, and Tittle 1973; Weitzman and Rizzo 1974). One of the first messages that is communicated to girls is that they are less important than boys. Textbook stories are most often about male characters (Weitzman 1975). Furthermore, guidance counsellors and teachers reinforce conformity to the traditional female roles by encouraging girls to take home economics and discouraging them from taking "male" subjects such as algebra, physics, and industrial arts (Blackstone 1976; see also Lefebvre in this volume). Girls are also socialized to utilize verbal ability, whereas boys are socialized to strengthen ability in logic. The tracking system often ensures that girls are excluded from rigourous sports and athletic competition.

Other studies have shown that, despite the discouragement they receive, girls consistently perform better in school (in reading, mathematics, and speaking) until they reach high school (Weitzman 1975: 12). During the secondary school period, girls' analytic ability seems to be lower than boys. Maccoby (1966) attributed this apparently lower performance on the part of girls to the fact that the typical measures of intelligence and achievement are strongly male-biased. Sherman (1967) further argued that the way analytic ability is defined, from a male perspective, leads women to believe that they do not have such analytic ability, and, as a consequence, they do poorly. This is an instance of self-fulfilling prophecy, in which belief leads to evidence for the belief.

These studies helped to dispel certain beliefs about girls' abilities, but the research adopted behaviourist subscriptions to quantitative, statistical modes of inquiry. The use of these models resulted in the reduction of women's and girl's behaviours to readily classifiable, simple behaviours (in this case the reduction of female performance in schools to categorizations of "independent" or "dependent" variables). In general, the studies of Maccoby (1966), Sherman (1967), and Weitzman (1975), adhered strictly to the methods of behaviourism. As a result of these methods, these accounts attempted to abstract from female experience by quantitatively measuring and categorizing women's behaviour into already established, male-defined group averages. In the final analysis, as Wine (1982) says, the research poked holes in many widely accepted myths regarding sex differences. However, it did not "seriously question male-defined dimensions themselves....It seems implicitly to be guided by the goal of demonstrating that women and men are essentially the same" (1982: 77).

In a similar way, although along different lines, feminist psychologists in the early seventies argued against the "women are inferior" theme in traditional behavioural circles and brought attention to the socialization/learning element of gender roles. For example, Horner (1972) discovered the "motive to avoid success." Horner's research stressed that popular notions of women involved the belief that femininity and individual achievement (which reflects intellectual competence) are mutually exclusive and contradictory. Belief in the incompatibility of femininity and success provides women with a motive for avoiding success. Because women expect that achievement will be followed by negative consequences, fear of success is aroused and inhibits their performance. Horner's studies were included in Bardwick's larger anthology on the psychology of women (1972). Mednick and Tangri's work (1972) followed the theoretical trend of Horner and Bardwick's behaviourist orientation. Mednick and Tangri's article examined the literature on sex roles and stereotypes. They concluded that liberation for women would come about only by changing women's choice of roles and aspirations (1972: 68).

Another area of feminist research in educational psychology deals specifically with the interaction between sex-role stereotyping and the socialization/learning process. Here again, concepts of a social learning model, "attitudes" and "behaviour" are central. Chetwynd and Harnett (1978) claim that the educational system generally reinforces and transmits societal stereotypes of masculinity and femininity. Fenemma (1976) and Sarah (1980) examine the school as a socializer by focusing on (a) the teacher as a model of sex-appropriate behaviour; (b) curriculum materials, (c) teachers' sex-differentiated expectations, (d) teachers' sex-differentiated attitudes and treatment patterns, and (e) the need for a change in societal attitudes and role assignments. Frazier and Sadker (1973) further elaborated on the pervasiveness of socialization by both the school and the family. They argue that notions of femininity enforced in the home are paralleled and perpetuated by the school (through teachers, books, peer interaction etc.). All of these authors emphasize that the school is one of the principal institutions of socialization. Its role in reproducing gender roles cannot be underestimated. These authors also conclude that in order to understand this socialization role fully, there must be more analysis of school practices, curricular materials, attitudes, reinforcements (both positive and negative) as well as expectations that perpetuate sex roles and negative female self-evaluations.

Confining their conceptualization of sexism within the rigid parameters of behaviourism, feminists were able to point to the psychological oppression created by the ideology of femininity by schools. Their research offers explanations of the nature and extent of the unequal treatment of girls and women in comparison to boys and men in the educational system. As Vaughter contends, "analyses of theoretical models from a social...perspective indicate that we need to get women out...of the deep, dark motives of the 'Feminine psyche' and into the social contexts within which her behaviour takes place" (1976: 144). However, the constraints of the behaviourist approach leave little room for explaining why gender roles have taken the forms they have historically, and why they have infiltrated the schooling system so extensively. The focus on attitudes, expectations, and behaviours, moreover, locates the problem of gender bias with the individual, rather than with the individual as part of the social structure. They thus tend to blame the victim for sexism rather than to supply sociological causes. Insights into the ideological and institutional structures which perpetuate sexism are ignored, as are women's subjective experiences of the educational processes. These difficulties stem largely from the fact that behaviourism itself is problematic for feminists' understanding of women and of sexism. The focus on the individual is itself a male construct, as Gilligan (1982) incisively pointed out; this individualistic, mechanistic orientation leaves no room to talk about how women negotiate socialization processes in their own ways. The only way in which this and other deeply rooted biases will be purged is through "an assault on the nature of the scientific method as used by psychologists and through the re-definition of both theory and practice" (Walker 1981: 121).

Liberal Sociology of Education

Contradictions in liberal thinking are also revealed in sociology of education's structural-functionalist theories. Structural functionalism (in the spirit of Emile Durkheim, Talcott Parsons, and Auguste Comte) views the school's structure in terms of its function in the wider society. Structural functionalism also emphasizes the patterns of schoolroom interaction which develop normative behavioral orientations required by the larger society. The dictum that the social structure is greater than the individual accents the primary and unproblematic nature of schooling and reflects only a secondary concern with the student, who is seen as the passive recipient of the school's practices. This model has methodologically "taken the form of empirical, usually quantitative, studies of the role of education in reducing or maintaining structures of inequality that co-exist with increasingly widespread equalitarian ideologies" (Karabel and Halsey 1977: 16).

Feminists have shown that the structural-functionalist model operates as a male one which maintains the sexual status quo much more effectively than it preserves an individual's rights or freedoms (see especially O'Brien 1984: 9). The rights espoused in this position are clearly male rights. Stanley and Wise (1983) argue that the functional approach is characteristic of most statistical studies. In such fields as educational administration and policy, the structural-functionalist model predominates. The use of the model creates distortions in both theory and practice according to Arnot (1981) as well as Stanley and Wise (1983). Social stability--including a social order that is essentially sexist--is all important for the liberal theorist. People should internalize the rules and norms of their culture. Divisions between males and females are viewed as necessary for social order.

The conflict theory of Bowles and Gintis (1976) expresses another manifestation of structural-functionalism. The general problems in this theory of conflict are beautifully summarized by Sarup (1978: 173): "The rationale for their epistemology is positivism, their methodology...is empiricism, and their ontology...is determinism." Above and beyond these broad criticisms, feminists have pointed to the nonexistence of gender in this conflict theory (e.g., Arnot 1981; MacDonald 1980). Furthermore, the failure of Bowles and Gintis to examine intraschool processes, social interaction, and teacher/student experiences led many feminists to turn to the "new sociology of education" for help in understanding gender production in education because this new movement dealt more directly with questions of power, ideology, and control. As such, the "new sociology of education" also moved the pendulum away from liberal-based theories to the adoption of what O'Brien (1984: 11) calls "socialist frameworks."

Socialist Theory of Education

Michael Young (1971), now considered the founder of the "new sociology of education", delineated the need to conduct research on the content of both what is taught and what is learned, and the effects of the teacher/student interaction on the process of teaching and learning (Karabel and Halsey 1977; Whitty 1985). Above all, the "new sociology of education" examines curricula of "school knowledge." This new sociology also radically rejects empiricist methodologies; rather it employs ethnography, ethnomethodology, phenomenology, and symbolic interactionism (Douglas 1980). It is concerned with how individuals "construct the social world through interpretation and action" (Woods and Hammersley 1977: 11). These studies also shift the emphasis from how the social structure determines the person to how individuals' intersubjective experiences shape their worlds. An example of this is Willis' (1977) study of "how working class kids get working class jobs." The "lads" resist the hegemony of schools by the dominant social class. The message is that there are "complex and creative fields of resistance through which class...mediated practices often refuse, reject, and dismiss the central messages of the school" (Giroux 1983: 260). These types of analysis display the ways in which individuals experience their socialization. They also reveal that the theories of socialization according to behaviourism are too simplistic and overly deterministic.

The issue of school curriculum has been a major item on the agenda of the "new sociology of education's" research (see, for example, Apple 1979; Bernstein 1977; Bourdieu and Passeron 1977). In those works, connections are made between the content of schooling and the power relations outside the school in the forms of economic, legal, political, and military institutions. For example, Anyon (1980) explicates the school as a form of social and cultural reproduction and hence of social and ideological control. Bernstein (1977) similarly shows how the structures and processes which underlie the social structure are transmitted through the family, work, and education. These processes, he argues, are affected by class structures, polity, division of labor, and the dominant codes through which the social order is regulated. The theorists emphasize class because ultimately the studies of this "new sociology of education" are, above all, concerned with social-class hegemony, not with gender hegemony.

Feminists have made general remarks about gender bias in these grand theories--structural functionalism and the "new sociology of education." Feminists have illustrated that the individual in both approaches is male. Both theories also employ male definitions of the social structure. Feminists further argue that the parameters of both the liberal debate about equality of opportunity and the socialist theorists's radical critique have been male-defined. Women and their experiences have not been adequately represented (Arnot 1980; Smith 1977; 1980). In the final analysis, feminists in the subfields of education are united in the belief that both the liberal and socialist models and the theories which embody them are inadequate for understanding women.

Gender Bias in Educational Methodology

> In opposing women's oppression we have to resort to women's experience as yet unformulated and unformed; lacking means of expression; lacking symbolic forms, images, concepts, conceptual frameworks, methods of analysis; more straight-forwardly, lacking self-information and self-knowledge (Smith 1979: 144).

Thus far, it has been argued that women have not and cannot be seen in traditional, classic educational theory. The theories of education lack concepts by which the reality of women's lives can be named, described, and understood (see especially Daly 1978a; 1978b; 1984; Vickers 1982; Miles 1982; Benston 1982; Wine 1982; Finn 1982; Spender 1981a). The omission of women in theories is one facet of the overall bias in scholarship; the androcentric values embedded in educational methodologies is the other. In this section I will highlight some of the feminist criticisms that have been made of educational methods. Two points should be noted here: (1) much of what has been said concerning the problems of method in education overlaps with critiques about methodology in all academic knowledge; and (2) feminist criticisms of methodology have sometimes been aided by recent criticisms of method in the philosophy and the history of science. Feminists' challenges to particular methodologies, in other words, have in some cases, borrowed or built on the work of nonfeminist, male critics. Because this review is only concerned with those analyses which have explicitly discussed gender, I will confine myself to feminist examination, while acknowledging the contributions of those nonfeminists (see especially Kuhn 1970).

Feminists criticize educational methods primarily because they are often characterized by dualistic models of human nature and intercourse (Smith 1977; Pierson and Prentice 1982; Spender 1982). Fashioned after scientific methods, they reflect dichotomy, duality, linearity, and fixity (Vickers 1982: 41). Feminists reject these methods in education--as elsewhere--because they cast reality into rigid, opposed, and hierarchical categories.

The following charges summarize other aspects of the feminist critique of educational methodology: (1) the use of empiricist methods, like the ideology of "objectivity" which lies embedded in them, has been associated with masculinity itself (Roberts 1976); (2) knowledge in these empiricist approaches is presented as a fait accompli with little or no recognition of the part played by the person in the process of producing such knowledge (Spender 1981a); (3) the way in which empirical methods are valued, and concomitantly, the way "hard" data is considered superior to "soft" data parallel the way the society values the masculine over the feminine (Malmo 1983); (4) the use of empiricist methods strips the social context away from the individual (Vickers 1982); and (5) the most visible observation is that most scientists are male, and this predominance has led to a bias in the choice and definitions of problems with which educational theorists have concerned themselves (Spender 1982). These problems are of a general nature, as are the charges that biases exist in the actual design and interpretation of theory (Gilligan 1982; Wine 1982), in knowledge (Smith 1980; Spender 1981a), and in language or discourse (Spender 1980). In particular, the assumptions of "objectivity" and "rationality," which underlie the methodological enterprise in education, have been questioned and challenged (Malmo 1983; Smith 1975; Wine 1982).

In response to these concerns, feminists have attempted to recontextualize women's experiences and generally have rejected the separation of knower and known in their research. They have argued that objectivity and subjectivity are interrelated modes of knowing:

> As women, we inhabit our world with a double consciousness. We are in and of our society but in important ways also not "of" it. We see and think in terms of our culture; we have been trained in these terms, shaped to them; they have determined not only the ways in which we have been able to perceive and understand large events, but even the ways in which we have been able to perceive structure and understand our most intimate experiencing. Yet we have always another consciousness. We are aware...of the reality of our own perceptions and experience; we are aware that this reality has often been not only unnamed but unnameable; we understand that our invisibility and silence hold the germs of both madness and power, of both dissolution and creation (Du Bois 1983: 112).

Feminists generally agree that new methodologies must be found to study women. In fields such as the "new sociology of education," feminists have found ethnography, ethnomethodology, and phenomenology useful alternative methods to the more widely used statistical, quantitative methods. Recent work in this field has also yielded exciting approaches with the help of symbolic interactionism (Smith 1977).

In the history of education, alternative methods involve dialectical approaches to women's history that acknowledge both the strengths and constraints in women's roles. "Opposing the notion that women's history was one of undifferentiated oppression,...authors ask for deeper and more inclusive investigations of ordinary women's lives" (Cott and Pleck 1979: 15; emphasis mine). These feminist historians also dispute "the conventional division of history into eras or periods. All such demarcations are arbitrary, in the last analysis, since historical change is constantly taking place" (1979: 15). They deny traditional periods or eras because history has made man as its subject and measure, hence, "its periodization has little to do with changes in women's lives" (1979: 15). Within the history of education specifically, Pierson and Prentice (1982) believe that feminist methods should avoid studying "women worthies." "We must recognize the flawed nature of analyses which assign importance to women only insofar as they have contributed to or supplemented the work or achievements of men" (1982: 110). These scholars outline some of the information sources feminists use to get at the actual experience of women in the past. They explain that

> historians of women...recognize the necessity to go beyond the prescription of and debate over roles wherever possible, in order to examine women's actual behaviour and their lives through whatever sources are available. New approaches have been discovered: official statistics and their categories have been challenged, different questions have been asked and put to old sources and new sources have been found (1982: 111).

In educational psychology, feminists have largely abandoned the use of empiricist models. Rather, they have begun to examine women's experience in its social context and to listen to women's experiences as women experience them (Gilligan 1982).

Most feminists argue that new, alternative methods are necessary in all fields of education. In Malmo's work (1983), it means "going beyond the other"; in Smith's formulation (1979), it is "doing a Sociology for women"; in Robert's anthology (1982), it is "doing feminist research"; in Wine's opinion (1982), it is moving "toward a gynocentric psychology." Like the critique of theory which accompanies it, feminists' call for new methods currently stands at the very front of the feminist agenda in academe.

New Visions

> It is no longer a sight merely a photograph, or fresco scrawled upon the walls of time, at which we can look with merely an esthetic appreciation. For there we go ourselves and that makes a difference.... The questions we have to ask and answer...during this moment of transition...may well change the lives of all men and women for ever...(Woolf 1938: 28).

Virginia Woolf's words are as true today as they were in 1938. Without taking the uniqueness away from Woolf's experience of transition, it is clear that feminist scholarship has reached a critical juncture in its evolution. The "moment of transition," to which Woolf refers, is evidenced presently in the mammoth feminist literature. Generally speaking, this literature argues that education and the other disciplines, like society at large, is patriarchal. Feminists' voices repeat over and over that all of the disciplines reverberate a desire to explain, justify, and maintain the sexual status quo of human and institutional relationships. Because such a desire is violating to women, the epistemological and experimental distortions which result are unacceptable for feminist scholarship. It is here, at this crucial point of rejection, that feminists have reached the crossroads in their work. They have found that when they added women to the established theories and methods of education (as elsewhere), the ensuing explanations are incomplete, inadequate, deficient, and insufficient. Hence, feminists argue that the time has come to generate concepts, theories, and languages that are firmly and richly grounded in the actual experiencing of women (Boxer 1982; Oakley 1977; MacKinnon 1982; Stanley and Wise 1983; Keohane et al. 1982; Finn 1982; O'Brien 1984; Griffin 1982; Abel and Abel 1983; Wine 1982; Miles 1982; Spender 1982; 1983; Roberts 1982; Gilligan 1982; Smith 1980; Hubbards 1979; Bleier 1984; Thibault in press). The foundation of this argument for new forms of discourse rests in the assertion that

> the circle must be broken because, if it lies anywhere, women's liberation lies outside of our encapsulement by sexist language, sexist ways of thinking, sexist styles of writing, sexist forms of argument, sexist ideas about criticism (Stanley and Wise 1983: 186).

The evidence also suggests that the structure and operation of education are irrevocably tied to larger processes in our society through which patriarchy is maintained. Yet feminists have been able, within limits, to survive there long enough to expose the features of gender bias discussed in this chapter. The fact that feminists are still pushing forward on epistemological and methodological fronts suggests that the structure and operation of education are not purely conspiratorial or successful in their attempts at domination. The knowledge which feminist scholarship brings to education, moreover, challenges male dominance, empowers women, and holds the potential of moving towards a new academy whose one redeeming feature will be an organization that makes feminism unnecessary. While the precise extent of the transformation wrought by feminist scholarship is clearly impossible to "measure," it is evident that feminists' efforts have made this chapter and indeed this volume academically possible.

Conclusion

Feminism has introduced the discipline of education to the "other half" of humanity and verges on a radical transformation of what we know and understand as education. If such an intellectual current is to thrive, however, it is vitally important that feminists acknowledge the obstacles that threaten our research. Our history has taught us the fragility of our hard-won gains and certainly the recent backlash and opposition to feminist scholarship stands as a potent reminder of the need to remain supportive of each other. A strong feminist network within the university, as well as one which has ties to the outside community, will be necessary to maintain feminist momentum in education. Forging support links across academic disciplinary boundaries is also imperative if we are not to be co-opted by our own disciplinary discourse and if we are not to lose the strength of a feminist community inside the university.

There has been widespread distrust of feminist ideas in education. Claims are made that feminist scholarship lacks academic depth and rigour, or, that there is not enough material to study. Others contend that we must maintain our loyalty to education lest we lose ourselves in an ill-defined area without "acceptable" criteria of research or clear academic standards. The most common retort has been that feminist research might or could be "biased," "trivial," or, "trendy." These notions will hopefully be mitigated by the extensive publication of educational literature by women, about women, and the recent proliferation of feminist studies' courses and programs--though again, retrenchment and financial cutbacks absorb a great deal of our optimism. Financial restraints often affect which authors and what books get published, as well as when and if women get hired in academia. In addition, these restraints affect feminist and nonfeminist curricula.

With these barriers in mind, feminist scholarship continues to press for dramatic changes, not only in educational theory, methodologies, language, and in educational structures, practice, and institutional form. Despite the fact that being female in male places means that these endeavours are painful, frustrating, and tiring, it also means that education will never be able to exercise its male hegemony with the same efficiency as it has done in the past.

Endnotes

1. A. Diller and B. Houston presented "A Gender Sensitive Perspective on Education: The Case of Women's Physical Education" at the Canadian Society for the Study of Education Conference that was held in Vancouver, B.C., in June, 1983.

2. The expression, "add women and stir method," was coined by Charlotte Bunch (1979) to refer to feminists' inclusion of women as subjects in classical, traditional theories. Bunch argued that this method is problematic because it assumes that the theories themselves and their underlying assumptions about human nature are unproblematic.

3. I essentially concur with Finn's definition of ideology (1981: 4) as a representation of reality at the level of ideas which systematically conceals much of that reality by mystifying it and by presenting partial truths as if they were whole ones.

References

Abel, E., and Abel, E. (eds.)
    1983   The Signs Reader: Women, Gender and Scholarship. Chicago: University of Chicago

Anyon, Jean
    1981   Social Class and School Knowledge. Curriculum Inquiry 11: 69-92.

Apple, Michael
    1979   Ideology and Curriculum. London: Routledge and Kegan Paul.
    1982   Cultural and Economic Reproduction in Education, ed. Michael Apple. London: Routledge and Kegan Paul.

Arnot, Madeleine
    1981   Cultural and Political Economy: Dual Perspectives in the Sociology of Women's Education. Educational Analysis 3: 64-89.

Astin, H., and Bayer, A.E.
    1973   Sex Discrimination in Academe. Pp. 75-93 in Academic Women on the Move, ed. A. Rossi and A. Calderwood. New York: Russell Sage.

Ayim, Maryann
    1983   "What's Wrong with High School English:...It's Sexist...Un-Canadian...Outdated?": A Book Review. Resources For Feminist Research 12: 20-22.

Bardwick, J. (ed.)
    1972   Readings on the Psychology of Women. New York: Harper and Row.

Benston, Margaret
    1982   Feminism and the Critique of Scientific Method. Pp. 47-67 in Feminism in Canada: From Pressure to Politics, ed. A. Miles and G. Finn.

Bernstein, Basil
    1977   Class, Codes, and Controls: Volume 3. London: Routledge and Kegan Paul.

    1982   Codes, Modalities, and the Process of Cultural Reproduction: A Model. Pp. 69-81 in Cultural and Economic Reproduction in Education, ed. M. Apple. London: Routledge and Kegan Paul.

Blackstone, T.
    1976   The Education of Girls Today. Pp. 199-214 in The Rights and Wrongs of Women, ed. J. Mitchell and A. Oakley. London: Penguin.

Bleier, Ruth
   1984   Science and Gender: A Critique of Biology and Its Theories of Women. New York: Pergamon.

Bourdieu, P., and Passeron, J.
   1977   Reproduction in Education, Society, and Culture. London: Sage.

Bowles, S., and Gintis, H.
   1976   Schooling in Capitalist America. London: Routledge and Kegan Paul.

Boxer, M.
   1982   For and about Women: The Theory and Practice of Women's Studies in the United States. Pp. 237-73 in Feminist Theory: A Critique of Ideology, ed. N.O. Keohane et al. Chicago: University of Chicago.

Brodribb, Somer
   1983   Canadian Universities: A Learning Environment for Women? Resources For Feminist Research 12: 70-71.

Bunch, C.
   1979   Visions and Revisions: Women and the Power to Change. Women's Studies Newsletter 7: 1-19.

Bunch, C., and Pollack, S. (eds.)
   1983   Learning Our Way: Essays in Feminist Education. New York: Crossing.

Chetwynd, J., and Harnett, C.
   1978   The Sex Role System. London: Routledge and Kegan Paul.

Clarricoates, K.
   1978   Dinosaurs in the Classroom: A Re-examination of Some Aspects of Hidden Curriculum in Primary Schools. Women's Studies International Quarterly 1: 353-64.

   1980   All in a Day's Work. Pp. 69-80 in Learning to Lose: Sexism and Education, ed. D. Spender and E. Sarah. London: Women's Press.

Coleman, James, S., et al.
   1966   Equality of Educational Opportunity. Washington, D.C.: U.S. Office of Education, Department of Health, Education and Welfare.

Cott, N., and Pleck, E. (eds.)
   1979   A Heritage of Her Own. New York: Simon and Schuster.

Daly, Mary
   1978a Beyond God the Father: Toward a Philosophy of Women's Liberation. Boston: Beacon.

   1978b Gyn/Ecology: The Metaphysics of Radical Feminism. Boston: Beacon.

1984 *Pure Lust: Elemental Feminist Philosophy*. Boston: Beacon.

David, M.
1978 *The State, the Family, and Education*. London: Routledge and Kegan Paul.

1981 Social Policy and Education: Towards a Political Economy of Schooling and Sexual Division. *British Journal of Sociology of Education* 2: 118-31.

Deem, Rosemary
1978 *Women and Schooling*. London: Routledge and Kegan Paul.

1980 *Schooling for Women's Work*, ed. R. Deem. London: Routledge and Kegan Paul.

1981 State Policy and Ideology in the Education of Women, 1944-1980. *British Journal of Sociology of Education* 2: 131-43.

Dewey, John
1966 *Democracy and Education*. New York: Free Press.

Douglas, J.
1971 *Understanding Everyday Life*. London: Routledge and Kegan Paul.

1980 *Introduction to the Sociologies of Everyday Life*. Boston: Allyn and Bacon.

Du Bois, B.
1983 Passionate Scholarship: Notes on Values, Knowing, and Method in Feminist Social Science. Pp. 105-17 in *Theories of Women's Studies*, ed. G. Bowles and R. Duelli-Klein. London: Routledge and Kegan Paul.

Eichler, M.
1977 Review Essay: Sociology of Feminist Research in Canada. *Signs* 3: 329-46.

1980 *The Double Standard*. London: Croom Helm.

Erikson, E.
1963 *The Childhood Society*. New York: Norton.

Federbush, M.
1972 *Let Them Aspire*. Ann Arbor, MI: University of Michigan.

Fee, E.
1976 Science and the Woman Problem: Historical Perspectives. Pp. 63-82 in *Sex Differences: Social and Biological Perspectives*, ed. M. Teitelbaum. New York: Anchor.

Fenemma, E.
1976 Women and Girls in the Public School: Defeat or Liberation. Pp. 51-71 in *Beyond Intellectual Sexism: A New Woman*, ed. J. Roberts. New York: David MacKay.

Ferguson, Janet (ed.)
　　1982　Who Turns the Wheel? Ottawa: Science Council of Canada.

Finn, Geraldine
　　1981　Why Althusser Killed His Wife. Canadian Forum Sept./Oct.: 23-24.

　　1982　On the Oppression of Women in Philosophy--or, Whatever Happened to Objectivity? Pp. 145-75 in Feminism in Canada: From Pressure to Politics, ed. A. Miles and G. Finn. Montreal: Black Rose.

Frazier, N., and Sadker, M.
　　1973　Sexism in School and Society. New York: Harper and Row.

Freud, S.
　　1959　Group Psychology and the Analysis of the Ego, tr. A. Richelieu. New York: Norton.

Friedenberg, Edgar
　　1965　The Dignity of Youth and Other Ativisms. Boston: Beacon.

　　1970　The Vanishing Adolescent. 13th ed. New York: Dell.

Gaskell, Jane
　　1977　Stereotyping and Discrimination in the Curriculum. Pp. 263-84 in Precepts, Policy and Process: Perspective on Contemporary Canadian Education, London, ON: Alexander Blake.

　　1981　Equal Educational Opportunity for Women. Pp. 173-93 in Canadian Education in the 1980's, ed. J. Wilson. Calgary: Detselig.

　　1983　The Reproduction of Family Life: Perspectives of Male and Female Adolescents. British Journal of Sociology of Education 4: 19-38.

Gillett, Margaret
　　1981　We Walked Very Warily: A History of Women at McGill. Montreal: Eden Women's Publications.

Gilligan, Carol
　　1982　In a Different Voice: Psychological Theory and Women's Development. Cambridge, MA: Harvard University.

Giroux, Henri
　　1983　Theory and Resistance in Education: A Pedagogy for the Opposition. London: Heinemann Educational Books.

Gordon, M., et al. (eds.)
　　1971　The American Family in Socio-Historical Perspective. New York: St. Martin's.

Griffin, Susan
　　1982　　The Way of All Ideology. Pp. 273-93 in *Feminist Theory: A Critique of Ideology*, ed. N. Keohane et al. Chicago: University of Chicago.

Grumet, M.
　　1981　　Pedagogy for Patriarchy: The Feminization of Teaching. *Interchange* 12: 165-84.

Hickerson, Nathaniel
　　1966　　*Education for Alienation*. Englewood Cliffs, NJ: Prentice Hall.

Holt, John
　　1964　　*How Children Fail*. New York: Delta.

Horner, Matina
　　1972　　Towards an Understanding of Achievement-Related Conflicts in Women. *Journal of Social Issues* 28: 157-75.

Howe, Florence
　　1984　　*Myths of Coeducation*. Bloomington, IN: Indiana University.

Hubbards, R., et al. (eds.)
　　1979　　*Women Look at Biology Looking at Women*. Cambridge, MA: Schenkman.

Hughes, Patricia
　　1982　　Towards the Development of Feminist Theory. *Atlantis* 1: 16-25.

Illich, Ivan
　　1970　　*Deschooling Society*. New York: Vintage.

Jagger, Alison
　　1983　　*Feminist Politics and Human Nature*. Totowa, NJ: Rowman and Allanheld.

Janeway, Elizabeth
　　1971　　*Man's World: Women's Place: A Study in Social Mythology*. New York: Delta.

Karabel, J., and Halsey, A. (eds.)
　　1977　　*Power and Ideology in Education*. New York: Oxford University.

Kealey, Linda, et al. (eds.)
　　1974　　*Women at Work, Ontario, 1850-1930*. Canadian Women's Educational.

Keohane, N.; Rosaldo, M.Z.; and Gelpi, C.B. (eds.)
　　1982　　*Feminist Theory: A Critique of Ideology*. Chicago: University of Chicago.

Kohlberg, Lawrence
　　1966　　A Cognitive-Developmental Analysis of Children's Sex-Role Concepts and Attitudes. Pp. 82-173 in *The Development of Sex Differences*, ed. E. Maccoby. Stanford: Standford University.

Kuhn, Thomas
　　1970　The Structure of Scientific Revolutions. Chicago: University of Chicago.

Laurin-Frenette, Nicole
　　1982　The Women's Movement and the State. Our Generation 15: 27-41.

Light, B., and Prentice, A. (eds.)
　　1980　Pioneer and Gentle Women of British North America. Toronto: New Hogtown.

Maccoby, E.(ed.)
　　1966　The Development of Sex Differences. Stanford: Stanford University.

MacDonald, M.
　　1980　Socio-Cultural Reproduction and Women's Education. Pp. 13-25 in Schooling for Women's Work, ed. R. Deem. London: Routledge and Kegan Paul.

MacKinnon, C.
　　1982　Feminism, Marxism, Method, and the State: An Agenda for Theory. Signs 7: 515-45.

Malmo, Cheryl
　　1983　Women's Experiences as Women: Meaning and Context, Vol. 1. University of Alberta Ph.D. dissertation (unpublished).

Mednick, S., and Tangri, S.
　　1972　The New Social Psychological Perspectives. Journal of Social Issues 28: 1-18.

Mies, M.
　　1983　Towards a Methodology for Feminist Research. Pp. 117-40 in Theories of Women's Studies, ed. G. Bowles and R. Dueli-Klein. London: Routledge and Kegan Paul.

Miles, Angela
　　1982　Ideological Hegemony in Political Discourse: Women's Specificity and Equality. Pp. 213-29 in Feminism in Canada: From Pressure to Politics, ed. A. Miles and G. Finn. Montreal: Black Rose.

Oakley, A.
　　1972　Sex, Gender, and Society. London: Maurice Temple Smith.

　　1974　The Sociology of Housework. London: Martin Robertson.

　　1977　Housewife. London: Penguin.

　　1981　Subject Woman. London: Martin Robertson.

O'Brien, Mary
　　1984　Education: A Review. Resources for Feminist Research 12: 3-17.

Perun, P.J. (ed.)
　1982　The Undergraduate Woman: Issues in Educational Equity. Lexington, MA: Lexington Books.

Piaget, Jean
　1968　Six Psychological Studies, tr. A. Tenzer. London: University of London.

Pierson, R., and Prentice, A.
　1982　Feminism and the Writing and Teaching of History. Pp. 103-19 in Feminism in Canada: From Pressure to Politics, ed. A. Miles and G. Finn. Montreal: Black Rose.

Prentice, Allison
　1977　The School Promoters. Toronto: McClelland and Stewart.

Prentice, A., and Houston, S. (eds.)
　1975　Family, School, and Society in Nineteenth-Century Canada. Toronto: Oxford University.

Riesman, David
　1970　Introduction. Pp. 7-19 in The Vanishing Adolescent, by E. Friedenberg. 13th ed. New York: Dell.

Roberts, J. (ed.)
　1976　Beyond Intellectual Sexism: A New Woman, A New Reality. New York: David MacKay.

Roberts, H.
　1982　Doing Feminist Research. Boston: Routledge and Kegan Paul.

Rosenberg, Rosalind
　1982　Beyond Separate Spheres: The Intellectual Roots of Modern Feminism. New Haven, CN: Yale University.

Sarah, E.
　1980　Teachers and Students in the Classroom: An Examination of Classroom Interaction. Pp. 50-63 in Learning to Lose, ed. D. Spender and E. Sarah. London: Women's Press.

Sario, T.; Nagy-Jacklin, C.; and Tittle, K.C.
　1973　Sex-Role Stereotyping in the Public Schools. Harvard Educational Review 43: 21-34.

Sarup, Madan
　1978　Marxism and Education. London: Routledge and Kegan Paul.

Shack, Sybil
　1975　Women in Canadian Education. Toronto: Gage Educational.

Sherman, J.
　1976　Problems of Sex Differences in Space Perception and Aspects of Intellectual Functioning. Psychological Review 74: 290-99.

Silberman, Charles
　1970　Crisis in the Classroom. New York: Vintage.

Smith, Dorothy E.
> 1975 Analysis of Ideological Structures and How Women Are Excluded: Considerations for Academic Women. The Canadian Review of Sociology and Anthropology 12: 353-69.

> 1979 A Sociology for Women. Pp. 135-87 in The Prism of Sex: Essays in the Sociology of Knowledge, ed. J. Sherman and E. Beck. Madison, WI: University of Wisconsin.

> 1980 Using the Oppressor's Language. Resources for Feminist Research 1: 26-41.

Spender, Dale
> 1980 Educational or Indoctrination? Pp. 22-32 in Learning to Lose, ed. D. Spender and E. Sarah. London: Women's Press.

> 1981a The Patriarchal Paradigm and the Response to Feminism. Pp. 155-75 in Men's Studies Modified: The Impact of Feminism on the Academic Disciplines, ed. D. Spender. London: Pergamon.

> 1981b The Gatekeepers: A Feminist Critique of Academic Publishing. Pp. 186-202 in Doing Feminist Research, ed. H. Roberts. Boston: Routledge and Kegan Paul.

> 1982 Invisible Women: The Schooling Scandal. London: Writers and Readers.

> 1983 Women of Ideas. London: Ark Paperbacks.

Spender, D., and Sarah, E. (eds.)
> 1980 Learning to Lose. London: Women's Press.

Stanley, L., and Wise, S.
> 1983 Breaking Out: Feminist Consciousness and Feminist Research. London: Routledge and Kegan Paul.

Thibault, Gisele
> in press The Feminist Academy: A History of Barriers to Feminist Scholarship.

Thibault, G., and Laidlaw, T.
> 1984 Review of Feminism for Girls: An Adventure Story. Resources for Feminist Research 13: 25-27.

Vaughter, Rossa
> 1976 Psychology: Review Essay. Signs 2: 120-46.

Vickers, Jill McCalla
> 1982 Memoirs of an Ontological Exile: The Methodological Rebellions of Feminist Research. Pp. 27-46 in Feminism in Canada: From Pressure to Politics, ed. A. Miles and G. Finn. Montreal: Black Rose.

Walker, B.
> 1981 Psychology and Feminism--If You Can't Beat Them, Join Them. Pp. 111-25 in Men's Studies Modified: The Impact

of Feminism on the Academic Disciplines, ed. D. Spender. Oxford: Pergamon.

Weisstein, Naomi
    1971   Psychology Constructs the Female. Pp. 63-81 in Roles Women Play: Readings towards Women's Liberation, ed. M. Garskoff. Belmont, CA: Brooks/Cole.

Weitzman, L.
    1975   Sex-Role Socialization. Pp. 105-45 in Women: A Feminist Perspective, ed. J. Freeman. Palo Alto, CA: Mayfield.

Weitzman, L., and Rizzo, D.
    1974   Images of Males and Females in Elementary School Textbooks. New York: National Organization of Women's Legal Defence and Education Fund.

Whitty, G.
    1985   Sociology and School Knowledge: Curriculum Theory, Research and Politics. London: Methuen.

Willinsky, John
    1984   The Well-Tempered Tongue: The Politics of Standard English in the High School. New York: Peter Lang.

Willis, Paul
    1977   Learning How to Labour: How Working Class Kids Get Working Class Jobs. Farnborough, UK: Saxon House.

Wine, Jerri
    1982   Gynocentric Values and Feminist Psychology. Pp. 67-89 in Feminism in Canada: From Pressure to Politics, ed. A. Miles and G. Finn. Montreal: Black Rose.

Wood, Caroline Sherif
    1977   Bias in Psychology. Pp. 117-35 in The Prism of Sex: Essays in the Sociology of Knowledge, ed. J. Sherman. Madison, WI: University of Wisconsin.

Woods, P., and Hammersley, M.
    1977   School Experience: Explorations in the Sociology of Education. New York: St. Martin's.

Woolf, Virginia
    1938   Three Guineas. Harmondsworth, UK: Penguin.

Young, M.F.D. (ed.)
    1971   Knowledge and Control: New Directions for the Sociology of Education. London: Collier-MacMillan.

GENDER BIAS IN ART EDUCATION

Alice Mansell

Gender bias in the acquisition of visual literacy (traditionally termed "art education") is the subject of this essay. Although a number of studies have begun to reveal the layers of bias in the study of art, most have proceeded from specific disciplines, such as criticism (Lippard 1976) or history (Parker and Pollock 1981). I shall analyse gender bias in art education, especially in regard to how research resources are utilized in the educational system. The effects of the narrow perspectives in the attainment of visual literacy colour and form the representation and meaning of art throughout our lives as students. To unravel the tangled layers of thought in art education, it is necessary to begin by analysing art curricula in Canada and the U.S. Then, by focusing on the component elements of Alberta's current art curriculum, I shall seek to expose the sources and kinds of judgment which have involved bias. Finally, strategies to reduce gender bias in the study of art will be suggested.

North American art education research has undergone a number of shifts in emphasis over the past decades. Its most recent materialization as a discipline-based study indicates the difficulties our society has in evaluating cultural and educational values. This curriculum is referred to as Discipline-Based Art Education, or DBAE (Di Blasio 1985: 197) and consists of an art program which attempts to acknowledge and integrate history, philosophy, criticism, and art practice. The new Alberta Art Curriculum Guides for secondary schools reflect this orientation (Alberta Department of Education 1985); attempting to analyze and quantify art, these guidelines appear to aim to make a science out of visual art. This discipline-based curriculum in art may reflect a necessary phase in understanding and evaluating visual, cultural meanings in North America. However, the urge to quantify judgments, without examining the source of those judgments, may result in further alienation or obfuscation. To prevent these possibilities, the DBAE curriculum and its component disciplines sources should be examined for gender bias. That bias affects artists, art educators, researchers, and consumers of visual culture.

Since the terms "art" and "art education" are used in this broad and complex field, a few comments on definitions are necessary. I have chosen "visual metaphor" to replace the term "art" for, as dictionary, popular, and academic definitions will attest, "art" is associated with ideas about beauty and pleasure. Such definitions usually exclude, for example, its many other functions across cultures and through time. "Visual metaphor" attempts to define art as visual information, both as form and as content. It can encompass popular as well as fine art, including pictures and objects of many media by creators of all persuasions.

One of the goals of the discipline-based curriculum is something called "visual literacy." This term assumes the importance of understanding the ways that visual images in fine, popular, and folk arts shape and are shaped by the values of Western culture. Visual literacy, or understanding, should include the perspectives of more than one class or gender. When only one perspective is given, that in itself needs to be stated. Art educators must begin to frame questions about the education of artists as image-makers, the education of researchers in the various discipline fields, and the formation of North Americans as we become visually literate through education. The scope of research into these three levels of visual literacy is daunting. However, the following analysis and questions may offer a preliminary guide for artists, students, and educators until our research advances further.

History of Art

The first component of the DBAE curriculum is history (Di Blasio 1985: 200). While this curriculum also contains theories and assumptions drawn from psychology, sociology, and other fields, the discipline of history is central to understanding the traditions and conventions of visual form in Western culture. The following four aspects of the history of art are important determinants of male tradition.

First, painting and sculpture are presented as the important artifacts in the study of art in post-industrial Western history (Janson 1971). The media of painting and sculpture dominate both student textbooks and standard reference works. Inherent in the references to these media are assumptions about size, venue, and purpose. Many of these paintings and sculptures may have been commissioned as public monuments; even works independently generated in the artist's studio were often designed with a specific exhibition milieu in mind. They tend therefore to reflect a particular value system; their content and form are often consistent with the male-dominated political systems that endorse them and the financial sources which support them. By contrast, the images made by women sometimes in different, sometimes more transient media, may remain unsupported and undocumented (Govier 1985: 69). For example, fibre works such as rugs display metaphors similar to those in paintings. Their art value is compromised by the designation of the media as craft media.

"Masterpieces" are often judged as exemplary visual metaphors based on their meaning, context, and form. Why have some messages about art and culture been chosen as the only important ones? Do they represent all people? Apparently not. Art in Context by Jack A. Hobbs (1975), a recommended reference for the new school curriculum (Alberta Department of Education 1985: 38), contains a chapter called "Men and Women." Yet, its sculptural and painted images of men and women were produced exclusively by male artists and are inappropriately presented as a balanced presentation of the images and ideals of both sexes. Hobbs chose not to include works by female artists and rationalized his choice as follows: "man" represents the male and female in all of humanity (1975: 142). He continually refers to women as seen by the male artist, implying that this constitutes a total view.

> Style and content together also describe the attitudes held toward men and women, telling us whether the people of a given time believed that a man should be athletic or elegant, or if a woman was considered a piece of decorative property or an object of worship (Hobbs 1975: 176).

In both of the latter references, the woman is described as an object (noun) while the man is described in adjectival terms. The genesis and rationales of historians' choices of works to include in texts may often reflect the gender bias of the dominant culture.

Secondly, the modernist tradition exemplifies how recent, mainstream, fine art has been defined. A mistrust of the humanistic functions of art is evident in this tradition. Its concentration on form or the purely visual qualities of colour, line, and space, and their evolution through time and styles implies growth very much resembling Piaget's model of growth and development in the child (Phillips 1975: 7). Many historians and critics, such as Greenberg (1982: 5), have interpreted the "progression" from cubism to constructivism and abstract minimalism as signs of growing sophistication, as intellectual control. Further, they often view the maturation of art as an articulation of the objective over the subjective, the mind over the body, sense over sensibility, and the analytical over the expressive (Gablik 1979: 174).

The urge to simplify, control, direct, and exclude--the "modernist law"--derives from a narrow perspective. It must be observed that the modernist tradition, with its accompanying beliefs in science and progress, expanded consideration of the forms of art. This tradition recognized the meanings and potentials of media and formal composition; however, its interpreters unfortunately did so by excluding all other art forms and their meanings (Greenberg 1982: 8). Their zealous exclusivity may be illustrated by the attempts of historians and critics to discredit the female artists who chose to make art, even according to the dominant rules of modernism. Even when women's works conformed to modernism's intellectual concern with form, they were condemned for showing concern only with physical, emotional, "feminine" expressions. For example, Helen Frankenthaler worked with staining canvas in an attempt to

> assert the notion of the flatness and 2-dimensionality of the surface of a painting....Her thorough understanding of the premises of modern formalist art with this innovation won her recognition, albeit only unequivocally in 1969, and only after two men, Kenneth Noland and Morris Louis, had acknowledged their debt to her in their own, later and different use of this procedure (Parker and Pollock 1981: 146).

Yet in a major retrospective catalogue for her show at the Whitney Museum of American Art, E.C. Goosen commented that

> no matter how abstract her paintings,...they never quite lost that hereditary connection with the world of nature and its manifestations. This is in direct contrast with that kind of art which is fed only by other art and derives itself from current aesthetic theory (as cited in Parker and Pollock 1981: 146).

The phrase, "that hereditary connection," might imply a condemnation of her femaleness. One might ask at this point why every individual who is a woman should represent or be genetically connected to all women? Why must an interpretation of her work be predicated on a stereotypical translation based on gender? Scholars are beginning to become more sensitive to this issue. Stephen Westfall observes, "an original member of the American Abstract Artists group, Alice Turnbull Mason remains an under-rated artist for all the usual reasons: she was American at the wrong time, she was a woman and she was modest by temperament" (1985: 141). A careful observation of works by women in particular might reveal a truer picture of history and art.

A third important aspect in art history involves the notion of normative humanity. When reviewing works of art in which a representation of lived experience is ostensibly expressed, the normative perspective of critics and historians is that of the male as an embodiment of universal humanity. In many interpretations, "public" and "private," "general" and "specific," "universal" and "personal" are terms used to describe opposite and exclusive phenomena--with implied value judgments favoring the first term in each pair. For example, Degas' portrayals of women and Cassatt's portrayals of women and children are evaluated quite differently. Degas, as "master," is claimed to represent women objectively, as she appears; Cassatt's representations of domestic interaction are seen as minor works influenced by the master (Canaday 1961: 227-28, Slatkin 1985: 105). One finds another example of the odd-couple syndrome in the critical literature concerning Frida Kahlo and Diego Rivera (Chadwick 1985: 90). Critics write that these artists' works represented different schools of intentions. And yet, since the two were a couple, their works are compared nonetheless. Kahlo's work is defined as surrealist, though she was not a member of the surrealists (Chadwick 1985: 90). Her works were of modest size in which her self-portrait appears amidst complex images of life as she perceived it. Rivera's works, on the other hand, were mural-sized depictions of the class struggles in Mexican life. By size and topic, Rivera's are judged more important by male critics (e.g. Bloch 1986: 104). Can a self-portrait or an autobiographical work by a man express ideas and ideals of a universal or a general, political nature? Why must a self-portrait of a women be deemed only self-indulgent, personal, and particular?

A fourth determining factor in the history of art it that of role model. In contemporary North American expressive painting, artists often are led to "quote" images or compositions from the designated "masters." There may be a number of sociological, financial, and aesthetic reasons for the choices of such "quotations" from the "masters", reasons which will not be examined here. However, many prejudices about intellectual engagement and appropriate role models are imbedded in these choices, and may exclude female participation, especially given the modernist preoccupation with size and with "big themes," such as were present in classical paintings of the eighteenth century (Janson 1971: 277). Are there myths for female artists in the "masterpieces" which provide vehicles for such "quotations"? Is the use of such vehicles another device that distances, obscures, or depersonalizes the artist's identification with certain roles? If a women artist wishes to employ the device of referring to recognized "master" works, are there images and themes which physically and psychologically offer a comfortable alter-ego image? Does the insertion of one's image (i.e., self-portrait) into pictures from other periods offer a distancing device which is incompatible with a contemporary female artist's vision? Does the acceptance of the validity of this device demand that a contemporary female artist subsume herself in the historically dominant, habitually male artist's persona?

These four areas of concern about the historical component of the DBAE curriculum represent a few of the many possible directions in which gender biases are repeated and multiplied in the contemporary education of visual literacy. Educators and critics supply translations of earlier visual metaphors to contemporary artists, students and the general public. These translations contain the values and perspectives of male historians. Their selection and presentation of "significant" images and artists can be particularly intimidating to visual artists. Too often a male perspective on visual metaphors is taken to be both normative and factual. Seeking clarity of analysis, art historians have also risked reducing the images, theories, and techniques to their perspective. Women's perspective has been ignored or vigourously denied in the history of art.

> Recent analyses of the 'enunciative apparatus' of visual representation--its poles of emission and reception--confirm that the representational systems of the West admit only one vision. It is the vision of the constitutive male subject. Or, rather, they posit the subject of representation as absolutely centered, unitary, masculine (Owens 1983: 58).

Philosophy

Philosophical assumptions in the DBAE curriculum are revealed in historical interpretations of the meanings and intentions of art as well as in texts on composition and technique. They also provide the rationale for art education in schools and colleges. There are two major areas in which philosophical assumptions have contributed toward gender bias.

The first philosophical assumption is that of isolated singularity. In historical interpretations of visual metaphors, individual works are often presented singly and with no context. Such isolation assumes that a work of art must stand on its own as a form. The ensuing analysis of its compositional structure and technical virtuosity no longer needs to seek its associative meanings, from which understanding and appreciation may derive. Conventional values related to clarity, focus, and control, as they apply to the form, may cloud the fact that reality, or actual experience as well as re-created experience, might not be expressed most satisfactorily by such a narrow, exclusive focus. In addition, by not attending to the associative meanings, critics may forget that a large population, whose ideas and values contribute to an ideology about art and life, may not be represented. Often the control of meaning, the lure of clarity and the habitual use of modernist formal criticism inhibit interpretation of a multitude of images from a variety of artists and contexts (Berger 1972). A pertinent Canadian example is Mary Pratt. Her depictions of food, such as "Red Currant Jelly," are analysed formally to ascertain their success as pictures rather than attending to the associative and sensual contexts of the images which may be more powerful than their "formal" qualities (Bennett and Hall 1984: 77).

Secondly, philosophical discourse about works of art is rooted in language. It may refer to language symbols as a logical and linear translation of images that are neither. Therefore, the imposition of structure based on discursive logic and linguistic meaning contributes further to the exclusion of visual meanings. Although the reference materials recommended in the Alberta Curriculum rarely refer to women artists, several sources of the translation of visual complexity to a series of simple, linear descriptions are evident. Georgia O'Keefe's work is described thus:

> Her marriage to Alfred Steiglitz, the American dealer and promoter of new art may have had something to do with her direction, but the highly personal from of abstraction she developed was derived more from an interpretation of nature than form any particular 20th century school of abstract art (Hobbs 1975: 222).

What purports to be a clear, careful description contradicts its reading of "powerful and evocative" images as purely formal relationships. Furthermore, in the translation of visual phenomena to a verbal mode, the values of the translator may interfere.

Since making and appreciating art relies on personal, "subjective" judgment, should not a diversity of interpretations be entertained? Should not the intention--if that can in any way be ascertained--and form of a work of art direct the method of its interpretation? In many instances, female viewers see in a different way; this suggests that different theoretical constructs need to be considered.

> One of the feminist goals is to reintegrate the esthetic self and the social self and to make it possible for both to function without guilt or frustration. In the process, we have begun to see art as something subtly but significantly different from what it is in the dominant culture. This is not said in a self-congratulatory tone. It remains to be seen whether different is indeed better. Success and failure in such unmapped enterprises are often blurred. Various feminists have already fallen into various traps along the way, among them: the adoption of certain clichés in images (fruit and shell, mirror and mound), materials (fabrics and papers), approaches ("nonelitist"), and emotions (nontransformative pain, rage, and mother love); a certain naïveté (also carrying with it a certain strength) that comes from the wholesale rejection of all other art, especially abstraction and painting; a dependence on political correctness that can lead to exclusivity and snobbism; and, at the other extreme, an unthinking acceptance of literally anything done by a woman. Beneath these pitfalls is a need for language--visual and verbal-- that will express the ways our art and ideas are developing without being sappy and without denying the powers of the individual within collective dialogue (Lippard 1984: 151).

The dialectical tradition of academia has reinforced the tendency to see works as either/or, rather than as variations or degrees or aspects of a more complex experience. "Objectivity" or "purity" are cherished values in traditionally male-oriented academic research; they should, however, not be considered the exclusive mode.

> What we are pointing to is a trend in art away from iconic modes of representation and towards the development of formal logical systems dealing with sets of pure abstract relations. Viewed this way, the history of art can be seen

as a process which has entailed the slow and laborious liberation of forms from their content (Gablik 1979: 45).

Criticism

Criticism in the DBAE curriculum directs viewers in their experience of appreciating a work of art (Feldman 1982: 211). Visual images are made more accessible to viewers. Criticism, most broadly defined, may include patronage, curatorship, and publication in settings as diverse as public and private galleries, museums, and collections, popular and scholarly magazines, monographs, and newspapers. These settings provide the pools of information from which historical models are invented and suggest the following concerns.

First of all, critics can engender bias through their role as gatekeepers. Critics and curators often choose works which quote from accepted art traditions. They select art they can recognize from their own education and experience. Only a few have the knowledge and courage to identify work that has not been validated, usually in the male-dominated critical literature. In the article, "Personal Bests" (Walker 1985), a variety of artists, curators, and critics have chosen artists they ostensibly believe are the best in Canada. In all cases, they are already "anointed," mainstream artists, and the great majority of them are male. Because women have been excluded from the social and political art groups by historical and critical choices, they have not been identified as part of accepted art traditions. Thus, critics accept only "exceptional" women and the few who "paint as well as men." Rosa Bonheur is an example of such an "exceptional" woman; like her male peers, she painted animals and the outdoor, active life rather than the domestic feminine scenes of her female peers (Greer 1979: 20). The situation continues in the same vein. The main change that has occurred in twenty years, according to Joan Murray, is not in the system, which she believes is still terribly unfair to women. It is in the women's work (see Govier 1985).

When choosing works that fit known categories, critics and curators often choose forms congruent with works of "recognized" quality. They prefer works that look expressive, that have expressionist-like marks, rather than works which construct or recreate personal experience. Marks refer to the way paint or charcoal, for example, is applied to the surface. This usually records the manner of its application (forcefully, quickly, etc. and carries with it ideas about emotional action or meaning. The German Expressionists used dramatic colour and gesture in paint application to reinforce the expression they wished to convey. Younger painters use the form of the mark-making process without necessarily tying it to an image to be <u>reinforced</u>. This is illustrated by a recent practice of young Canadian and American painters to quote colour and paint marks from European expressionist painters of the preceding several decades. These quotations of distinctive marks, like the quotations discussed in the history section, further distance meaning from the individual artist. Such graphic quotations also prejudice the accessibility of artists who experiment with new forms to enhance meaning. Joyce Wieland's painting, "Paint Phantom," uses the colour and direction of paint strokes to reinforce the disturbing dream-like quality of the two figures in this picture. Her palette and style of mark-making have evolved to emphasize the psychological impact of implied tension between the nude female and the male/animal figure locked in an embrace. These contribute to a visual and psychological confrontation which is stronger and more unsettling than the impressionist marks and colours used by the "younger" painters in the Toronto 84 exhibit. In the latter, "the expressive marks" became formal devices which refer to the "current style" (see Burnett 1984: 88).

A second concern arises from the tension between analytical and personal responses of art critics. Critics often adopt models of analysis from other disciplines and schools to structure or give credence to what often is a personal judgment of quality or even of taste. They tend thus to analyse, simplify, and quantify an image which is essentially a qualitative endeavour in both procedure and perception. Neglecting to fit analysis to the genesis of the work and denying ambiguity and complexity lead to this question: if the critic is disturbed by the content of a work, why must it be rejected or devalued as personal, minor, or subjective? These terms need not be derogatory; they unfortunately retain that stain from seventy years of modernist purification.

> The critic has assumed an unprecedented importance, reconsidering and assessing the significance of the art produced while elaborating the theories and premises upon which modern art are based. The critic of modern art is a central element in 20th century art practice, one who conditions the reception of works of art. It is through the discourse of critics, however, that ideology operates to

> protect the dominant system and stamp the work that women produce, even within radicalist practices, with its stereotypes and values (Parker and Pollock 1981: 136).

Thirdly, critics respond to works that have been made public in galleries and publications. The exposure and value given such works is based often on commercial appeal. Their acceptability contains an implicit valuing of pleasure and decoration, involving a denial of works whose function may be to question our values in art and life. Are these critics then responsible for the North American viewers' predilection for fine arts as beautiful possessions? Has the tradition of determining art value primarily on the basis of independent and creative curatorship been displaced by a validation in the marketplace? Perhaps the artist as promoter in this context reinforces certain traditional gender-role interpretations further.

Market Value

The manner in which market value militates against the inclusion of women artists is revealed in statistical accounts of the number of women artists included in major museum and gallery shows and in the concomitant critical analysis and acceptance of such works (Robinson 1986: 168; Crean 1985: 30). Men's works and shows outnumber women's ten-fold or more. The private galleries follow suit. Further, in the context of this climate, the female artist as promotor of her own work neither looks nor acts like what curators, critics, or consumers have subconsciously identified as the artist. A recent article in Arts Magazine alludes to the difficulties a photographer encountered when including women in group photos of artists done in the manner of the Irascibles-Abstract Expressionist Painters of the forties and fifties (Greenfield-Sanders 1985: 103).

Art Practice

Art practice is the actual studio involvement with materials and techniques, the meaning of which results in a visual metaphor or a work of art. Here gender bias may affect the school and college curricula in several guises. First, interpretation and instruction by a majority of male studio instructors, functioning as translators, formulators of assignments, and role models may affect the manner in which females interpret form and content both in making and understanding works. If the translator of works does not seek to understand an artist's intentions, will students? Thus a woman who intends to communicate a feminist message in her art may well have her intended meaning completely ignored or even radically altered because male translators deny her intention. "As for women artists, it is clear that their experience has been mainly available to the world of art in translation, that is translation by men" (Feldman 1982: 208). Feldman also says: "Perhaps greatness has been defined in such a way that excludes what women, for example, make and do" (1982: 205). Secondly, does the focus on certain compositional and media forms carry assumptions about their values? Does the production of large, analytical, sculptural constructions, for example, enjoy greater attention than the development of small, layered, fibre works? During my experience in both secondary and post-secondary classes, female students have not been encouraged to make pictures and forms about their experiences, but have rather been led to objectify universal ideas in clearly articulated, often large paintings and sculptures. A female student who wishes to express a visual image of domestic life is often advised to change to something "bigger, or more important."

> Within traditional studio offerings at all levels of art education, the status and values that have been attached to male-dominated art forms is reinforced and taught as a not so hidden curriculum. Painting, sculpture, drawing, and print making are offered with pride, while jewellery making, weaving, needlework, ceramics, and crafts are offered somewhat apologetically or in certain college art departments, offered in art education rather than in studio programs (Collins and Sandell 1984: 36).

And thirdly, does presenting female artist-teachers working often as anomalies or exceptions in the traditional "fine arts" offer potentials for alternative perspectives or does it merely reinforce the exclusivity of male value judgments of both form and content?

Strategies to Reduce Gender Bias in Art Education

Finally, we may employ the preceding analysis of the sources of gender bias in art education to formulate strategies to reduce such bias both now and in the future. These strategies can be implemented through the present, discipline-based system.

Every educator must attend to the present gender bias in the historical component by being aware of the historical analysis of art as interpretation, and as such, open to further interpretation. Therefore, an effort must be made in the classroom and in curriculum development to obtain more equitable representation of gender both as sources of art and as images represented in works of art. The articulated need for more and different resources (i.e., slides and texts) may motivate historians to conduct further research on more women artists. Such research may, in fact, uncover previously unknown artists.

In the same manner, philosophical assumptions about what art is and what it does should be examined in curricular rationales and in resource materials dealing with composition and media. Students and teachers need to be made aware of a variety of proceses whereby assessment and interpretation of works may be carried out. The ability to match systems of analysis to systems of creation must be encouraged. Further, observation of works may require reassessments outside of narrow, mainstream, fine art perspectives. Fresh perspectives likely will make visual art more accessible to the general population, the majority of whom are women.

The use of art criticism, as it is available in the contemporary media, will need to focus on several issues. The first is the necessity for more female interpreters of historical and philosophical sources. Secondly, translation of works must attempt to deal with more than commercially viable fine arts. A variety of arts and artists, especially in the contemporary and regional milieu, should be represented. The promotion of an expanded type of criticism by artists, educators, and critics will undoubtedly promote a more creative curatorship of a more representative gallery of art.

Finally, in the schools and colleges, the means and goals of the "making of art" or the training in the manipulation of materials and meanings need to be examined. For example, do the goals of promotion and support of art and artists exhibit a narrow gender bias, one implemented through a certain selection of media, process, size, and meaning? Students need to be guided in the analysis and utilization of form and content as it best articulates their own developing ideas and experiences. Therefore, instructors must present a balanced sensibility and exhibit a sensitivity to the needs, ideas, and experiences of students of both genders.

Art educators can ultimately filter out the layers of gender bias in the education of artists, in the appreciation of consumers, and in the research of scholars. If the aim of our art curriculum is to promote visual literacy in these groups, then we must consciously include the perspectives and visual metaphors of women in all aspects of art education.

References

Alberta Department of Education
    1985   Alberta Art Curriculum and Teacher Resource Guide for Art 7, 8, and 9. Edmonton: Department of Education.

Bennett, B., and Hall, C.P.
    1984   Discovering Canadian Art. Scarborough, ON: Prentice Hall.

Berger, J.
    1972   Ways of Seeing. Harmondsworth, UK: Penguin.

Bloch, L.
    1986   On Location with Diego Rivera. Art in America Feb.: 102-23.

Bringhurst, R.; James, G.; Keziere, R.; and Shadbolt, D.
    1983   Visions: Contemporary Art in Canada. Vancouver, B.C.: Douglas and McIntyre.

Burnett, D.
    1984   Toronto Painting 84. Toronto: Art Gallery of Ontario.

Canaday, J.
    1961   Mainstreams of Modern Art. New York: Simon and Schuster.

Chadwick, W.
    1985   Women Artists and the Surrealist Movement. London: Thames and Hudson.

Collins, G., and Sandell, R.
    1984   Women, Art and Education. Reston, VA: National Art Education Association.

Crean, S.
    1985   This Magazine.

Di Blasio, M.K.
    1985   Continuing the Translation: Further Delineation of the DBAE Format. Studies in Art Education 26: 197-205.

Elsen, A.E.
    1981   Purposes of Art. 4th ed. Toronto: Holt, Rinehart and Winston.

Feldman, E.
    1982   The Artist. Englewood Cliffs, NJ: Prentice Hall.

Gablik, S.
    1979   Progress in Art. New York: Rizzoli.

Govier, K.
    1985   Venus as Victim. Canadian Art 2: 65-69.

Greenberg, C.
    1982   Modernist Painting. Pp. 5-10 in *Modern Art and Modernism*, ed. F. Frascina and C. Harrison. New York: Harper and Row.

Greenfield-Sanders, T.
    1985   The New Irascibles. *Arts Magazine* 60: 102-10.

Greer, G.
    1979   *The Obstacle Race*. London: Secker and Warburg.

Harper, J.R.
    1977   *Painting in Canada: A History*. 2nd ed. Toronto: University of Toronto.

Herrera, H.
    1983   *Frida: A Biography of Frida Kahlo*. New York: Harper and Row.

Hobbs, J.A.
    1975   *Art in Context*. New York: Harcourt Brace Jovanovich.

Janson, H.W.
    1971   *A Basic History of Art*. New York: Abrams.

Kuspit, D.
    1983   Gallery Leftism. *Vanguard* 12: 22-25.

Lippard, L.R.
    1976   *From the Center*. New York: Dutton.

    1984   *Get the Message: A Decade of Art for Social Change*. New York: Dutton.

Owens, C.
    1983   Feminists and Postmodernism. Pp. 57-77 in *The Anti-Aesthetic: Essay on Postmodern Culture*, ed. H. Foster. Port Townsend, WA: Bay Press.

Parker, R., and Pollock, G.
    1981   *Old Mistresses: Women, Art and Ideology*. New York: Pantheon.

Phillips, J.C.
    1975   *The Origins of the Intellect: Piaget's Theory*. San Francisco: Freeman.

Reid, D.
    1973   *A Concise History of Canadian Painting*. Toronto: Oxford University.

Robinson, W.
    1986   Male Bias under Attack. *Art in America* Jan.: 168.

Slatkin, W.
    1985   *Women Artists in History*. Englewood Cliffs, NJ: Prentice Hall.

Walker, S.
    1985   Personal Bests. *Canadian Art* 2: 41-51.

Westfall, S.
1985 Alice Turnbull Mason: Home-Grown Abstraction. <u>Art in America</u> Oct.: 140-44.

RE-VISIONS OF THE PAST

Eliane Leslau Silverman

I do not want to claim too much for the re-visions that have taken place in the historical writing of the last fifteen years. No grand revolution has yet occurred. Nor do I want to claim too little, for it is also true that major and fascinating changes in the literature are transforming the historical profession and the historian's craft. Sexism, of course, still persists in the profession, from the paucity of women in departments of history to outright ridicule of what historians of women do. Sexism underlies the facile question, "Well, why don't we have men's history?" It is also manifested by leaving women right out of the story of change over time. The exclusion of women from history departments will probably alter as demographics pressure depleted departments to hire female Ph.Ds. More universities, like the University of Alberta and the University of Western Ontario, are making a concerted effort to hire women (see Head 1985: 2, n.2). As their numbers grow, they will seem less anomalous and the work they do will also seem less bizarre or marginal. Still, until now women's history and the integration of women into the story of the past are not much more the subjects of what historians teach than they were when I took what I believe was the first graduate seminar in women's history in the United States at the University of California at Los Angeles in 1965. Our first assignment was to read every textbook in American history, seeking out references to women, certainly, but also searching for some significance assigned the presence of women. We were not surprised to find none. We are taken aback, nearly twenty years later, to find that two major 1983 Canadian textbooks written by renowned historians include no mention of women (see Van Kirk 1984). One can also read two books published in 1984 on the Canadian west (Berton, Friesen) and imagine the prairies to have been inhabited solely by men. Less overtly sexist, but no more informed about the state of the historiography, are requests for talks like the one just asked of me--which I declined--on "The Contribution of Jewish Women to Canadian Life" that manifest ignorance of the subtlety of historical writing on women, in stark contrast to the specificity of the parallel talk on men which was to focus on Jewish labour between 1910 and 1920.

Less and less, however, can the expanding discipline of women's history be ignored as the body of literature grows larger and more sophisticated and as questions about the nature of gender grow more pressing. Indeed, here is precisely one of the problems: part of the recalcitrance against women's history derives from the difficulty of including a new field in lectures when professors are entrenched in and perfectly comfortable with what they know. A possible solution lies in creating bibliographies for professors specifically geared towards the courses they teach; many professors do acknowledge a desire to incorporate the new materials but hesitate to do so because of such logistical difficulties. Universities could commit themselves to providing these professors with undergraduate or graduate researchers to present them with new bibliographies, right down to such details as library call numbers and primary sources available on their campuses, to facilitate more representative lectures and course syllabuses. Certainly such a development would signal university administrations' commitment to preparing their students with the best that academia can offer; right now that intellectual obligation lies in part in acknowledging the presence of women in their midsts and in their pasts.

We also need openly to admit that women as historians and as subjects in historical literature arouse a degree of anxiety. The depth of some male resistance to feminist ideas--often those very ideas that motivate the search for gender as an element in history--should not be underestimated. Henry James (1984: 293) has Basil Ransom say in <u>The Bostonians</u>,

> The whole generation is womanized; the masculine tone is passing out of the world; it's a feminine, a nervous, hysterical, chattering, canting age, an age of hollow phrases and false delicacy and exaggerated solicitudes and coddled sensibilities, which, if we don't soon look out, will usher in the reign of mediocrity, of the feeblest and flattest and the most pretentious that has ever been. The masculine character, the ability to dare and endure, to know and yet not fear reality, to look the world in the face and take it for what it is...that is what I want to preserve.[1]

James has Ransom alert us to the anxiety, sometimes the sheer terror, with which some people have responded to the introduction of women into the historical literature, university history departments, and the public word. Basil Ransom has something else to say: when Verena Tarrant laughs that the social system has no place for women, he responds in a less outmoded way than one might think, "No place in public. My plan is to keep you at home and have a better time with you there than ever" (James 1984: 294). There is some reason for this fear. Historians, of all people, know how tenuous are the balances of power which are traditionally understood as hierarchic and which always seem chillingly to suggest a power struggle. I hope to indicate below that precisely these notions of individuation, separation, territoriality, and conflict are part of what a new scheme might alter, with women's history elucidating richer, denser conceptions of the web of connections that women have known in private life, in the public realm, and even in universities.

The writing of women's history is no doubt motivated in part by the feminist activism of students and teachers alike. Women who learn more about their history become more conscious of their identification with their gender and often more desirous of altering the status of women. Naomi Black (1984: 467) addresses herself to the sometimes ambivalent relationship of women to feminism. She writes that feminism

> has become a contested and often a pejorative term. The majority of women today are inclined to define themselves out of it, even while supporting goals contributing to women's equality and autonomy. As an ideology, feminism seems to mean a belief in the distinctive situation and experience of women, combined with a refusal to allow women to be judged inferior or lacking in comparison with men or by male standards.

Black's definition of feminism requires that we develop new criteria for historical significance; it also demands collectivization, or at least a knowledge of living in a community outside academia. A remarkable number of women's history organizations, some within established learned societies such as the Canadian Historical Association, and others, more interdisciplinary, like the Canadian Research Institute for the Advancement of Women and the Canadian Women's Studies Association, have sponsored conferences and journals which recognize that women's lives and their histories are entwined with each other, and with men's and children's too. These groups often discuss openly the kinds of lives that women scholars actually live. They cannot always go far away for research. Sometimes women scholars cannot get jobs. Their children tug at them. Their students ask much of their time and energies. They are, in short, enmeshed in relationships. Freud's suggestion that the two great quests in life are for love and work--for relationship and creativity--is borne out by the way women historians do their work (see especially Ruddick and Daniels 1977). We often feel the need to speak not just to our scholarly community but also to the other communities we inhabit. By thinking about our own lives in this way--the autonomy we seek, the forms we create, our arrangements, our narratives--we have to address the meaning of gender in our writing as well. Natalie Zemon Davis, in an interview about her writing, says that "it isn't possible for me to write without joining the issues in some way....I am not in this business just to satisfy other historians (MARHO 1983: 116). Linda Gordon puts it another way. "There has got to be a tension between historical empathy and rootedness in one's own present, a rigourous defense both against presentism and against the illusion that the historian remains outside history (MARHO 1983: 77). These recognitions are an important part of what women's history has introduced into the profession, the knowledge that intimate questions of birth, copulation, and death--having bodies, in short--are historically significant, belonging therefore in our scholarship. Thus, for example, feminist historians have frequently written about marriage, the context in which one often finds women. Phyllis Rose, writing about five Victorian marriages, sees the marital relationship, not merely as a relationship of power, but as two narrative constructs, the way two people create their lives. She writes:

> We tend to talk informally about other people's marriages and to disparage our own talk as gossip. But gossip may be the beginning of moral enquiry, the low end of the platonic ladder which leads to self-understanding. We are desperate for information about how other people live because we want to know how to live ourselves, yet we are taught to see this desire as an illegitimate form of prying. If marriage is, as Mill suggested, a political experience, then discussion of it ought to be taken as seriously as talk about national elections (Rose 1984: 9).

One sees the results of that sort of enquiry in the titles of history courses at a variety of universities. No longer limited to the male past, contemporary historians teach courses such as the following:

At Mt. Holyoke College:
"Bonds of Intimacy in the Ancient World";

"The Politics of Reproduction in the Twentieth
Century";
"Women, Spirituality, and Power";
"Women and Men: An Historical Inquiry into the Social
    Relations of the Sexes";

At Tufts University:
"Gender and Economics in Pre-Industrial Europe";
"Growing Up Female in America";
"Witchcraft and Society";

At The University of Calgary:
"Contemporary Issues in Canadian Feminism";

At Hampshire College:
"Gender and Public Policy";
"The Problem of Motherhood and Work in the Twentieth
    Century."

The dramatically changed content in such courses is often reinforced by a highly charged process in the classroom. Just as much of the writing is impelled by an understanding of the importance of context and of connections, the lecture hall and seminar room become just such a contextual setting to which students come not for answers but to be part of the quest in which students and professors alike are engaged. This process frequently begins with self-disclosure by the professor, who thereby legitimates the students' attempts to extrapolate from the complexity of their own lives to the past. If our lives are a mass of ambiguity, ambivalence, and confusion--as well as the narrative form we choose also to impose on them--were other women's lives any simpler? Students are compelled into a degree of identification with the subjects. They then learn to transmute this identification into intellectual enquiry.

The nature of historical enquiry which seeks to understand gender as a critical component of our work has changed since 1970. Initially, scholars responded to a body of literature which was concerned with what men have done and the activities and institutions that interested them. They attempted to find women who fit into those activities, but soon realized that most women quite simply did not fit. It was discovered that there were masses of women whose names we did not know--never would--and that women's lives were dominated by sexist structures. That sort of enquiry became a literature on oppression: what have men done to women? Such enquiries on oppression proved less than satisfactory as women were rendered passive recipients or merely reactors and even victims. Scholars then searched for signs of women's rebellion against male norms and male impositions, finding it in female societies, in women's organizations, and among deviant women. What came of all this was an appreciation of women as they perceived themselves qua women--as workers, as friends, as mothers, as daughters, and within social and political institutions (Cott and Pleck 1979: 9-24; Scott and Chafe 1980: 3-17; Degler 1983: 67-85; Silverman 1982: 515-33).

Anthropologists, literary critics, and sociologists who very much influence the work of historians are simultaneously exploring the ways that women inhabited a realm which was sometimes concentric with the world of men, at other times intersected it, and was at still other times entirely separate from it.[2] A new framework marked the beginning of a historical scholarship which recognized the frequent intersection of gender, race, and class as variables. It saw that a woman might be identified both with her gender and her class or race and that these identifications might be either in conflict or congruent (see Newton, Ryan, Walkowitz 1983; Pugh 1983). Such scholars often used the everyday, material lives of women and men as data, studying social rituals, or gendered uses of language, or how technology was employed and perceived, they record and analysed such details as how it felt to get a sewing machine or how parents talked to their children. Some historians (e.g., Lasch 1972; Kelly 1984), often drawing from cross-cultural and interdisciplinary data, began to speculate that the realm of women, especially after industrialization, could be styled the private realm and the world of men the public domain.

Indeed, one found suggestions in the work especially of psychologists that whatever men did was by definition public or political, while women's work was by definition private and affective, the work of the emotions, of relationships, of creating a context in which to raise gendered selves who would take their private or public place as adults (Chodorow 1978; Gilligan 1982). Historians, increasingly interdisciplinary, discovered a separate sphere of women. They found dichotomies, most importantly, in the difference between the public and the private worlds which, although perhaps auxiliary to each other, represented nonetheless two spheres, those of male power and of female deviance, of the "real" political activities of men and the marginal concerns of women. Men's interests constituted the measure of women's competence, development, and interactions. Henry James alerts us once again to how much we as scholars are heir to a tradition which polarized women and men when in The

Bostonians, written a hundred years ago, he had Olive Chancellor muse that "the age seemed to her relaxed and demoralized, and...she looked to the influx of the great feminine element to make it feel and speak more sharply" (1984: 108). Olive, resisting and probably fearing men's public power, hoped to replace it with the "great feminine element" (James 1984: 108).

The scholarship that emerged from a conceptualization of male and female realms was most important, perhaps, for restoring women to historical significance (Carroll 1976; Bridenthal et al. 1984; Lerner 1979). We could study women on their own terms, and hope to record their experience in fidelity to their lives as they lived them, recognizing and documenting the presence of both the private and public spheres. I wish to suggest, however, that at this point we need to re-view even this fascinating way of organizing the past. We need now to ask: is the conceptualization of a public/private dichotomy simply another of the polarities that we think about when we think of women and men, as we were taught by our culture, in our schools and universities, and that we perpetuate as teachers? Is this dichotomy another duality like natural versus civilized, or unconscious versus social, or mind versus body, or dominant versus submissive? Do we want to continue to dichotomize as we have been taught to do? Or, are we ready to think of gender not as polar opposites but instead as a continuum along which we may find separate realms, but whose impact may be different in different times and places, and whose borders are far from clear? So, for example, Jane Lewis (1984) points out that an ideology of nineteenth-century England which decreed that the public world of work should remain separate from the private world of the home weighed more heavily on middle class women than on those of the working class, the women who went out to work for pay. The ideology of separate spheres in this instance was influential, but altered itself to suit altered circumstances (Lewis 1984; Giddings 1984).

We need to think less of dichotomies and less of gender as the creation of biological differences, but more about gender as the product of social relationships in distinct and always changeable societies. Indeed, as historians, we must examine our discipline especially carefully just now and listen for the lessons it has taught us. We may, in fact, need to unlearn the capacity to dichotomize feeling and thought, experience and its recounting. We historians need to be cognizant that in the creation and the re-creation of the moment, in the living and the telling and the re-telling, the viewing and the re-viewing, we are both those who listen and those who are listened to. We hear; we speak; we write. We constitute and re-constitute. In our living and our work, we must engage in examining experience, feeling, and thought in new ways. Instead of seeking essential qualities in the sexes, we are beginning to ask what in the relations of the sexes makes them appear the way they do. The asymmetries of the genders, we will see, are bound to socially specific forms of inequality and hierarchy and will be found to be a function of class, of time, and of place. Gender becomes a personal and a political fact with nuances that the historian must subtlty assess instead of easily categorizing.

So, for example, Naomi Black writes that political scientists and historians have assessed the League of Women Voters as politically immature, with the women involved in it "uninterested and incompetent, associated with deviant practices and marginal issues and attitudes" (1983: 586). Furthermore,

> analysts have emphasized the need to obtain for women the resources and experiences that would enable them to approximate men's levels and types of political involvement. Ideally, women would then become indistinguishable from all other (male) citizens. This would occur when women had matured politically; men, and existing processes of politics, would remain the same. Assimilation or integration of women into politics is the goal, while men continue to be the model (Black 1983: 586).

She proposes instead that the mechanisms of the political world may be both unresponsive to women's modes and inadequately defined by scholars and that the League's nonpartisan role as "training ground, springboard, influencer of policy agendas and public awareness" must also be considered political. In concluding that "non-partisanship is not a substitute for politics but part of it" (Black 1983: 599), she is clearly directing us to a reconsideration of the public/private dichotomy. The League of Women Voters cannot be relegated to the private realm of women merely because its politics did not proceed like those of, say, a political party. Black's analysis, instead of dismissing women as merely private--and thereby politically immature--cautions us to seek a continuum of female, and perhaps male, activities along which private and public realms are not so glibly separated.

Let us return to Phyllis Rose's <u>Parallel Lives</u> for an extension of Black's insight. Black indicates that the private realm is enmeshed in the public sphere. Rose points out that the public realm is embedded in the private. She writes that we have learned to read about the perils of public lives but that "there was no equivalent or even vaguely similar series of domestic portraits" (Rose 1984: 5). She finds marriage to be not only "a subjectivist fiction with two points of view often deeply in conflict, sometimes fortuitously congruent..." but also a political construct.

> On the basis of family life, we form our expectations about power and powerlessness, about authority and obedience in other spheres....I believe marriage to be the primary political experience in which most of us engage as adults, and so I am interested in the management of power between men and women in that microcosmic relationship. Whatever the balance, every marriage is based upon some understanding, articulated or not, about the relative importance, the priority of desires, between its two partners. Marriages go bad not when love fades--love can modulate into affection without driving two people apart--but when this understanding about the balance of power breaks down, when the weaker member feels exploited or the stronger feels unrewarded for his or her strength (Rose 1984: 7).

Rose's conclusion reminds us emphatically that marriage, an institution both private and public, shares with politics, which is also private and public, a mode of expression wherein "equality consists...in perpetual resistance, perpetual rebellion" (1984: 270).

Finally, my own research in progress on the National Council of Jewish Women of Canada suggests that if gender is both a personal and a political fact, then the public and the private realms are inhabited in a variety of ways by women and men. The twentieth-century, middle class, Jewish women I am studying defined themselves entirely self-consciously as wives and mothers, that is, as private people.[3] And yet, they immersed themselves in work that can only be called political as they attempted to alter the powerlessness and pain of the old, of immigrants, of domestic servants, of children. These women thus moved themselves into the public realm even while asserting that they were doing such work while being wives and mothers too, or perhaps first. Like other immigrant women, they created the institutions and even the artifacts, such as styles of dress and foods, of ethnicity. They knew that as women they must participate in the life of their community, the Jewish and the Canadian, or the ethnic part of the community's life would die. These Jewish women said that they were merely behaving in consonance with their Jewish tradition; they were doing, quite simply, what they must do, devising survival strategies for themselves and for other Canadians; maintaining community. The matters that concerned them often became known as "women's issues." And yet it was precisely their involvement in such questions that removed them from the private realm to a recognition of their marginality, of their inequality, sometimes of their inferiority. That involvement constituted activity in the public realm. If our understanding of "public" precludes their involvement or labels it peripheral or immature, then there is simply something wrong with our definition of what matters in the public realm.

The instant after I wrote that last sentence, I read an announcement for the 1987 Berkshire Conference, the major United States conference on women's history. Its theme will be "Beyond the Public/Private Dichotomy: Reassessing Women's History." There can be no complacency among us. With the introduction of gender as a part of the history we write, we know that we must keep reinventing ourselves and our past. From our marginality, women as scholars and activists point to the need for cooperation, for relationship, for a context in which we can be in both public and private spheres. We need to seek, not further polarities, not disjointed individualism, not more battles, but a community in which our work can grow towards greater breadth. A private realm that is not blindly privatized and inured to the world beyond, an intellectual climate which nurtures rebellious creativity, a political milieu which allows us to give voice to our humanity, and colleagues in our universities who acknowledge our work will create a scholarship rich in its exploration of human possibilities.

Endnotes

1. The Bostonians was first published in serial form in 1885 and then in book form the following year.

2. See, for example, Rosaldo and Lamphere 1974; Faderman 1981; and Bernard 1981. Note also the renewed interest in first person accounts as exemplified by the reprinting of the 1935 volume by Margaret Llewellyn Davies (ed.), Life as We Have Known It in 1975. See Silverman 1984 for the influence of such work.

3. These women's papers are housed in the National Council of Jewish Women headquarters in Toronto and in the Archives of the Canadian Jewish Congress in Montreal.

References

Bernard, Jessie
    1981   The Female World. New York: Free Press.

Berton, Pierre
    1984   The Promised Land: Settling the Prairies. Toronto: McClelland and Stewart.

Black, Naomi
    1983   The Politics of the League of Women Voters. International Social Science Journal 35: 585-603.

    1984   The Mothers' International: The Women's Co-operative Guild and Feminist Pacificism. Women's Studies International Forum 7: 467-76.

Bridenthal, Renate; Grossman, Atina; and Kaplan, Marion (eds.)
    1984   When Biology Became Destiny: Women in Weimar and Nazi Germany. New York: Monthly Review Press.

Carroll, Bernice (ed.)
    1976   Liberating Women's History. Chicago: University of Illinois.

Chodorow, Nancy
    1978   The Reproduction of Mothering. Berkeley, CA: University of California.

Cott, Nancy, and Pleck, Elizabeth (eds.)
    1979   A Heritage of Her Own: Toward a New Social History of American Women. New York: Simon and Schuster.

Davies, Margaret Llewellyn (ed.)
    1975   Life as We Have Known It. New York: Norton.

Degler, Carl
    1983   What the Women's Movement Has Done to American History. Pp. 67-85 in A Feminist Perspective in the Academy: The Difference It Makes, ed. Elizabeth Langland and Walter Gove. Chicago: University of Chicago.

Faderman, Lillian
    1981   Surpassing the Love of Men: Romantic Love and Friendship Between Women from the Renaissance to the Present. New York: William Morrow.

Friesen, Gerald
    1984   The Canadian Prairies: A History. Toronto: University of Toronto.

Giddings, Paula
    1984   *Where and When I Enter: The Impact of Black Women on Race and Sex in America*. New York: William Morrow.

Gilligan, Carol
    1982   *In a Different Voice: Psychological Theory and Women's Development*. Cambridge, MA: Harvard University.

Head, Tina
    1985   Mixed Bag at CAUT Women's Workshop. *Canadian Association of University Teachers Bulletin* 33 (Feb.): 2.

James, Henry
    1984   *The Bostonians*. New York: Bantam.

Kelly, Jan
    1984   *Women, History, and Theory*. Chicago: University of Chicago.

Lasch, Christopher
    1972   *Haven in a Heartless World*. New York: Basic Books.

Lerner, Gerda
    1979   *The Majority Finds Its Past*. Oxford: Oxford University.

Lewis, Jane
    1984   *Women in England, 1870-1950: Sexual Division and Social Change*. Brighton, UK: Wheatsheaf.

MARHO
    1983   *Visions of History*. Manchester: Manchester University.

Newton, Judith; Ryan, Mary; and Walkowitz, Judith (eds.)
    1983   *Sex and Class in Women's History*. London: Routledge and Kegan Paul.

Pugh, David
    1983   *Sons of Liberty: The Masculine Mind in Nineteenth Century America*. Westport, CN: Greenwood.

Rosaldo, Michele, and Lamphere, Louise (eds.)
    1974   *Women, Culture and Society*. Palo Alto, CA: Stanford University.

Rose, Phyllis
    1984   *Parallel Lives*. New York: Vintage.

Ruddick, Sara, and Daniels, Pamela
    1977   *Working It Out*. New York: Pantheon.

Scott, Anne, and Chafe, William
    1980   What We Wish We Knew about Women: A Dialog. Pp. 3-17 in *Clio Was a Woman*, ed. Mabel Deutrich and Virginia Purdy. Washington, DC: Howard University.

Silverman, Eliane Leslau
    1982   Writing Canadian Women's History, 1970-82: An Historiographical Analysis. *Canadian Historical Review* 63: 515-33.

1984   The Last Best West: Women on the Alberta Frontier 1880-1930. Montreal: Eden.

Van Kirk, Sylvia
1984   What Has the Feminist Perspective Done for Canadian History? Pp. 43-58 in Knowledge Reconsidered: A Feminist Overview. Ottawa: Canadian Research Institute for the Advancement of Women.

ON THE TREATMENT OF THE SEXES IN SCIENTIFIC RESEARCH[1]

Yvonne Lefebvre

Introduction

Less than one-fifth of North America's scientists are women. Men dominate grant panels and decide where scientific research dollars go. Three examples illustrate the consequences of this male control over the funding of medical research. Osteoporosis, a disease that afflicts about forty percent of women by age sixty and costs the U.S. $3.8 billion annually, is poorly funded (Osteoporosis-Consensus Conference 1984). So too, premenstrual syndrome (PMS) attracts few research dollars and these only in the last few years. PMS, in fact, is still seen largely as a figment of women's imaginations. Again, male grant panels direct the vast majority of research funds for contraception, which can harm the body's chemistry, to the investigation of methods to be used solely by women.

Scientists in molecular biology, my own sphere of interest, focus much research on the search for the understanding of the "master" molecule, not on the interaction of molecules. The whole is conceived as under the control of one. This conceptualization reflects an authoritarian, male view of the world's organization, not the relatedness of a female view. Or, to take another example: recent studies that show sex differences in brain organization have been used, largely by male investigators, to explain differences in learning between men and women and especially the lesser mathematical abilities of women. Yet the difference in learning abilities <u>between</u> the sexes is, in fact, small compared with the differences <u>within</u> each sex.

These instances drawn from the life sciences demonstrate that scientific research suffers from gender bias. Because science is a male-dominated profession, we can see not only that women suffer, but that truth suffers too. To lessen gender bias, we need more women doing scientific research. But women's presence alone is not sufficient. Women must lead the scientific community. They must seek the instances where biased treatment of the sexes occurs. And they must eradicate it.

I, myself, would never have believed that gender bias pervaded so many levels of scientific research until very recently. I thought that gender bias began and ended with the predominantly male panelists' decisions of which research was to be funded. Then two things happened. First, I was asked to contribute to this volume. I remember saying to a friend that although I thought that there were not enough women doing science, I really did not believe that women could do a different kind of science. How could we, I argued, fight for equality, on the one hand, and yet, on the other, say that we had something unique to contribute? She pointed out that because men and women are currently products of different cultures, they are different, and they think differently. I began to think about so-called subjective input into "objective" science.

My awareness of gender bias was increased a second time at the 1985 International Congress of Biochemistry in Amsterdam. There Margareta Baltscheffsky, Chairperson of the Women's Caucus, presented "Why Should Women Do Science Anyway?" She argued for women's participation for two reasons: (1) <u>without science, women lose</u>: some women miss an opportunity for personal fulfillment by not participating in scientific careers; and (2) <u>without women, science loses</u>: over half of the available pool of talent is left out and the quality of science is thereby diminished. Contemporary science is simply not representative. To illustrate the last point, she mentioned that four times as many male rats as female rats are used in biochemical experiments. My ears pricked up at this example. In my research I have always employed male rats. Like many other scientists, I wished to avoid complications in interpretations of the data, complications introduced by female hormonal cycles. Obviously, any good researcher designs the least complicated experiment and, equally obviously, the male rat has the simplest hormonal system. But how universally applicable can I say my discoveries are when I have investigated less than fifty percent of the population? As a good scientist, I am obliged to state explicitly in all of my scientific publications that my results come from male animals or, better yet, to continue my investigation and find out if the same mechanisms operate in females at all stages of the estrous cycle. My blindness to the importance of this point I attribute to my professional upbringing by male scientists. After Baltscheffsky spoke, I began to question the validity of drawing conclusions about molecular mechanisms in both sexes after having studied only one.

Many scientists still scoff at the idea that gender bias can exist in scientific research. Similarly, any suggestion that women can contribute something unique to science meets with extremely stiff resistance (e.g., see Black's comments on Gould in this volume). The major reason for this resistance, I submit, is science's alleged objectivity. The scientific method consists of observation, hypotheses based on that observation, followed by rigourous testing of such hypotheses by further observation and by still further experimentation. This process is supposed to guard scientific inquiry from subjectivity. This objectivity is also supposed to produce what Charles Dickens' Mr. Chadband might have called "The Light of Terewth."

Nonscientists, however, have been questioning the objectivity of science for some time. T.S. Kuhn, in The Structure of Scientific Revolutions (1970), questioned whether science is autonomous, that is, whether it is logical, such that answers are forced upon it by ineluctable law. Since then some social scientists have tried to identify the political and social factors which affect the growth of scientific knowledge. Scientists themselves, though, have not recognized the subjective element in science. Evelyn Fox Keller wrote recently: "Working scientists may agree that political pressures affect the uses and even the focus of scientific research; but they fail to see how such pressures can affect their results, the description of nature that emerges from their desks and laboratories" (1985: 6). Ruth Bleier (in press) uncovered another example of how scientists' values, beliefs, and expectations influence what they actually see. The Aristotelean belief was that women contributed nothing to reproduction except for the incubating womb. Convinced of this erroneous notion, microscopists of the seventeenth and eighteenth centuries claimed that inside sperm they had seen exceedingly minute forms of men, complete with arms, heads, and legs. This is what they expected to see and they saw it. Scientists' unwillingness to acknowledge the subjective aspect of science is a classic case of "there being none so blind as they who do not want to see."

The contemporary women's movement and ideology of feminism were born in the 1960s. Barely were its eyes open when feminism found inaccuracies and omissions in historical documents, in literature, and in psychology. The avid feminists of the sixties vehemently damned these flaws, saying they arose from women's lack of participation in scholarly activity. Why has science not been investigated in the same way? Again the supposed objectivity of science is the reason. Evelyn Fox Keller (1985: 7) writes that there is a deeply rooted popular mythology that says objectivity, reason, and mind are masculine qualities, whereas subjectivity, feeling, and nature are feminine characteristics. Rather than risk being caricatured as males, girls and women have refrained from the practice of science. The kind of enquiry needed to ferret out gender bias in scientific research has not been undertaken, then, because science is considered objective and therefore not prone to untruth; and because of its masculine quality, women have not become scientists. The few feminists who have strayed into science are beginning to question the myth of objectivity in science and to shrug it off.

Evidence of Gender Bias in Scientific Research and Alternatives to the Bias

Beyond the very obvious kinds of gender bias in the granting of funds and in the selection of animals used in research, there are deeper, more subtle kinds of gender bias which I hinted at in the Introduction.

One scientific area especially prone to gender bias is brain research. Most people have heard of the nineteenth-century neuroanatomists and craniologists who measured the human brain to prove the biological superiority of the white male brain and temperament. Yet differences in the structure and function of the brain are still being used to explain presumed sex differences in ability to learn. Ruth Bleier (in press) reports that scientists who investigate prenatal hormonal effects on the developing brain and hemispheric lateralization of cognitive functions always stop just short of making assumptions that their data cannot support. She cautions, however, that such scientists can rely on their readers to supply what she believes to be the intended, relevant cultural meaning to their scientific work.[2]

Some assumptions that guide our reasoning in science are even more subtle. Evelyn Fox Keller (1985: 129) has considered this more abstract aspect of gender bias, and I would like to lead you through one of her arguments. One of the assumptions all scientists share is that the "universe they study is accessible; that it is represented by concepts shaped only by the demands of logic and experiment." "Laws of nature" are encoded in logical structures that require only the discernment of reason and the confirmation of experiment. She then goes on to demonstrate that the very concept "laws of nature" introduces into the study of nature a metaphor indelibly marked by its political origins. "Laws of nature, like laws of the state, are historically imposed from above and obeyed from below." Laws resemble authoritarian states and control by a governing body. An example of how this concept of the laws of nature influences our framing of questions is the central dogma of molecular biology: like an authoritarian government, DNA is conceptualized as a controlling macromolecule in cellular organization; information flows unidirectionally, from DNA, much as in a totalitarian state.

What Fox Keller proposes is that we replace the concept of law with the concept of order. The concept of order, she believes, is wider than that of law and also free from its coercive, hierarchical, and centralizing implications. "Order is a category comprising patterns of organization that can be spontaneous, self-generated or externally imposed; it is a larger category than law precisely to the extent that law implies external constraint."

Fox Keller concludes that an interest in order would imply far-reaching changes in our conception of science because it would imply a shift in the focus of scientific enquiry from the pursuit of the unified laws of nature to an interest in the multiple and varied kinds of order actually expressed in nature. Priorities would shift from hierarchical models of simple, relatively static systems towards more global models of complex dynamic systems. She observes that in physics such a change may already be taking place. New mathematical techniques now make it possible to replace traditional, time-dependent equations with those better suited to describing the emergence of particular kinds of order. In biology too, Keller believes that there is a resurgence of interest in complexity.

Gender bias in the construction of scientific theories is so indirect that it will require much exploration. Evelyn Fox Keller's argument is that the ideological pressures are directly related to the commitment of modern science to masculine concepts. How can this be changed? The first step is to allow more than the ideologies and self-interest of one sex to determine the nature of scientific research.

The Major Source of Gender Bias, Reasons for It, and Ways to Correct It

In this section I shall examine women in the "hard" sciences (e.g., mathematics, physics, chemistry, and geology) and in the more descriptive life sciences (primarily various types of biology).

At the first possible opportunity, many females withdraw from participation in science. This withdrawal occurs in high school when curricular options are first offered. Joan Scott, in Who Turns the Wheel? (1982: 23), reports that two to three times as many boys as girls were enrolled in high school physics in four provinces. More boys than girls were also enrolled in chemistry but the difference was smaller than for physics. Fewer girls than boys were also enrolled in pure mathematics. On the other hand, more girls than boys take biology. This may reflect, as Scott points out, the tendency of schools to require at least one science course to graduate. Biology is often perceived by students, according to another widespread myth, to be the least difficult of the sciences.

The same general pattern continues at the undergraduate level, as exemplified in The University of Calgary's Fact Book (for the years 1982-83; 1983-84; 1984-85). During the last three academic years for which statistics are available, at The University of Calgary, an average of 9 percent of those enrolled as physics majors were women. More women concentrated in chemistry (an average of 35 percent) and mathematics (pure: 29 percent; applied: 30 percent) although they seldom comprised much more than one third of the majors. An interesting exception to this pattern occurs in statistics, where an average of 75 percent of the undergraduate majors were women. However, the total number of students who majored in statistics during these three years was small (17) and thus the high percentage of women in this area may not be statistically significant. In the majors I have grouped together under life sciences, as many women as men are enrolled. Yet it is perhaps enlightening to note that while 55 percent of those concentrating in cellular and microbial biology are women, women constitute only 37 percent of the undergraduate majors in biochemistry. The same goal aspirations can be achieved with both majors, yet more women select biology than biochemistry.

The statistical picture for women in graduate programs appears fairly bleak (The University of Calgary's Fact Book [1982-83; 1983-84; 1984-85]). When the number of males and females enrolled in graduate studies in physics at The University of Calgary is compared, about the same ratios as seen in undergraduate programs reappear at both the M.Sc. (average of 11 percent) and Ph.D. levels (13 percent). The same holds true in geology and geophysics graduate degree programs, where 35 percent of the M.Sc. and 26 percent of the students are women. The number of women enrolled in mathematics and statistics drops dramatically to less than one quarter of the total enrollment while the women enrolled in chemistry drops slightly at the M.Sc. level (30 percent) and again at the Ph.D. (27 percent). If the life sciences in biology and medical sciences are considered, it is interesting that the percentage of women in biology graduate programs drops (M.Sc. 32 percent; Ph.D. 25 percent), while that of women in the medical sciences stays higher, at over 50 percent. (I was unable to determine how many students in chemistry graduate programs were enrolled in biochemistry.) It appears that the trend for fewer women to be enrolled in the so-called hard sciences persists in graduate school, whereas many women are still enrolled in life sciences graduate and professional programs.

I have been unable to obtain statistics for the number of women awarded postdoctoral fellowships in Alberta. However, Margareta Baltscheffsky at The International Congress of Biochemistry reported that in her study of biochemists in Sweden, it was clear that girls and women were not treated any differently than their male counterparts as far as awards were concerned until their postdoctoral years, when women were not awarded postdoctoral fellowships. Whether this bias also occurs at the postdoctoral level needs to be investigated.

Let us now examine the number of women in faculty positions. Only 18.5 percent of the full-time faculty at The University of Calgary are women; similarly women comprise only 19 percent of the faculty at the University of Alberta. Women continue to be underrepresented as faculty members of the "hard" sciences, just as they are from the secondary through graduate levels of education. At The University of Calgary, there is a single women among the faculty members in the physics department. In mathematics, statistics, and computer sciences, 2 out of 63 faculty are women. In chemistry 4 of 35 faculty members are women, while in geology there is a solitary women among 28 faculty. In the life sciences, where as many women as men are being trained to the Ph.D. level, women are still not assuming positions as independent researchers. In the department of biology, 3 out of 42 faculty are women. In medical biochemistry, 2 of 22 academic staff are women. In conclusion, the outcome in all sciences is the same: women never participate fully in the lifeblood of science itself, its research.

The reason for this lack of participation by women is likely the same for both the "hard" and "softer" sciences. Although in the "softer" sciences the withdrawal of women occurs later, many girls and women cannot see themselves pursuing scientific careers. One of the reasons most often cited is the stronger mathematical ability of boys. Anne-Marie Decore (1984: 35) found that the statistics of female performance in mathematics at the University of Alberta did not support this claim. I hope that the discussions and arguments provoked by possible sex differences in test scores on verbal, mathematical, and visual-spatial tasks will now end. The so-called irrefutable evidence does as much to lock males into roles as females. In <u>Who Turns the Wheel?</u>, Meredith Kimball (1982: 59) concluded, after reviewing the evidence of gender differences in ability and biological explanations for these differences, that "a disproportionate amount of energy has been spent examining biological explanations that have very little or at best mixed evidence to support them. We have been asking the wrong questions far too long." Kimball poses the important question: "Why is it that the difference in participation of men and women in scientific fields is so large when sex differences are so small?"

If inherent deficiencies in female abilities do not deprive them of the potential to achieve in science, what does? According to Linda Fischer (1982: 63), it is socialization that affects the involvement in science by young girls. Socialization does this by (1) imposing roles on a growing female child which discourage activities contributing to the development of those features which facilitate the learning and practice of science and (2) giving the female child an image of a scientist which may appear at odds with the image of the person she wants to be.

I shall not rehearse the entire area of stereotyping here, as it is common knowledge how pervasive the sex-role stereotypes in our

North American society are. Suffice it to say that most children and adults appear to believe that becoming a scientist involves the adoption of a whole, particular lifestyle rather than simply training to do a job. The most consistent features of the stereotypical scientist are intelligence and masculinity.

Jan Harding (1985: 159) believes that not only values but cognitive style separate women from science. Her research shows that even girls who do science perceive it quite differently from boys. The girls are more interested in seeking relationships in the natural world and are more concerned with the relevance of science to human needs. She has suggested that strategies for change should proceed on three fronts: (1) to challenge stereotypes with long-term planning, involving everyone concerned including the young people; (2) to reorganize the curriculum to ensure that curricular choices do not exclude individuals from essential areas of experience; and (3) to change curricula to facilitate the entry and continued involvement of girls in science and technology by presenting course offerings within the framework of our present social context. One way to achieve these goals is to attempt to reform the way science is taught in schools, emphasizing its practical applications in order to attract more girls. But the real revolution lies in the notion that the girls' perspectives on the world should be fully incorporated into the way we do science.

At the University of Alberta, a task force on Women in Scholarship, Engineering, Science, and Technology (WISEST) has been very active in trying to influence girls in secondary school, where choices are being made. Margaret-Ann Armour presented their strategies for change in a paper presented to the Third International Conference on Girls and Science and Technology (1985: 124). In May, 1984, WISEST also sponsored a provincial conference, "Steps to a Scientific Career"; 120 female high-school students joined teachers, women scientists, and women engineers in a program which included plenary sessions featuring distinguished women speakers, panel discussions, a careers fair, and a series of mini-symposia in which the scientists and engineers presented summaries of their work. In another ongoing program, high-school students spend six weeks during the summer as members of university research groups--girls in the sciences and engineering, boys in home economics. WISEST has also been working on the design of a presentation suitable for use in the Grade 9 classroom. A lesson on skin care, for example, has been developed and presented by a team of male and female scientists to students in junior high schools.

The work of WISEST is to be applauded and should be attempted in other communities as well. Professional scientists need to work with those involved in school curricula planning so that relatively minor but relevant changes could be implemented immediately and more foundational changes could be planned for the future.

WISEST has also founded the UAWS, University of Alberta Women in Science and Engineering, to provide support, encouragement, information, and role models to help students set and reach their goals. Distinguished female scientists have addressed the group and several meetings have taken the form of panel discussions on topics such as choosing a research director, coping with a family and a career, as well as science and gender. Young women are encouraged to consider what they would like to be doing in twenty years time and to design a career path which is most likely to lead to such a goal.

The programs implemented by WISEST at the University of Alberta should be copied everywhere. At The University of Calgary, for example, we have had a Women Scholars series. This was set up as a forum for interchange between university women here and visiting women scholars. Visiting women scientists from other universities came to speak about their lives as women and scientists; I, for one, derived much encouragement, support, and insight from their visits.

For some time now, I have been concerned about the very real withdrawal of women in the life sciences from academia after they have completed their graduate studies. The training period for a Ph.D. is for all a most challenging time. However, for women, it is not only a time when their intellectual and creative abilities are on the line. Female doctoral students realize that because of the ticking of their biological clocks they are compelled to make life decisions concerning both their careers and their family lives. At least partly because of the few role models available to them, very few women view having both as possible. We need to address this problem on two fronts. First, graduate students need to be made aware by being shown examples of women who have succeeded in doing both, that it is possible to have a successful career and to help raise a family. And, secondly, and perhaps more important, we need to make it easier for both men and women to participate in family life while pursuing their careers. In Canada such attempts are in their infancy.

The Equal Opportunities Committee of the Canadian Biochemical Society (CBS) has begun to approach granting agencies for changes in procedures which give women who want to have children no opportunity to do so while continuing with their careers. Most granting agencies in Canada will now allow postdoctoral fellowships to be taken up at any time after the Ph.D. rather than only immediately after obtaining a Ph.D. This allows both men and women more flexibility in planning their personal lives.

It is also very important that steps be taken to ensure that women graduate students are trained and groomed for faculty positions in the same way that men are. The CBS is considering a counselling service to deal with this problem.

Will More Women Scientists Guarantee the Elimination of Gender Bias in Scientific Research?

I believe that it would be naive to expect that male scientists should or could, without pressure, be expected to lead the scientific community in seeking both to eradicate gender bias in science and to formulate new ways of doing science. But can we expect the women who are doing science to effect these changes? Ruth Bleier, in the Introduction to Feminist Approaches to Science (in press), describes how contributors to that book disagree about who will effect the changes in science.

Vivian Gornick interviewed several hundred women scientists for her book, Women in Science (1983: 172). Among women scientists she found radical, liberal, and conservative feminists, as well as open-minded fellow-travellers and secret sympathizers. She found very few antifeminists among these women scientists. And there was not one scientist in her thirties or forties who did not acknowledge the influence of the women's movement on her own working life. But Gornick concluded that once women actually conduct research, the women work exactly like men. She was unable to observe how women organize their thoughts differently, or ask different kinds of scientific questions, or apply different methods of investigation.

Who will initiate changes aimed at eliminating gender bias in scientific research? Namenwirth (see Bleier in press) forecasts that pressures for changed in scientific practices and thinking will come from people who are outside of science, from the feminist movement, rather than originate from within, even from women scientists, because the latter are not alienated from the thinking or authoritarian voice that characterizes contemporary science. She believes that eventually feminist and other radical attitudes about ways to do science will come to seem less strange and threatening to scientists. On the other hand, Rose and Hrdy (see Bleier in press) believe that the presence of more women and feminists in the sciences will itself provide the force for change. If women constituted nothing less than half of the members of laboratories, Rose proposes, the daily interaction and the work would necessarily be different. Bleier (in press) notes that the study of primates, primatology, is the lone example in the natural sciences of dramatic changes having already taken place under the influence of feminist viewpoints. This is related in part to the critical mass of women and feminists within that field, a situation which does not exist in any other area of the natural sciences. Both Hrdy and Haraway (also in Bleier in press) agree that two related factors were responsible for effecting a major destabilization in long-held beliefs and assumptions: the entrance of large numbers of women into field primatology and their individual and collective feminist consciousness. Women primatologists were able to recognize that aggressiveness on the part of female primates was a sustained and natural characteristic and not aberrant behaviour as it has so often been categorized by men primatologists (see Hrdy and Haraway in Bleier, forthcoming). Women primatologists identified with the female primates under observation and with their problems at the same time that these scientists began to be aware of and to articulate problems that women confront in their world. Consequently, they began to formulate questions that had never been asked before concerning the behaviour and coping mechanisms of female primates. These new questions, observations, and interpretations transformed a body of beliefs that had been central to primatology. The presence of numerous women did make an impact on the research of primatology.

While I agree that women scientists, with the exception of primatologists, do not currently do a science that is different from that of men, I believe that fundamental changes can come from within science and that feminist scientists will lead these changes, as they have in primatology. After all, the feminists I have quoted in this paper were, for the most part, scientists. We need more women scientists to form a critical mass (so to speak), but without a desire for change and a feminist perspective, women will simply follow established paths of scientific research. The result of women scientists striving to rid the scientific disciplines of gender bias will be better science.

Endnotes

1. Many friends and colleagues have helped me to clarify my ideas while writing this paper, through sometimes heated but always enjoyable discussions. I want to thank especially Suzanne Kurtz for our jogging talks and Catherine Warren, who has forced me to take the next step in my thinking several times in the last sixteen years. Thanks too to my sister, Fleur-Ange, and my two graduate students, Betty Golsteyn and Gillian Howell, who, by sharing their struggles, enabled me to understand the universality of women graduate students' problems. Ruth Bleier kindly provided me with a preprint of the Introduction of her new book, <u>Feminist Approaches to Science</u>, and I thank her for this enlightening courtesy. Finally, thanks are due to Andrew Brown, who spent many hours helping me to refine my thinking and therefore my writing.

2. For example, readers supply the notion that women are inherently inferior in mathematical skills. I shall return to this point when discussing why young girls do not prepare themselves for careers in scientific research by taking more mathematics courses.

References

Armour, M.-A.
    1985 Women into Science, Engineering, and Technology: Strategies for Change at the University of Alberta. Pp. 124-31 in Contributions to the Third GASAT Conference. London: University of London.

Bleier, R. (ed.)
    in   Feminist Approaches to Science.
    press

Decore, A.-M.
    1984 Vivre la Difference: A Comparison of Male and Female Academic Performance. Canadian Journal of Higher Education 14: 35-58.

Fischer, L.
    1982 Science and the Environment of Young Girls. Pp. 63-74 in Who Turns the Wheel?, ed. Janet Ferguson. Ottawa: Science Council of Canada.

Gornick, V.
    1983 Women in Science: Portraits from a World in Transition. New York: Simon and Schuster.

Harding, J.
    1985 Values, Cognitive Style, and the Curriculum. Pp. 159-66 in Contributions to the Third GASAT Conference. London: University of London.

Keller, E.F.
    1985 Reflections on Gender and Science. New Haven, CN: Yale University.

Kimball, M.M.
    1982 Sex Differences in Intellectual Ability. Pp. 45-59 in Who Turns the Wheel?, ed. Janet Ferguson. Ottawa: Science Council of Canada.

Kuhn, T.S.
    1970 The Structure of Scientific Revolutions. Chicago: University of Chicago.

Scott, J.
    1982 Is There a Problem?: Enrolment and Achievement Patterns among Girls in High School Science in Canada. Pp. 23-32 in Who Turns the Wheel?, ed. Janet Ferguson. Ottawa: Science Council of Canada.

Osteoporosis-Consensus Conference
    1984 Osteoporosis-Consensus Conference. Journal of the American Medical Association 252: 799-802.

University of Calgary, Office of Institutional Research
 1982-83 Fact Book. Calgary: University of Calgary.

 1983-84 Fact Book. Calgary: University of Calgary.

 1984-85 Fact Book. Calgary: University of Calgary.

EPISTEMOLOGY AND WOMEN IN PHILOSOPHY: FEMINISM IS A HUMANISM

Petra von Morstein

Research in any intellectual discipline is determined by the methods of investigation in terms of which a discipline is defined. With the exception of philosophy, intellectual disciplines range over specific areas of topics, with some amount of overlap and interdisciplinary complementation. The concern of philosophy, however, is not with what we know and may come to know in any one specific area of enquiry, but with the conditions necessary for the possibility of human knowledge, its scope and limits. Thus philosophy is the investigation of experience, belief, understanding, knowledge, reason. Philosophy thereby concerns itself in principle with anything that can be experienced, believed, understood, known, explained: the empirical world and any aspect of it; science in general; any natural or social science (in particular, mathematics); law; religion; morality; politics; art; psychology.

Gender Bias and Points of View in Philosophy

Philosophy is gender-biased if only because the history of philosophy has been man-made. Human experience was investigated and explained almost exclusively by men. If male and female points of view systematically differ, and if a method of investigation is determined by a point of view, we must infer that Western philosophy, until this century, may have established explanations of what man perceives, knows, understands, believes. We can further infer that we have learned about human experience only in so far as such philosophical explanations are compatible with women's point of view. The fact that philosophers have referred mostly to man or men in their questions, statements, and examples is consistent with this account. By itself, it can therefore not be taken as a manifestation of gender bias.

Points of view are untransferrable. To integrate different points of view in any method for investigating human experience presupposes that they are mutually intelligible and can be shown to be so. Without addressing the question of whether there is a difference between male and female points of view, various philosophers in the history of Western philosophy did, however, hold that individual self-consciousness entails interrelation or communication with other self-consciousnesses. Leibniz, Kant, Hegel, and Heidegger all espoused some form of interrelatedness. Both Hegel (1977)[1] and Heidegger (1962)[2] held that for a self to exist is to be immediately and prereflectively aware of the existence of other selves. These two require special attention from feminist philosophers because, according to both, cognitive modes of consciousness presuppose or entail affective modes of consciousness. According to Hegel,[3] the primary intentional mode is desire; according to Heidegger,[4] care. The existence of other selves is thus part of every single self's "facticity."[5] Every point of view is necessarily different from every other; every point of view is untransferrably owned and therefore eludes complete conceptual representation. But, every point of view is also necessarily incomplete because it entails interrelatedness with other points of view. There cannot be a problem of the existence of other minds: this position, forcefully argued by some contemporary feminist philosophers (e.g., Sherwin, oral communication)[6] is firmly rooted in the history of philosophy.

Bias against a person or group of persons consists of eliminating their point(s) of view as irrelevant. Of course, no one can actually take every point of view into account. Hegel thought one could solve this problem only in terms of the Absolute Spirit; his insistence on the necessary interrelatedness of all points of view in history as a condition for the existence of any self constitutes a persuasive apology for the Absolute Spirit.[7]

The most one can actually do is to be open in principle to any point of view. Indeed this openness is necessary for the complete being and authenticity of any self. Such openness must be a criterion for the lack of gender bias in philosophy. By this criterion we can, for instance, assume that Heidegger's ontology and epistemology of caring in Being and Time (1962) is not gender-biased. But I shall not argue his or any other such case here. Rather, I shall address myself to the more general question of gender bias in philosophical method. It is assumed that any results that may ensue from the investigation of gender bias in philosophical method will illuminate problems of gender bias affecting current academic scholarship in philosophy. I shall also focus on some questions concerning the foundations of gender bias in philosophy scholarship and point to some of the possible consequences of such bias in the practice of academic philosophy.

Philosophical method itself became a topic in philosophy with Descartes. Spinoza held that philosophy must proceed more "geometrico," and he put forward philosophical arguments in favour of this mathematical method. For Hume philosophical enquiry had to proceed by analogy with experimental inquiry in science. Kant aimed at bringing metaphysics onto "the sure path of science." Hegel relied on dialectical processes; Husserl, on phenomenological reduction. Bergson's philosophy proceeded from intuition; Bradley's, from pure immediate feelings; Wittgenstein's, from the uncovery of nonsense in language; Heidegger's, from the truth that shines forth from any particular being as it immediately presents itself to the perceiver. All of them aimed to establish the foundations and limits of knowledge and truth.

For philospshers, to investigate knowledge must be to investigate human knowledge. There is only the human perspective to assume. The constitution of human persons as subjects must underlie all philosophy whether or not we can have a clear and distinct idea of subjectivity. But philosophy has fallen away from the human subject again and again, and for it to return to the subject sometimes requires a revolution in philosophy. For example, Kant (1965: 42) revolted against Plato when he wrote: "It was thus that Plato left the world of the senses, as setting too narrow limits to the understanding, and ventured out beyond it on the wings of the ideas, in the empty space of the pure understanding." Kant induced a philosophical revolution, which he himself compared to the Copernican revolution, and showed that knowledge by pure reason alone is impossible, that we cannot know objects as they are in themselves but only as they must appear to us by virtue of the nature of human subjectivity. Philosophy built on the notion of pure objectivity must be dogmatic and engender contradictions. It is self-deception and can be self-destructive.

Kant called for and accomplished a revolution in philosophy. Few explicit calls by philosophers for revolution in philosophy are so well-documented. Here is another, recent one: "The 'discovery' of the sex/gender system...calls for a revolution in epistemology....We can detect sex/gender...in what the problems of philosophy are supposed to be" (Harding 1983: 311-12). How exactly the sex/gender system affects and has affected epistemology is nowadays under investigation; explorations have just begun. It is obvious that especially epistemology and ethics in philosophy reflect it. Philosophy is, after all, "the business of reason" but tradition has man exercise reason, and woman live by the senses, feeling, and intuition. Traditionally man is believed to be rational and woman irrational.

This commonplace and effective prejudice about woman and man's natures in philosophical tradition forms the foundation of the following explorations. The duality which it maintains corresponds to the dualities of culture/nature, mind/body, abstract/concrete, knowledge/intuition. Philosophy, the business of reason founded on love for knowledge, has been traditionally masculine. It is then reasonable to assume that until the recent arrival of feminist philosophers, philosophy was restricted to and narrowly limited by, male points of view, that is, those of "men of reason." But I have already indicated reasons, despite the deplorable monosexuality of the history of philosophy, against this assumption.

I aim to show that the feminist revolution in philosophy, whose goal is to reconstruct philosophical problems and methods by integrating women's points of view and the content of women's experiences into epistemology, has allies in the history of philosophy and that women in philosophy need, for the sake of their cause, to resuscitate features of philosophical works of the past that have been ignored or maligned.

Historical Sources for Feminism

I start with a remark of a male philosopher who, justly or unjustly, is known as one of the most fervent misogynists among Western philosophers of the past twenty-five hundred years. Nietzsche, in Beyond Good and Evil states:

> A philosopher: that is a human being, who constantly experiences, sees, hears, suspects, hopes, dreams extraordinary things; who is struck by his own thoughts as if from the outside, from above and beneath; who is

> perhaps himself a thunderstorm, pregnant with new flashes of lightning; a doomed human being around whom it is always roaring and grumbling and tearing, and all is sinister. A philosopher: ah, a being who runs away from himself, who is often afraid of himself--but who is too curious not always to return to himself (para. 292, my own translation).

It is amusing that the philosopher is both "he" and "perhaps a thunderstorm, pregnant with new flashes of lightning." But it is not my concern in this paper to point out the explicit or implicit sexist opinions held by philosophers or their use of gender-biased language. Rather I hope to show that it is wrong for a feminist in philosophy to reject a male philosopher and his work on the grounds of his sexist opinions or language alone.

I am committed to the passion of the philosopher that Nietzsche describes, that is, both to the inevitability of philosophy, and to the suffering inevitably connected with it. The passion for the extraordinary is the passion not to settle in familiar and established schemata and explanations. It is the passion to confront the theories at hand with every new experience (and every experience is necessarily new) and to be prepared to discover their inadequacy or deceptiveness. This is the passion always to return to oneself, because it is one's own experiences with which one is most intimately acquainted. I am also convinced that knowledge is based on experience. This is a common enough view. A less common view holds that the original, irreducible basis of knowledge is concrete, felt experience. This experimental basis of knowledge can be expressed in the first person, as my immediate acquaintance with what is present in my consciousness. The immediacy of every experience as an inner, mental occurrence entails its unfamiliarity, its extraordinariness. What is now present in my consciousness, an "appearance immediately given," is marked by strict particularity. Yet the concepts I use to determine and communicate it are necessarily general. Any concept can represent a number of particular experiences; no concept can represent any one experience fully. This may lead one to ignore or eliminate unconceptualized, or indeed, unconceptualizable aspects of particular experiences: it is just this that revolutionary philosophers, for instance, Kant, Nietzsche, and women in contemporary philosophy, find has been done.

Strictly speaking, every single representation in a person's consciousness is a new experience, a "new flash of lightning." By virtue of its immediacy, no exhaustive, inductive, or formal account can be given of it. Every single experience is therefore the experience of something as extraordinary: it does not completely--if at all--fit into the order supplied by the concepts available for describing what is experienced. To be able to recognize and accept the extraordinary nature of every single experience, it is, however, necessary to possess the order inherent in our conceptual framework and explanatory devices. Otherwise we would be unable to speak; indeed we would be incapable of the passion of the philosopher. We would be like many species of nonhuman animals who live in a world perceived and recognized, but uninterpreted. The interpreted world, described and explained, is a condition for the possibility of philosophy, but it is not the world in which we exist. Rilke (1984: 151) similarly express our alienation:

> and already the knowing animals are aware that we are not really at home in our interpreted world.

The passion of the philosopher is to remain unsettled, to question concepts in the necessarily unfamiliar light of every new experience. To experience "extraordinary things" is not to be surrounded by weird objects and fanciful creatures. To experience extraordinary things is to experience human reality. The passion for the extraordinary is the passion for concrete human experience, from my and any point of view. I cannot have your experiences, whether you are a woman or a man; nor can you have mine. The uniqueness of our individual experiences in itself is not and cannot be a manifestation of gender bias. Only the incapacity or unwillingness to acknowledge the other point of view as necessarily interrelated with mine, a lack of openness to the other point of view, can be a manifestation of gender bias (or some other form of discrimination). Whether a male philosopher in the past did or did not hold sexist opinions or used sexist language need not and should not affect our research in philosophy nowadays. But the openness or lack of openness of their work to women's points of view determines their work's acceptability and usefulness in our present work. A philosopher's sexist opinions may be inconsistent with such openness but need not affect its philosophical potential.

The Epistemological Revolution of Feminist Philosophies

The epistemological revolution induced by feminist philosophers is committed to a version of epistemological empiricism which integrates concrete experiences as immediate and necessarily extraordinary. The various paths that can be and have been taken from this basic approach I cannot discuss within the scope of this paper. The fact that the history of philosophy has been made by male philosophers has, according to some feminist philosphers (see especially Harding and Hintikka 1983) at least two major consequences: (1) that it was a male-dominated point of view that determined accounts of reality, and (2) that philosophy fell away from concrete, felt experiences. The second consequences can be seen as a function of the first. For, the claim is that philosophy could not have been severed from concrete, felt experience had it been guided by a female point of view. There is, however, a danger lurking behind this position. If we assume a noncontingent difference between the male and the female points of view, it follows that "each sex can speak about but not for the other." That is indeed a view put forward by the report of the Social Sciences and Humanities Research Council (SSHRC) On the Treatment of the Sexes in Research (Eichler and Lapointe 1985). I consider this view dangerous indeed because it yields sexual discrimination as a logical consequence. I quote point A 3.4.4 of this report in full:

> Each sex can speak about but not for the other. If it is impossible to obtain information about members of one sex directly from themselves, and one must therefore use information about them from the other sex, it must be clearly indicated that at best these responses convey the opinion of one sex about the other, rather than the reality experienced by the other (Eichler and Lapointe 1985: 12).

This position necessarily results in the establishment of two distinct epistemologies: his and hers. From my perspective as a philosopher, I can in no way accept such a dichotomization of epistemology.

For the feminist approach to epistemology not to be self-defeating, male and female perspectives must be understood as constitutive factors of the human perspective. In order for this to be possible, both perspectives may have to be modified. I will show that both distinct perspectives, as tradition has led us to describe them, are antihuman. To put it more technically: women and men's points of view stand in contradiction to human nature if they are not taken as interrelated, but as distinctly separated. Feminism, only now entering the history of philosophy, must therefore envisage the task of eliminating the basis of this contradiction. Let me elaborate.

Knowledge by Acquaintance and Description

Self-reflection distinguishes humans from nonhumans. It involves two dimensions of knowledge: acquaintance and description. Think of a human perceiver whom I will call "I." Note that my use of the first person singular pronoun entails the capacity for self-reflection. It is by virtue of this capacity--let us call it "self-consciousness"--that I am a person and as such distinct not only from nonhuman animals (with the possible exception of dolphins and chimpanzees), but also from the Spinozistic God and the Kantian bearer of intellectual intuition. What I have in common with at least many species of mammals is the capacity for sense perception. In both animal and human perception, appearances of outer objects, of one's surroundings, are immediately present by way of sensations and awareness. Sensations are not given in perception, they are, as Kant says (1964: 202), the "mere matter of perception." Rather, prior to any determination through concepts, appearances (i.e., representation of objects in the environment) are given as unified and related. It is by virtue of such inner representations that both nonhuman animals and I are "at home" in the world and capable of orientation. There is much physiological and behavioural evidence that, in principle, their and my perceptual representations of the outer world are the same. I will assume that this is so, that nonhuman animals and I have the same perceptual constitution, and that the representations of objects in perception are a function of this constitution. Thus, there can be no guarantee that we perceive the world as it is in itself. The notion of reality as being independent from perceivers is noncontradictory, to be sure, but it must remain without any, even hypothetical, content for us. Reality is determined by the interrelation between perceiver and perceived.

On this nonconceptual (or preconceptual) level of experience the difference between me and nonhuman animals is that I am immediately aware of my inner representations as mine. I can ask the question: "What is my representation a representation of?" But I cannot ask, "Is this representation (this perceptual image, say) mine or yours?", in the way in which I can ask, "Did you or I take this photograph?", or even, "Is it my or your stomach that's rumbling?" For the immediate mental content of experiences there can be no intelligible question of ownership. Such immediate awareness of ownership necessarily accompanies my inner representations of objects. In

William James' phrase (1890), my experiences have for me the feeling of "warmth and intimacy" that your experiences cannot have for me. Immediate awareness of ownership and the capacity for self-reference mutually entail each other. Nonhuman animals cannot be aware of their inner representations as their own.

When I say "I" there is no way of mistaking the reference; self-reference cannot misfire. If I shout "I" from a crowd you may be unsure who said it; but once you know who said "I", you cannot ask, "Whom did you refer to?" There can be no doubt. But when I say "you," "she," "this," "that," "now," "here," I must supplement any such reference with a descriptive one. This descriptive reference may answer your question, but will still preserve your entitlement to doubt. Only self-reference is indubitably certain. I am saying nothing, note, of self-description. That is another matter.

May the preceding argument suffice to show that nonconceptual perception--with the component of self-awareness in my case, and without it for nonhuman animals--entails cognition or recognition of representations as unified and related. Such cognition is immediate; unity and relatedness are given--they are not imposed. Kant, the revolutionary philosopher, realized this, but could not render the cognitive aspect of our "sensible and empirical intuition" compatible with other views of his. On the one hand, he held (1964: 65-7) that mere perception is Anschauung, "intuition"--we do not perceive chaotic multitudes of elements, but organized units--and that the unity of understanding presupposes the unity of intuition. On the other hand, he believed that there is no knowledge without reason, and that "understanding is...the faculty of knowledge" (emphasis in original, 1965: 156) in that we, by means of concepts, impose order on the multitude of representations, each of which is ordered in itself and unified with "I." Truth and falsehood enter the scene with concepts, as if unity can be known only if it can be analyzed. In a contemporary philosophical idiom, we may say that Kant rejected the possibility of knowledge merely by acquaintance, and allowed only for knowledge by description. Indeed he went so far as to say that the contents of mere perception are "nothing." He wrote in a letter to Herz:

> [If I had the mentality of a subhuman animal, I might have intuitions but]...I should not be able to know that I have them, and they would therefore be for me, as a cognitive being, absolutely nothing. They might still...exist in me (a being unconscious of my own existence) as representations..., connected according to an empirical law of

> association, exercising influence upon feeling and desire, and so always disporting themselves with regularity, without my thereby acquiring the least cognition of anything, not even of these my own states (as quoted by Bennett 1966: 104-5).

Kant admitted that "only our sensible and empirical intuition can give to concepts sense and meaning" (1965: 163), but by denying nonconceptual and preconceptual cognition, he could find no way of accounting for the unity of intuition. In his view intuition is strictly passive and, without concepts, blind. Passivity alone, however, precludes cognition, which must be active. For example, I may indeed be passively affected by things given in my perceptual field, by way of merely having perceptual sensations. But such passivity precludes awareness; I do not then attend to what is given in perception. An act of attention is necessary for mere intuition. Attention is self-active; it originates in the self, again and again. It is what Husserl called the Ichstrahl, "the glancing ray of the Pure Ego" (1969: 267-70 [para 92]). Kant, unfortunately, devoted only one footnote to attention and did not explore it.

The capacity for self-reflection, for reflecting on my inner perceptual representations, is necessary for conceptual determinations. But such self-reflection also presupposes the possession of concepts. I can reflect on what is given in my consciousness only by means of concepts. Conceptual knowledge is indeed reflexive. Mere intuitive, nonconceptual knowledge is not. Because the cognition of nonhuman animals is without self-awareness--and is therefore nonreflexive and exclusively nonconceptual and unprejudiced--their preception is <u>unrestrictedly</u> open to their environment:

> With all its eyes the natural world looks out into the Open. Only our eyes are turned backward, and surround plant, animal, child like traps, as they emerge into their freedom. We know what is really out there only from the animal's gaze; for we take the very young child and force it around, so that it sees objects--not the Open, which is so deep in animals' faces. Free from death.
> ....
> Never, not for a single day, do we have before us that pure space into which flowers endlessly open. Always there is World and never Nowhere without the No: that pure unseparated element which one breathes without desire and endlessly knows (Rilke 1984: 193).

To conceptualize an inner representation is necessarily to restrict it. A statement cannot fully capture a particular experience. As Eliot (1963: 208) wrote:

> We had the experience but missed the meaning. And approach to the meaning restores the experience. In a different form, beyond any meaning....

Any one, inner representation can be appropriately expressed by any of a number of concepts, just as any particular object can be appropriately described in more than one way. Any one concept can be used to express any of an indefinitely large number of inner representations. To refrain from self-reflection and conceptualization of experiences would be to refrain from behaving as a person; one might cease to be a person.

Issues of truth and falsehood can be raised only with regard to conceptually restricted experiences. As descriptions, statements are true or false. What is immediately represented in consciousness is neither: it is known by immediate acquaintance. However, I can be true or false to my inner representations. Truth to my felt experiences on the preconceptual level entails the unity of the "I" that intuits with the "I" that thinks. To be false to my felt experiences is to be split between the "I" that intuits and the "I" that thinks, such that the latter, as it were, oppresses or suppresses the former. If knowledge is indeed self-reflexive, truth and falsehood cannot be subject merely to the verifiability or falsifiability of statements by objective criteria. In other words, objective proof is necessary, but not sufficient for truth. It is further necessary that I make my statements about the world, on the basis of my inner representations, _as_ the "I" of my inner representations. Thus, verification by objective proof _and_ the authenticity of a statement are conjointly necessary and sufficient for its truth. For a statement to be authentic, the felt quality of my experience must accompany it. This requirement has to be added to the Kantian condition for the possibility of knowledge that "it must be possible for the 'I think' to accompany all my representations" (1965: 152). My intuition, as mine, can be neither objectified nor transcendentalized. To account for the unity of intuition _and_ thought, all we can say is that my descriptions must be mine and felt to be so. This is not what Kant, as a man of reason after all, could envisage.

If the concepts that I use dissociates me from my felt experiences, I must question and revise them. If the way I speak in everyday discourse with my friend, lover, colleague, or chance acquaintance, or if the way in which I talk or write about philosophy dissociate me from my experiences and thereby from myself, I may still provide descriptions of the world that stand up to the conditions of public verification. But if they are not true to myself, their truth is incomplete. No speech-act, in whatever sphere of discourse, can be completely detached from its speaker and her or his point of view. To speak and act in dissociation from my felt experiences, from myself, is to succumb to self-deception and potential self-loss.

Authenticity, however, is no licence for idiosyncrasy or arbitrariness. It, too, is a necessary, not a sufficient truth-condition.

The unity of felt experience or intuition presupposes the integration of concrete, particular experiences in the epistemological endeavour. The principle of the unity of intuition is authenticity. Authenticity is a subjective and therefore unanalysable but empirical principle. Authenticity is truth to experience, not truth derived from experience. For statements to be authentic, experience must, as it were, be present in them.

Integrating Felt Experiences into Feminist Epistemology

Feminist epistemologists propose, in a variety of different ways, the integration of concrete, particular experiences and require truth to felt experience. I have shown how felt experiences (i.e., my representations) are, for "I," connected with self-awareness, the capacity for self-reflection and conceptualization of my representations. Self-awareness and self-reflection, as well as language-possession, constitute human nature. Better still, they distinguish persons from nonpersons. It is easy to see now that the feminist and the existentialist (especially Heideggerian) approaches to epistemology are alike in many important ways.

How, if at all, should the duality of male and female experiences enter into feminist epistemology? I do not doubt that in many respects male ways of experiencing the world are markedly different from female ways of experiencing the world (how females and males experience, for example, everyday circumstances, human physiology, parental relations, friendships, love relations, sexuality, morality, intellect, professional routines, and challenges); that such differences are deeply rooted in history and tradition as well as in biology; that these different ways made feminism necessary. The world has been dominated mainly by men in the past. Even a glance at history yields the schema of male points of view as those of the oppressors and of female points of view as those of the oppressed. Thus the duality of male and female perspectives generates the paradox of the Hegelian master-slave relation. For the master to aim at the oppression of the other is to aim at the destruction of the other as a self; the consequence would be the loss, for the master, of the I/you distinction in relation to the other as slave, and thereby the loss of the capacity for self-reference and self-reflection. The slave in turn would be forced to dissociate the "I" that thinks and acts from the "I" that feels and experiences. Thus the duality of male and female perspectives, as a duality of oppressor and oppressed, stands in contradiction to human nature. If feminists maintain such a duality, they make the mistake that they might condemn Hegel for: the mistake of looking at the world in terms of never-ending, adversary human relations. To ground the notion of female experience in the history of male domination and oppression is self-defeatist. For feminism to be effective, this duality must be overcome.

Women are more commonly given to being consistent with the human factor of self-awareness and less inclined to dissociate their thinking from concrete felt experiences than men. I see one of the feminist tasks in philosophy, and elsewhere, to be that of alerting men to such consistency and of preventing the dissociation of our thinking from our felt experiences. Both oppressors and oppressed must be freed from oppression in order to be able to be free to themselves. The feminist resistance against oppression must be resistance against the effects of oppression both on the oppressed and on the oppressor. Such resistance must be initiated by the oppressed; the oppressor who resists oppression ceases to be one.

Even in the ideal case of successful resistance against oppression, the contents of male experiences and female experiences may continue to vary. But experimental differences between the sexes need not undermine the unity of the human perspective any more than the necessary difference between my and your experiences does. As we have seen, conceptual expressions of inner representations must be restrictive. Common knowledge can only be of common factors of individual experiences. What you and I accept as common knowledge must be true to your and my experiences, and it can only be _felt_ to be so by you and by me. Common human knowledge must be true to both men's and women's experiences. There may be no way of strictly and universally distinguishing between women's and men's experiences.

I submit that feminism in philosophy should continue to strengthen the form of humanism that existentialism manifested in objection to traditional forms of humanism. Feminist approaches to epistemology must resist previous theories of knowledge that do not allow for the fact that every experience has a necessary component which eludes anticipation and analysis. The revolutionary Kant went so far as to show that sensations, as the matter of perception, cannot be anticipated: "[Appearances contain]...the real of sensation as merely subjective representation, which gives us only the consciousness that the subject is affected, and which we relate to an object in general" (1965: 202). Furthermore, "sensation is just that element [in the appearances] which cannot be anticipated" (1965: 202-3). If the felt qualities by virtue of which my experiences are necessarily my own cannot be described and, therefore, not be anticipated, we must not ignore them for this reason, but let them show themselves. Not to do so, and to treat entities--ourselves and our environment--by fitting them into our theories is to simplify "things," as they show themselves in our experiences. In <u>Will to Power</u>, Nietzsche said that truth, built only on thought, is "the kind of error without which a certain kind of creature could not survive" (para. 493, my translation).

We can know objects (the world) only as we experience them. Because experience cannot be fully anticipated, we cannot fully formulate--describe, analyse, predict--our world. Description, analysis, and prediction are secondary and restrictive in relation to existing entities, including ourselves as subjects, as they show themselves in our experiences. Existence precedes description and supercedes it, too. Or, as existentialists say, "Existence precedes essence." Thus we have to think of the world-in-experience (there is no other) as necessarily unfixable, becoming, and therefore elusive of formulation. Nietzsche, in <u>Will to Power</u>, writes that

> Knowledge and becoming are mutually exclusive. Thus knowledge must be something different: a will to make known must precede it; it must be through a kind of becoming that the illusion of being is generated (para. 517, my translation).

We must think of the world as becoming, because it must be the world-in-experience; the experiencing, self-aware, "I" is systematically elusive. I cannot begin and continue, and therefore I cannot <u>be</u>,

> ...when I am formulated, sprawling on a pin,
> When I am pinned and wriggling on the wall, (Eliot 1963: 15).

But to be an experiencing "I" is to have to ask "the overwhelming question"--"What is the 'I'?"--and to wait for an answer. It is, in Heidegger's phrase, part of our "facticity" (1962: 58). Problems of ontology, the question of being, are a constituent of our being; our being is "being-in-the-world," is subject-object relation. Formulation alone cannot constitute knowledge. To rely exclusively on formulation and analysability is to ignore how entities do and can show themselves. Formulation is interdependent of looking and seeing: "to let that which shows itself be seen from itself in the very way in which it shows itself from itself" (Heidegger 1962: 58).

Restriction is necessary for common knowledge. But it is a step to be taken differently again and again in the process of knowledge, along with the process of becoming. Knowledge is a process, not a state. To fix individuals in a formulated phrase is to oppress them directly; to structure our environment is to oppress them indirectly. Nietzsche, of course, was right: a certain stability of beliefs is necessary for our survival. But this stability does not mean that our beliefs can capture the nature of what is and is shown in experience.

For a person to be oppressed, she or he must be treated as a fixed object, not as a subject, a self. People of oppressed groups are prevented from developing as selves, from choice, from becoming. Given the history of a male-dominated world and women's oppression, and given women's concrete experiences of resisting and overcoming oppression, the following consequence for women in philosophy is obvious and overwhelmingly urgent: concrete human experience must be the original basis of common knowledge and limit its possibility. This is why "being-in-the-world" for a person (Dasein in Heidegger's terminology) is being circumspectively related within one's environment. Propositional knowledge can only supplement the caring which is necessary to let human beings show themselves as they do and to be able to disclose themselves in experiences. Caring and concern characterize the primary cognitive mode for Heidegger. Concepts without intuitions are blind. Concepts without intuitions generate oppression.

Women in philosophy, from the points of view of people in the process of overcoming oppression, must resist and reject the present, rigid opposition to the notion of ineffability. Philosophy in the analytic tradition denies the possibility of nonpropositional knowledge, of "merely" intuitive understanding, and of the ineffable aspects of human experience. In analytic philosophy, the man of reason thrives and flourishes while the person of feeling has a life, if at all, only outside the profession. Even Kant had one life in analytical philosophy and another life outside. As a man of reason, he was so respectable that as a European philosopher he was not subsumed under the arbitrary, pejorative heading of "continental philosophy." But his struggle over the ineffable aspects of experience and knowledge is hardly discussed in Anglo-American commentaries.

For women in analytical philosophy to succeed, they had to work like men of reason. As experiencing, feeling persons women were thus oppressed. The professional experience, with or without public success, was a continuation of an oppressed life. For example, I found myself adopting the "adversary method" (see especially Moulton 1983) that is so characteristic of analytical philosophical investigation, against myself, inauthentically. Was I oppressed into becoming an oppressor?

But the revolution in philosophy, especially in epistemology and ethics, by women in North American philosophy is a revolution in analytical philosophy, and cannot, as I hope I have shown, be a revolution in all of the history of philosophy.

Conclusion

It is indeed deplorable that the history of philosophy before the second half of this century, with the exceptions of the German medieval philosopher Hildegard von Bingen,[8] and the eighteenth-century English philosophers Anne Conway (1982) and Mary Wollstonecraft (1982), is exclusively man-made. But this is no reason for women in philosophy to reject the works of individual male philosophers, even if they held sexist opinions and used sexist language. Only if a philosopher's method generates blindness against what is to be experienced should it be rejected.

For a woman to attempt to bring the ineffable back to philosophy in an analytic philosophy department would be for her to take the risk of isolating herself and fuelling the established adversarial method. For women in Anglo-American philosophy to increase their effectiveness in this respect, they should admit that various male philosophers in the history of philosophy have taken indispensable steps on the revolutionary path. I do not hesitate to receive Kant, Hegel, Kierkegaard, Schopenhauer, Nietzsche, Bradley, Heidegger, and Sartre into the revolutionary group. I would also consider Husserl and Wittgenstein, even Rousseau, as candidates to help the feminist philosophical cause. To be sure, I would not want to be married to any of these male philosphers, though I am--I must admit--quite fond of Kant. They all, to varying degrees, display at least some openness to a female point of view.

It is incumbent on feminist revolutionaries in analytical philosophy to work towards terminating the utter isolation of this tradition from central aspects of its own history. Feminist philosophy cannot afford to be as ahistorical as the analytical tradition against which it rebels. It also cannot tolerate any proposal to dichotomize epistemology into two gender-specific ways of knowing. Feminism must be a humanism.

Endnotes

1. See 'The Truth of Self-Certainty,' especially 109-13.
2. See especially Part One, Division One, IV and V, 149-224.
3. In particular, see 1977: 105, 109f., 217-21.
4. See 1962: Part One, Division One, VI, 225-73 and Division Two, III, 349-82.
5. For example, see Heidegger 1962: 234-8.
6. Susan Sherwin presented "Philosophical Method and Feminist Method; Are They Compatible?" at the Annual Conference of the Canadian Society for Women in Philosophy, October, 1985 in Vancouver, B.C. To my knowledge this paper is so far unpublished.
7. See, for example, the Preface (1977: 1-45) and 'Spirit' (1977: 266-409).
8. Hildegard von Bingen lived from 1098-1179 and wrote Physica; Cause et Cure; Orde Virtutum; and Scivias.

References

Bennett, Jonathan
    1966   *Kant's Analytic*. New York: Cambridge University.

Conway, Anne
    1982   *The Principles of the Most Ancient and Modern Philosophy*, ed. Peter Loptson. The Hague: Martinus Nijhoft.

Eichler, Margrit, and Lapointe, Jeanne
    1985   *On the Treatment of the Sexes in Research*. Ottawa: Social Sciences and Humanities Research Council of Canada.

Eliot, T.S.
    1963   *Collected Poems 1909-1962*. London: Faber and Faber.

Harding, Sandra
    1983   Why Has the Sex/Gender System Become Visible Only Now? Pp. 311-24 in *Discovering Reality*, ed. Sandra Harding and Merrill B. Hintikka. Dordrecht, Holland: Reidel.

Hegel, G.W.F.
    1977   *Phenomenology of Spirit*, tr. A.V. Miller. Oxford: Oxford University.

Heidegger, Martin
    1962   *Being and Time*, tr. J. Macquarrie and E. Robinson. New York: Harper and Row.

Husserl, E.
    1969   *Ideas*, tr. W.R. Boyce-Gibson. London: George Allen and Unwin.

James, William
    1890   *Principles of Psychology*. 2 vols. New York: Holt.

Kant, Immanuel
    1965   *Critique of Pure Reason*, tr. Norman Kemp Smith. New York: St. Martin's.

Moulton, Janice
    1983   A Paradigm of Philosophy: The Adversary Method. Pp. 149-64 in *Discovering Reality*, ed. Sandra Harding and Merrill B. Hintikka. Dordrecht, Holland: Reidel.

Rilke, Rainer Maria
    1984   *The Selected Poetry of Rainer Maria Rilke*, tr. Stephen Mitchell. New York: Vintage Books.

Wollstonecraft, Mary
    1982   *Vindication of the Rights of Women*. Harmondsworth, UK: Penguin.

WHERE ALL THE LADDERS START: A FEMINIST PERSPECTIVE ON SOCIAL SCIENCE

Naomi Black

> Now that my ladder's gone,
> I must lie down where all the ladders start,
> In the foul rag-and-bone shop of the heart.[1]

Definitions of feminism vary, but all focus on women's autonomy, their claim to define their own options.[2] The key concept for feminism is therefore self-determination and, by implication, feminist research must take especially seriously the scholar's necessary task of self-definition. The conditions of academic enquiry reinforce the necessity. The female scholar is always likely to be forced to justify her presence in a setting where women are still relatively few, with their acceptance conditional on conformity to the existing modes of behaviour and enquiry. The feminist can expect more serious challenge and can anticipate hostility or, at best, indifference. The response of some feminists has been to reject participation in any of the established scholarly structures, whether institutional or analytic, choosing instead some version of radical action-research in the context of women's community politics. Others, however, have opted for a self-consciously feminist scholarship which still relates to the conventional mainstream pattern. I am concerned here with a subcategory of such research, what could somewhat dramatically be called "feminist social science." Less provocatively, it could be called "a feminist approach to social science."

"Feminist social science" sounds like a contradiction, a paradox. It fits the label Ann Scales applies to "feminist jurisprudence": a "historically threatening attitude" (1980: 375). That is, it looks like a political stance, which could therefore be dismissed as irrelevant to the conduct of research. But the scholarly tradition to which this term could refer is, nonetheless, a recognizable one. Furthermore, I think it can be developed to give guidelines to the feminist researcher. I shall discuss it here with special reference to political science, for this is the field in which my particular research belongs, and consequently the field about which I most need guidance. Political science, as I understand it, overlaps political sociology, political philosophy, and some areas of history. The general argument is, of course, applicable to all fields of social science, and extensible into other areas of research; I shall be referring to the study of literature and of pure science.

Feminist scholarship starts, in general, from the recognition of sexism in research. At the simplest, this is the realization that women are virtually absent in most accounts of human existence. Gaps must be filled, incompleteness identified and compensated for. This stage is now summed up by women's-studies scholars somewhat contemptuously as "add women and stir"; women enter history as what was going on "meanwhile." The nonfeminist scholar, however sympathetic, is likely to conclude that, using existing methods and categories, such research really produces little that is qualitatively new. A comforting, related line of analysis suggests that changes in modern social science could make incorporation of women's activities and concerns easier. For instance, political science's recognition of the political nature of social movements means that it can study the Women's Movement; Jo Freeman won a prestigious thesis prize on this basis, admittedly in International Women's Year (Freeman 1975).

A second stage of scholarship, which may be the first to be genuinely feminist, shifts attention to standards and techniques, finding a more serious sexism in the failure to apply to the study of women the criteria supposedly in general use. In political science at this point Susan Bourque and Jean Grossholtz (1974) showed how even eminent scholars have "fudged" footnotes, misusing earlier studies and disregarding evidence in their discussions of the supposed indifference of women to political participation. Thus, for instance, the few volunteered remarks of foreign-born Chicago women in a 1923 survey continue to be a major basis of statements that nonvoting women believe "woman is a flower for men to look after" and "a women's place is in the home" (Bourque and Grossholtz 1974: 256).

Though feminist in perspective and intentions, most such early critiques of social-science scholarship in effect merely ask for adherence to the academy's professed standards. Virginia Sapiro phrases it as follows:

> Accusations of sexism--whether levelled at the field as a whole or at an individual's work--are accusations of poor scholarship. Scholars cannot make assumptions about women or ignore gender where it is relevant without violating their own canons of research (1979: 264-65).

This transforms "accusations of sexism" into relatively benign enquiries that do not question methods or goals.

Yet feminist political scientists in practice learn that neither gaps nor distortions in accepted wisdom can easily be remedied by use of the available approaches or data. They find themselves led to the use of relatively marginal sources such as oral history and participant observation. This in turn, along with increased sophistication in the use of such "soft" material, produces reasoned defences of it, justifications that seek an independent rationale in terms of scientific goals. Feminists in social science thus acquire a deep distrust of the standards and procedures of the systems of enquiry in which they were trained. As political sociologist Thelma McCormack puts it, they begin to suspect a sort of "malevolence of method" (1981: 10). The criteria of "generality" and "objectivity" come to look like effective devices for maintaining male control, obstacles to truth rather than instruments for discovering it. There can be no doubt that such reactions are encouraged by the way in which the academic establishment as a whole still ignores or repudiates the findings of feminist scholars, pushing them into the isolated though fruitful enclaves of Women's Studies.

In the terminology now increasingly used for feminist ideology, we can see that some feminist scholars at this point turn to arguments like those of social feminism. In this long-established tradition of theory and activism, women's entitlement to equal attention and equal treatment is essential--as for all feminism. In addition, the notion of differentiated female values and experience serves social feminists as the basis of criticisms of existing social arrangements. The contrast is with the different versions of what I call "equity feminism," versions which emphasize women's similarity to men. Generally speaking, equity feminism aims to incorporate women into the existing versions of scholarship and society, while social feminism tries to transform all involved. In the social-feminist analysis of scholarship, a new mode of scholarly discourse is prophesied, seen as derived from and supportive of a new, transformed social realm.[3]

We can see the two sorts of feminism operating in the feminist discussions of political-science scholarship. The application of academic standards to the study of women continues to be basic to the feminist project. At the same time, there is more fundamental criticism. Indeed, certain scholars among the earliest feminist critics, such as Bourque and Grossholtz and their successors Murray Goot and Elizabeth Reid (1975), had already questioned assumptions based on the male monopoly of politics. Is it reasonable, they asked, to consider a state to be democratic if it denies the vote to women, as Switzerland did for so long? Do the similar votes of married men and women really mean that women are voting as ordered by their husbands? Should adult, experienced women be seen as "immature" because they make different choices, political as otherwise, than the equivalent men? By the eighties such social-feminist perspectives had become a significant feature of most, though not all, feminist critiques of social science.

For instance, in 1981 Virginia Sapiro prepared a lengthy "Research Frontier Essay" on women and politics for the prestigious <u>American Political Science Review</u> and concluded reassuringly that "political science can only benefit by expanding its views [to include women]" (1981: 713). In the same journal issue, Irene Diamond and Nancy Hartsock responded with a strong statement of disagreement:

> In sum, we are not saying, as Sapiro does, that recent scholarship in women's studies can show that political science has been studying the actions of only half of humanity, and that the subject matter of political science should be expanded. Instead, we are suggesting that the focus on the activity of only half of humanity is fundamental to what has been understood as political life for the last 2,500 years....To include women's concerns, to represent women in the public life of our society might well lead to a profound redefinition of public life itself (1981: 721).

Expanded to the whole of social science, this approach criticizes the mode of enquiry that has become enshrined as the scientific method. Catharine MacKinnon states the most far-reaching implications:

> Feminism does not see its view as subjective, partial, or undetermined but as a critique of the purported generality, disinterestedness, and universality of prior accounts. These have not been half right but have invoked the wrong whole. Feminism not only challenges masculine partiality but questions the universality imperative itself (1983: 537).

Such a perspective is a powerful solvent for the pretensions of sexist theory. An interesting, sometimes important critical literature has developed in its wake (Sherman and Beck 1979; Spender 1981; Harding and Hintikka 1983). Attempts to develop positive guidelines and models of procedure have been more difficult. MacKinnon, for instance, is disappointing. Although she makes a convincing case for the argument that "aperspectivity is revealed as a strategy for male hegemony" 1983: 537), all she can suggest for guiding alternative research is the substitution of the concept of female "desire" for male "power." As Judith Kegan Gardiner points out (1983), MacKinnon herself retains such assumptions as the use of the heterosexual dyad in defining female sexuality. More important, in the context of philosophy of science, she continues the "binary thinking" that lumps all female experience together as "difference" contrasted to the universality claimed by males; there is no allowance for the diversity among women (or, a point not made by Gardiner, for diversity among men). Gardiner concludes somewhat ruefully that she also lacks "substitute models to offer"; she regrets that she can recommend nothing more precise than continued attempts to conceptualize female specificity (1983: 736).

Both MacKinnon and Gardiner can be seen as working from a social-feminist perspective, in that women's values and experience provide their criteria for judging theory. At the same time, their modes of analysis are equity-feminist ones--accepting mainstream demands for grand theory and master concepts. They thus opt for one of the two ways in which feminists have attempted to restructure social science. Now the distinction is no longer that of the source of criteria, nor of the goal of the endeavour. Rather, it relates to a contrast familiar in philosophy of science, corresponding in a rough way to deductive as opposed to inductive approaches. For feminists, it has meant a choice: emphasizing either language and the construction of grand theory, or experience and a critique of the processes of enquiry. Both are easily encompassable within equity feminism; both present major problems from a social-feminist perspective.

MacKinnon can be understood better when we realize that she is operating in the first, deductive mode; she is among those North American feminists strongly influenced by the mainly French emphasis on language, seen as the repository of values and the shaper of human experience. The goal is to purify language and ideology, breaking free of the established patriarchal ("phallo-centric") fashions of apprehending reality.

The anglophone feminist's response to such efforts is likely to be mixed, divided between admiration and skepticism. For France, a nation where the highest prestige comes from election to the editorial board of a dictionary, an assault on language seems appropriate for challengers to the establishment; the more so with a language as deeply sexist as French. Yet the analytic modes of this deconstruction are male-generated and male-dominated, and not by men sympathetic to feminism. In addition, it is reasonable to apply to feminist theory its own critique of conventional scholarship, asking about social consequences: French feminism has been exceptionally faction-ridden and elitist. This is the country where the hegemonic, linguistically oriented "Psych et Po" actually trademarked the term "Women's Liberation Movement" (Sauter-Bailliet 1981; Kauffmann-McCall 1983).

Such criticisms are, of course, ones made from within a perspective of social feminism. In contrast, feminists committed to some version of North American equity feminism are unhappy with any analysis relying on female specificity. Carolyn Heilbrun, who has written approvingly of androgyny (1973), praises the French approach as "full of possibility and high intelligence," calling it a "brave undertaking," in spite of doubts that it "will eventuate in great advance for women" (1979: 21). Heilbrun is less satisfied with the alternative approach, which she labels "American," and correctly describes as "more empirical, less theoretical" (1979: 209). For her, such attempts are fatally constrained by the assumption that there is an "irreversible distinction between the sexes": "Womanhood must be reinvented by those who can imagine, not by those who wish to reconstruct their gender prison" (1979: 210). Her own position is clear: "So far, it is men who have told stories." She continues, "But perhaps women have not told stories because there were no stories to tell. There was only the dailiness of life, the attention to food, clothing, shelter, the endless replication of motherhood" (1979: 210).

Heilbrun therefore calls for the female appropriation of male experience and records, the consequent "reinvention of womanhood" as what manhood is, "a condition of risk, and variety, and discovery" (1979: 212). Her account embodies that equity version of feminist criticism which accepts existing (male) standards as a basis for changing the situation of women, through scholarship and through action.

In contrast, the most distinctive form of social-feminist critiques of social science, which focuses on content, highlights precisely the "dailiness of life" that Heilbrun discards as uninteresting. When anthropologists report that "women have not told stories," the response is not, agreeing with Heilbrun, that women as such lack a subject for narrative. Instead, there is offended distrust of the account of women's lives supplied by conventional techniques of enquiry and analysis. At the extreme, this approach concentrates on the subject or content of research, and aims at an atheoretic, direct examination of "the everyday world as problematic." The phrase is Dorothy Smith's; she is a Canadian sociologist who has tried to delineate a "sociology for women" (1979). Her analysis underlines the difficulties of this approach, which is nevertheless the one I shall attempt to adapt here.

Smith states explicitly the feminist conviction that modes of analysis are aspects of domination and, in particular, that systems of even intellectual order serve those who exercise social control. Her argument is framed in reference to sociology but applies to all social science and certainly to dimensions of the humanities:

> This implication that the actualities of the everyday world are unformed and unorganized and that the sociologist cannot enter them without a conceptual framework to select, assemble, and order them is one that we can now understand in this special relationship of a sociology constituted as part of a ruling apparatus vis-à-vis which the local and the particular, the actualities of the world which is lived, are necessarily untamed, disordered, and incoherent (1979: 174).

The recommended solution, a seductive one, is simply to go directly to the "local and the particular, the actualities of the world which is lived" (1979: 174).

Dorothy Smith is surely correct in stating that images of domestic disorder are part of the cultural control of women in a context where the everyday world is seen as a female domain. The socially dominant position of the "trained" researcher plays a role in the assumption that only general principles developed elsewhere can make any sense out of the domestic. But Smith attributes too much power to the investigator, who is less an imposer of order than one who may mistakenly report something which is not substantiated by reality. The system of control in turn is weakened by such inaccuracy—a possible partial explanation for the emergence of feminism. That is, perhaps women do tell unheeded but significant tales in spite of scholarly denial that it is possible. The feminist vision insists precisely on the objective reality of daily life; the more sophisticated feminist makes this assertion in full awareness of the existence of distorting simplifications of what is often fluid and ambiguous. The dominant observers are ignorant and arrogant; their privileged position make them perceive a tamed version of reality. But their power, although great, is inadequate to reshape the world entirely into the pattern of their perceptions.

At the same time the aspirations of the dominated are misleading. They are tempted to read resistance into their own situation even when it is characterized, most often, merely by complexity and potential (Rupp 1981). Accordingly, the feminist researcher may well have reason to hesitate as she seeks a focal point. Smith's proferred solution seems to represent that of the feminist critics who are prepared to say, with enticing and deceptive simplicity, women must begin where they are. In fact, she goes further. Here are her specific instructions:

> How our worlds are determined by processes which do not appear fully within them is a matter for investigation and inquiry, not for speculation. Making the everyday world our problematic instructs us to look for "inner" organization generating its ordinary features, its orders and disorders, its contingencies and conditions, and <u>to look for that inner organization in the externalized and abstracted relations for economic processes and of the ruling apparatus in general</u> (1979: 184, emphasis added).

Smith thus recognizes the existence of structures that are not directly observable in everyday life, and that have a wider range than the immediate activities of women. Even a naive social science must recognize the ways in which humans attempt to make sense of the temporal and spatial aspects of their lives, in the context of other times and places they have experienced or anticipate. This context must necessarily be expanded to include notions of connected, relating, encompassing, similar, or different lives, though this is in practice difficult and bound to be incomplete. This source of the markers and definitions necessary for the process is the key question, and one with which all theories of induction are still struggling.

Dorothy Smith, who seems to waive structure, in fact stipulates one. But hers is not a feminist framework. "The externalized and abstracted relations of economic processes and of the ruling apparatus in general" cannot be derived from women's "everyday world," nor were they. Marx and his followers teased this conceptual model out of careful observation of that everyday world which is most characteristically male: the paid labour force in advanced capitalism.

Its components are particularly difficult to trace in operation within domestic life, as a generation of Marxist feminists can testify. Smith herself cites a far more persuasive example of induction, drawn from Kurt Vonnegut--derivation of the nature of war from street-level experience of the bombing of Dresden. But she cites it as an argument for the ruling framework she prefers (1970: 177-78).

Smith has in fact imposed Marxist abstractions on the specificities of women's life. Marxist feminists who emphasize the Marxist aspect of their beliefs more heavily than she does move on to praise the "problematic of everyday life" as the locale where Marxism can best be perfected: "The women's movement has reinvented Marx's method and for that reason can be a force for revolution [and] a model for the rest of the left" (Hartsock 1979: 66). The priority of the interests of "the left" over those of women is clear: it is already implicit in the priorities of analysis in Smith's account. Like the conceptual categories used to sort their experience, women are secondary. They can enter history only because they can be assimilated into the systems of production defined by and in terms of men. Such a derivative equity feminism can produce only limited autonomy at either the theoretical or the practical level.

Still, however illogically, Smith and analysts like her do insist on the independent interest and importance of women's activities. Such analyses in practice point to the diversity that is the concrete expression of women's shared situation. Even when constrained by Marxism, feminism directs attention to life as experienced by women--in this case, their versions of class differentiation. In addition, even though some Marxist feminists have put their major energy into adapting the notion of domestic labour to the categories of use and exchange value, others have been able to suggest reconceptualizations of the household as units which challenge as well as support capitalism (Fox 1980; Rapp 1982). Searching among women's activities for resemblances to the class struggle, some feminists have identified even dimensions of consumerism as elements in proletarian resistance to the bourgeoisie (Rowbotham 1977). Attention to the everyday thus leads them to attribute value to the same differentiated activities and values which characterized the starting point of the social feminists whom they often despise as being conservative. Like the social feminists, they come to see domestic activities and values as a basis of women's intervention in and transformation of the public realm.

What is closer to the family, after all, than the slogan, "From each according to his ability, to each according to his need"? The feminist need only add "or her" twice, and the focus on daily activities inserts women into even conventional Marxist analysis:

> If, to paraphrase Marx, we follow the worker home from the factory, we can once again perceive a change in the _dramatis personae_. He who before followed behind as the worker, timid and holding back, with nothing to expect but a hiding, now strides in front while a third person, not specifically present in Marx's account of the transaction between capitalist and worker (both of whom are male) follows timidly behind, carrying groceries, baby, and diapers (Harding and Hintikka 1983: 291).

Marxists, or at least some of them, were looking at the "third person," however grudgingly.

In the context of non-Marxist enquiry, the impact of a focus on women's activities has more drastic implications, though again not adequate as a guide to research. In the conventional assumptions of social science research, women's lives are paradoxically seen, on the one hand, as so trivially varied that no generalizations are appropriate and, on the other hand, as explicable by a simple reference to biology. Women's lives have been seen as fragmented by involvement with the contingent and the immediate, but for reasons that are constant across the lifetimes of individuals and of the species. What feminism then does is to cast doubt on accepted accounts both of the nature of women's activities and of the reasons underlying them. This is most obvious in the studies of the family (Thorne and Yalom 1982) but is now beginning to have some impact on areas such as political behaviour (Flammang 1984). As a result, more researchers now look seriously at the activities of those who had been dismissed because they were believed to exist rather than to create or to reflect. Certainly it was inappropriate that behaviourists should have excluded such activities from their generalizations, as in practice they had. Even the first stages of feminist scholarship therefore transformed the subject matter of research. It continues to have an escalating effect as the cumulation of reports on daily life increases.

At this point the optimist might see a convergence of feminist and nonfeminist perspectives: the conventional researcher has been exposed to an opening up of subject matter, and perhaps the feminist can be persuaded that some version of scientific method is irreplaceable. If a transformation of mainstream scholarship is not imminent, perhaps it is nonetheless irresistible in the longer run.

Responding more pessimistically, the current phase of feminist critiques focuses precisely upon discussions of the likelihood and the desirability of real change, and on the usefulness of feminist acceptance of some version of existing methodologies.

Feminist scholars who turned to women's experience as the basis of knowledge encountered right there a set of new reasons to deter them from any search for truth. They valued the everyday, so long neglected as an academic subject, and they expected to use their research findings as a basis for feminist action--for increasing their own autonomy and the autonomy of women in general. Their imaginative use of the data of daily life uncovered a previously undescribed richness and complexity. If only to counter assumptions about the triviality of domesticity, such data had to be sorted into patterns. This was easy enough; it was not twisting evidence to show that women cope, adapt, resist, influence, respond to widely differing social structures. Women are thus demonstrably rational, even political, and admirable within the restricted sphere that they have historically occupied. But--and here is the rub--in every system with some differentiated structure of authority, women turn out to be relatively disadvantaged. Always, there is some division of labour based on gender, and where there is a difference in autonomy, women have less (Rosaldo 1974; 1980).

Feminist explanations were able to move from the biologistic to the more sophisticated, but they were not able to offer hope for change. For instance, feminist research on violence, grounded in women's actual experience of it as a persistent dimension of everyday life, was certainly less complacent than previous discussions but could not suggest how things might improve. For Susan Brownmiller (1975), the consequence was a theory that based social structure on male capability for rape. Such research could easily produce despair. It implied that the only hope was some violent, unprecedentedly radical, revolutionary transformation. Yet history, especially when enriched by women's experience, seems also to show that the advocacy of violent, drastic change has been a characteristically male mode, that it has not worked well when tried, and that such methods damage women even more than men.

The feminist scholar accordingly might well wish to reject the whole process of observation, generalization, theory, policy, even in the absence of alternatives. Such a scholar could come to suspect that such methods would, even if they did not co-opt one or, at the least, disarm or mislead. "How can we make a rigorous case for social justice when history has been unjust, and our methods of empiricism tie us to past and present history?" asks Thelma McCormack (1981: 5). Her response shows that difficulty of answering the questions she poses. Her first suggestion--to take as a model areas such as peace research, which introduce and control their own normatively designated agendas--is equivalent to the feminist insistence on the primacy of everyday activities. Next, McCormack argues for the acceptance of the causal impact of values as well as behavior, again something already central to feminist research as discussed here. Finally, she opts for future-oriented research because it has produced "consciousness-raising" (1981: 11). Here she discards conventional criteria for the selection of research methods; she can do so safely enough, since futures research, and specifically her preferred technique of simulation, have acquired a degree of scientific legitimacy. This is no help to the feminist researcher who has only McCormack's plausibility to rely on in response to her own uncertainties. Nor have peace research or futures research yet had any significant impact on the everyday world. The message so far has been unencouraging; does she dare to trust any conclusions that may be more heartening? She is on mined ground, and injunctions to look more closely at her own and other women's experience are not adequate guidance.

To this discouragement the intellectual establishment offers its most appealing version of co-option. Women and their scholarly and practical significance are admitted to the Whig progressions of social change. A would-be dispassionate social science, recognizing that it is value- and even bias-laden, aware it is a social system, can see feminism as merely the latest in the expanding, improving definitions of proper subjects and practitioners of scholarship. Emancipation advanced towards the final stage of liberation, both intellectual and practical. Feminist critiques then become the charges voiced by an excluded group--but in a setting where similar claims have, if reluctantly, been responded to before. That is, should we not recognize that women are not the first on whose behalf assertions of universality and abstraction have been challenged, nor the first to react to imposed stereotypes of emotionalism and incompetence? On these grounds, some men are prepared to act as women's champions, calling on a tradition in which non-white, non-Western, impoverished, and otherwise "alien" men have already been assimilated into the process of enquiry as well as its findings (Ruthven 1983). Previous group claims have already eroded the earlier pretensions of undifferentiated universality, both in respect to theory (hence the move to probabilism and contextuality) and in practice (hence the extension of ranges of accepted techniques, starting points, and focuses). How are women different, except as so often, in being the last group to get in line?

This is an argument sympathetic to feminism, if perhaps it is excessively aware of its own graciousness. It has produced a certain amount of good will and even progress. Yet a social feminist would have to respond that women are different in this as in so many other contexts and that the implications of the difference are not trivial.

We may see the failure of the analogy by looking at a simplified version of the nineteenth-century British and American emancipation of black slaves into the ranks of the free citizens and scholars. It is an appropriate if banal example, given the role of abolitionism in providing political training and theoretical analogues for some of the most important of British and American feminists. In these campaigns the common slogan, "Am I not a man and your brother?" was central, and its meaning was crucial. Brotherhood is the assertion of male autonomy. Historically, it has entailed female dependence. The less common slogan, "Am I not a woman and your sister?" meant only that black women were assimilated to the role of white. One of the grievances voiced by white men on behalf of black men is still the prevention of the establishment of the patriarchal family among Afro-Americans. Black nationalists in America assert that their women cannot be feminists, since female strength and independence threaten racial cohesion (Hull, Scott, and Smith 1982; Giddings 1984). Adult males can consider themselves entitled to rule at least over women and as certainly worthy of scholarly activity as well as scholarly attention. Law and even science could become relatively colour-blind when men could identify across the boundary of race.

The male identification once made, citizenship is clearly established in principle, even though practical problems remain in a deeply sexist society. But for women, even the theoretical identification is impossible. Most reductively and inescapably, women are defined in biological terms; as such, they cannot vanish into the mass of men. In any case, men do not wish such assimilation, which could cost each of them control over their own women--and neither do most women, however much they deplore the control. So that the incorporation of minority men into scholarship, as into politics, was a far easier process than the incorporation of women, and one which is not really a valid precedent.

For men, women's claims for equal treatment represent a demand that men relinquish entitlement to define women's status. Inside as well as outside the academy this means, for all men, the loss of a superior claim to knowledge and control. That perceptive observer, William J. Goode, has written of how "boys and grown men have always taken for granted that what they were doing was more important than what the other sex was doing" and he sees men as feeling threatened by "a loss of centrality." It is their "sense of superiority" as "superordinates" that feminism challenges (1982: 140, 145). Feminism, of course, denies that even the most superior of men have authority over women. Given how little influence most humans have in this world, it is not surprising that men should cherish their ascribed advantages over women. Nor is it surprising that women's claims become more irksome when the various castes and classes of males increasingly deny limits related to assigned characteristics.

At the same time, it is obvious that women are to be found, however unevenly distributed, in all categories of age, physical well-being, sexual preference, wealth, religion, even occupation. Everyone, however segregated by choice or obligation, is involved in a relationship with women, if only by filiation. That is, everyone had a mother, and the world as a whole is half female. As a result, the feminist demand for autonomy is fundamental in a way no previous challenge has been. Rejection of male monopoly of knowledge is the most important insubordination of all.

The feminist thus concludes that women's dependence and exclusion are different in kind than any other sort. Not only does it still mean an expectation that women will each be dependent on specific individual men, but it includes a continuing general entitlement of male authority to define and intervene in women's lives. This constitutes a conceptually important difference from the treatment of even the worst-oppressed minority. For instance, even under slavery white ministers were not normally imposed on black churches as male priests and popes are on laywomen and nuns. Even today the conditions of women's education, nutrition, health, child-bearing and child-rearing, sports, religion, government, dress, immortality, and sanity are still defined by groups composed of and dominated by men.

The feminist will also note that sexual asymmetry, which includes women's exclusion from scholarship and from power, is the most ancient as well as the most pervasive of social structures. Present in our mythic heritage, it is a feature of all but legendary regimes and, possibly, a few, relatively small recorded ones. So that if the scholarly establishment's stated willingness to admit women to the expansion of knowledge is welcome, more is needed.

Stephen Jay Gould, a scientist as sympathetic to women as can be imagined, shows both the possibilities and the limitations of the incorporations of women into the "rise of man," in this case scientific man. In a review of Ruth Bleier's Science and Gender (1984) he states succinctly the liberal justification of the equal participation of women in science:

> The reason for opening science to women is not that they will do it differently and better but that good scientists are hard to find and it seems perversely absurd to place social impediments before half the human race when that half could, person for person, do the job as well as the half granted access (1984: 7).

This is an argument compatible with feminism, though falling short of the assumptions of social feminism. However, Gould also cites another argument, which begins to move him onto more debatable ground: "Both the content of [scientific] theories and (in a much deeper way) the very character and methodology of research reflect the strong biases of patriarchy and thereby compromise good science" (1984: 7).

But Gould does not think that the involvement of women in scholarship is likely to affect its methodology: the revisions that Bleier sees as related to female experience "are now making great headway...and men are doing most of the work" (1984: 7). Specifically, he denies the importance of something he calls the "culture of feminism": "We desperately need more women as equal companions in this effort, not because the culture of feminism grants deeper vision but because we need as many good scientists as we can get" (1984: 7).

Gould's position is that, in spite of its defects, science as a social and intellectual system has been able to advance by its own volition. That means, of course, through the actions of its leaders--and women are now allowed to join that liberating group. Patriarchal bias is henceforth to be recognized as a scientific flaw. But Gould will not admit that women's experience, which in practice affects science only through women, may have nonrandom characteristics that may push both methodology and theory in specific directions related to that experience. Nor does he admit that women may be uniquely placed to dispute judgments made by men.

For "science" we may read "scholarship" or at the very least "social science." Gould doubts the impact of something he labels "feminist ways of thinking." By this he means, not feminist, but female in the sense used by social feminists. Paternally he tells women scientists: "We [sic] must dismantle our adversary's false tools, not use them to tell more congenial (but equally speculative) stories" (1984: 7). Women's viewpoint is thus reduced to yet another partial perspective, even if, somewhat illogically, one that makes them natural supporters of the "methodological revisions" already undertaken by men. The gap is bridged by Gould's own definition of "good science." His perspective, unusually humanistic for a scientist, is in fact sympathetic to just those shifts of theory and methodology that can be derived from female specificity. But he retains the authority of the male practitioner, and his general argument could be used in defense of a more conventional version of "good science," against the preferences of the feminist scientists and of Gould himself.

A feminist approach to social science therefore has to move beyond incorporation into the process of enquiry as it has developed under the patriarchy. Women's autonomy as individual researchers certainly increases as their opportunities for scholarship expand. But their autonomy even as scholars is limited unless there is some way to change the overall environment, of thought as well as of institutions, that leaves male-defined limits on women. Some possibility of transformation must exist, and there must be some way of deriving it from the areas of life (and thought) that are not simply extrapolations of the existing systems of male domination.

This line of argument suggests that a feminist perspective on social science has to be a social-feminist focus on what differentiates women's experience and values from men's. The guidance it gives for scholarship is to look for and at these differences, as a basis of organizing principles for research. Other scholars, it is assumed, will continue to study those areas in which men and women are alike. It is hoped that these studies will proceed with greater rigour and realism than they have in the past, with an awareness of the androcentric nature of most of what has been and is represented as generalizable. As many feminist critics have now pointed out, studies of shared aspects of life should, even by the existing canons of scholarship, recognize the many areas in which male and female experience are similar. But the deliberately feminist researcher will feel that her distinctive contribution to knowledge is most likely to result from defining and examining those areas in which women's lives and values differ from men's. Through the understanding of these areas, she can make the largest possible contribution to the social project of feminism: a transformed society influenced by women's experience, values, and definitions.

The content and locus of women's specificities are not easy to articulate. In addition, the identification of an intellectual style or approach with a particular sex is as risky as any other dimension of the differentiation insisted on by social feminists. Nevertheless, we may risk a metaphor. The notion of a feminist approach to social science can be modelled by an extended contrast between the (female) kitchen and the (male) study. The contrast is specific: it is not just the hurly-burly of daily life that is set against the life of the mind, but the ideal of the old-fashioned kitchen where women, with children underfoot, attend to cooking, clothing, feeding, and cleaning. The life of the mind, in turn, is envisaged as the quiet, isolated room inhabited by the solitary scholar who is undisturbed by the rest of the world, and, at the extreme, indifferent to his own hunger or fatigue. Even when he does not rely on someone else, usually female, to provide for his bodily needs, he is without responsibility for those needs in others, deliberately detached from the variable and contingent routines of normal daily life. He personifies at the same time the noble goals of exactness and objectivity, and their extension into sterility and irrelevance. If his work necessarily starts and is carried on in some particular real place, it aims at going (again metaphorically) as far as possible away from it. In contrast, in the work world of women the subjective dominates, and knowledge is immediate, limited, and above all, specific.

It is less than obvious that an understanding of society is more easily generated in the isolation of the study than in the dense social interaction of the kitchen. What is lacking in the kitchen, of course, is legitimacy and certain resources necessary for the pursuit and communication of knowledge. That is, women lack privacy, self-confidence, and independence, both intellectual and economic; this is the message of Virginia Woolf's <u>A Room of One's Own</u> (1928). More recent feminists now argue for the values of both private and shared workspace. The private "room"--_her_ study?--would be indispensable for completion of enterprises generated in and enriched by the life of the kitchen. In _Silences_ (1965), Tillie Olsen explicitly extends Virginia Woolf's theme to point out the value of the activities that have prevented women from being heard.

This is what a feminist perspective on the social sciences is about. The kitchen is where "all the ladders start."

Endnotes

1. W.B. Yeats, "The Circus Animals' Desertion."

2. "Feminism" is a contested and often a pejorative term. As an ideology, it seems to mean a belief in the distinctive situation and experience of women, combined with a refusal to allow women to be judged inferior or lacking in comparison with men and male standards. In respect to public policy, feminism demands as a minimum that women not be disadvantaged in contrast to men. Feminist organizations can be defined in terms of activity intended to produce an increase in women's autonomy (Gordon 1976; Berg 1978). I am using "autonomy" here as suggested by Evelyn Fox Keller: "the psychological sense of being able to act under one's own volition instead of under external control." She adds the important corollary that "this does not mean, or even suggest, that one's actions are not influenced by others, or that one has no need of others" (Keller 1985: 97).

3. Particularly in relation to suffragism, historians now generally distinguish between "social" or "maternal" feminists and "political" or "equal rights" feminists. I am suggesting use of the distinction as a more general classification of feminist theories. What is usually called "liberal," "Marxist," "socialist," or "anarchist" feminism is then interpreted as an equity-feminist version of liberal, socialist, Marxist, or anarchist theory. All attempt to fit women into the assumptions of a preexisting system. The so-called "radical" feminism, in contrast, I see as a descendant and variant of social feminism in its insistence upon the priority of gender relations and women's self-definition. For social feminism see Lemons 1975; for the more modern versions see Michel 1979.

References

Berg, B.
    1978   The Remembered Gate: Origins of American Feminism. New York: Oxford University.

Bourque, S., and Grossholtz, J.
    1974   Politics as Unnatural Practice: Political Science Looks at Female Participation. Politics and Society 4: 225-66.

Brownmiller, S.
    1975   Against Our Wills: Men, Women, and Rape. New York: Simon and Schuster.

Diamond, I., and Hartstock, N.
    1981   Beyond Interests in Politica: A Comment on Virginia Sapiro's "When Are Interests Interesting? The Problem of Political Representation of Women." American Political Science Review 75: 717-21.

Flammang, J.
    1984   Political Women: Current Roles in State and Local Government. Santa Barbara, CA: Sage.

Fox, B. (ed.)
    1980   Hidden in the Household: Women's Domestic Labour under Capitalism. Toronto: Women's Press.

Freeman, J.
    1975   The Politics of Women's Liberation: A Case-Study of an Emerging Social Movement and Its Relation to the Policy Process. New York: David McKay.

Gardiner, J.K.
    1983   Power, Desire, and Difference: Comment on Essays in Signs Special Issue on Feminist Theory. Signs 8: 733-36.

Giddings, P.
    1984   When and Where I Enter: The Impact of Black Women on Race and Sex in America. New York: William Morrow.

Goode, W.J.
    1982   Why Men Resist. Pp. 131-50 in Rethinking the Family: Some Feminist Questions, ed. B. Thorne and M. Yalom. New York: Longman.

Goot, M., and Reid, E.
    1975   Women and Voting Studies: Mindless Matrons or Sexist Scientism? Beverly Hills, CA: Sage.

Gordon, L.
    1976   Women's Body, Women's Rights: Birth Control in America. New York: Grossman.

Gould, S.J.
    1984   Review of R. Bleier, Science and Gender: A Critique of Biology and Its Theories on Women. New York Times Book Review Aug. 12: 7.

Harding S., and Hintikka, M. (eds.)
    1983   Discovering Reality: Feminist Perspectives on Epistemology, Metaphysics, Methodology, and Philosophy of Science. London: D. Reidel.

Hartsock, N.
    1979   Feminist Theory and the Development of Revolutionary Strategy. Pp. 56-77 in Capitalist Patriarchy and the Case for Socialist Feminism, ed. Z. Eisenstein. New York: Monthly Review Press.

Heilbrun, C.
    1973   Toward a Recognition of Androgyny. New York: Alfred A. Knopf.

    1979   Reinventing Womenhood. New York: Norton.

Hull, G.T.; Scott, P.B.; and Smith, B. (eds.)
    1982   All the Women Are White, All the Blacks Are Men, But Some of Us Are Brave. Old Westbury, NY: The Feminist Press.

Kauffmann-McCall, D.
    1983   Politics of Difference: The Women's Movement in France from May, 1968 to Mitterand. Signs 9: 282-93.

Keller, E.F.
    1985   Reflections on Gender and Science. New Haven, CN: Yale University.

Lemons, J.S.
    1975   The Woman Citizen: Social Feminism in the 1920s. Champaign-Urbana, IL: University of Illinois.

MacKinnon, C.
    1983   Feminism, Marxism, Method, and the State: Towards Feminist Jurisprudence. Signs 8: 635-58.

McCormack, T.
    1981   Good Theory or Just Theory? Toward a Feminist Philosophy of Social Science. Pp. 1-33 in Another Voice: Feminist Perspectives on Social Life and Social Science, ed. M. Millman and R.M. Kanter. New York: Doubleday/Anchor.

Michel, A.
    1979   Le feminisme. Paris: Presses Universitaires de France.

Olsen, T.
    1965   Silences. New York: Delacorte/Seymour Lawrence.

Rapp, R.
    1982   Family and Class in Contemporary America: Notes Toward an Understanding of Ideology. Pp. 168-87 in Rethinking

the Family: Some Feminist Questions, ed. B. Thorne and M. Yalom. New York: Longman.

Rosaldo, M.B.
    1974   Women, Culture, and Society. Pp. 17-42 in Women, Culture, and Society, ed. M.B. Rosaldo and L. Lamphere. Berkeley, CA: University of California.

    1980   The Use and Abuse of Anthropology: Reflections on Feminism and Cross-Cultural Understanding. Signs 5: 389-417.

Rowbotham, S.
    1977   Hidden from History: 300 Years of Women's Oppression and the Flight Against It. London: Pluto.

Rupp, L.J.
    1981   Imagine My Surprise: Women's Relationships in Historical Perspective. Frontiers 5: 61-70.

Ruthven, K.K.
    1983   Male Critics and Feminist Criticism. Essays in Criticism 33: 263-72.

Sapiro, V.
    1979   Women's Studies and Political Conflict. Pp. 353-65 in The Prism of Sex: Essays in the Sociology of Knowledge, ed. J. Sherman and E.T. Beck. Ann Arbor, MI: University of Michigan.

    1981   Research Frontier Essay: When Are Interests Interesting? The Problem of Political Representation of Women. American Political Science Review 75: 701-16.

Sauter-Bailliet, T.
    1981   The Feminist Movement in France. Women's Studies International Forum 4: 409-20.

Scales, A.C.
    1980   Towards a Feminist Jurisprudence. Indiana Law Journal 56: 375-444.

Sherman, J., and Beck, E.T. (eds.)
    1979   The Prism of Sex: Essays in the Sociology of Knowledge. Ann Arbor, MI: University of Michigan.

Smith, D.
    1979   Toward a Sociology of Women. Pp. 135-87 in The Prism of Sex Essays in the Sociology of Knowledge, ed. J. Sherman and E.T. Beck. Ann Arbor, MI: University of Michigan.

Spender, D. (ed.)
    1981   Men's Studies Modified: The Impact of Feminism on the Academic Disciplines. London: Pergamon.

Thorne, B., and Yalom, M. (eds.)
    1982   Rethinking the Family: Some Feminist Questions. New York: Longman.

Woolf, V.
    1928   A Room of One's Own.   London: Hogarth.

SUBJECT INDEX

Achievement, psychology of, 26-28
Art value, 107-109

Bias: definition, 148; gender bias: definition, xiii, 2, 28, 48, 134, 168
Biological arguments, xiv-xv, 25, 30, 45, 51, 72-73, 123, 131, 134, 179-80

Careers and family lives, 119-20, 140, 183-84
Classroom socialization, 65-74, 78, 109-110, 111-12, 118, 120-21
Contextualization: interrelatedness, connectedness, xx, 7, 53-54, 85, 119-21, 148, 153, 155, 161, 174
Co-option, 11-12, 88, 178-79

Dichotomization of epistemologies, xviii, 123, 134, 153
Domestic, private realm, xvii, 4, 7, 47, 70-72, 103, 107, 110, 122-23, 125, 173, 175, 184, 186
Dualities, 3-4, 45-46, 53, 73, 118-19, 122-26, 150, 158-59

Epistemological empiricism, 81-82, 153
Epistemological revolution, xiii, 149-50, 153-63

Felt experience, xvii, 151, 157-58
Female difference, xiv, xvi, xviii, xix, 110, 119, 122, 171, 172
Femininity, xvi, 6, 26-27, 45-46, 49-50, 59, 70, 72-73, 77-80, 102, 118-19, 123
Feminism: anglophone, 145, 171; categories: 185 n. 3; definition, 119, 167, 185 n. 2; equity, 169, 172, 175; French, 53-54, 171-72; social, 169-72, 175, 179, 181-83
Feminism and existentialism, 160; and historical philosophy, 150-52; and humanism, xix-xx, 50, 66-69, 160, 163; and liberalism, 75-81; and marxism, 174-76; and new sociology of education, 67-68, 82-83; and post-structuralism, 48, 53; and the scientific method,

14, 29-30, 133-43, 170, 176, 181-82; and sociology of knowledge, 2, 6-7, 10-11

Future expectations, 13-15, 34-38, 54, 86-88, 171, 182

Gatekeepers, 6, 9, 11, 22, 97, 107
Gender: definition, xiv, 123; as a continuum, 124, 148, 153, 183-84

Hermeneutics: definition, xvii
Heroines, heroism, 49
Human nature, xiv-xv, 103, 150, 153
Humanism, xix-xx, 50, 67-68, 73, 75-76, 160, 163

Ideologies, xvi-xvii, 14, 46-48, 54, 60-70, 72-73, 89 n. 3, 119, 134-36, 169
Insubordination, xvi, 180
Interpretation, xvii-xviii, 5, 8, 30, 35-36, 45, 48, 51, 55, 82, 84, 101, 103, 105-106, 109, 111, 132

Language and art, 101, 105-106; and education, 67; and literature, 47-53; and philosophy, 151; and values, 171
Laws of nature, 135
Literary canon: redefinition, 48; genres, xix, 45, 47, 50, 52

Male and female rats in science, 132-33
Malestream/mainstream research, 3, 5-6, 10-14, 16, 28-31, 45-47, 51, 54-55 n. 6, 66, 74-75, 100ff., 171
Masterpieces, 47, 101, 104
Men as subjects, 28-29, 65-66, 74, 101, 104; as researchers, xvi, 5, 65, 147, 153, 172, 180
Methodologies, xiii-xx, 10-11, 27, 34-38, 45, 51-54, 64, 66, 73-74, 77, 83-86, 88, 122, 147, 149, 168-73, 177-78, 180-82
"Modernist law," 102, 105
Molecular biology: central dogma, 131
Morality, 28-29

Objectivity in scholarship, xv, xvii, xix, 2, 27, 47-48, 84-85, 93, 106, 132-36, 149, 157, 168-69, 173-74, 183
Omission of women, xv, 2-4, 26, 31, 45-48, 64-65, 74-75, 83, 109, 117-18, 133, 168, 180

Subject Index

Passion in research, xiii, 148, 152
Patriarchy, 19, 48, 50, 52-53, 60, 63, 87, 93, 179, 181-82, 187
Percentage of women trained in sciences, 136-37
Political, xiii, xvii, 3, 21-22, 55-56, 61, 67-68, 70, 75-76, 83, 90, 92, 95, 101, 103, 106-7, 120, 122, 124-26, 133, 136, 168-70, 177
Power, xvii-xviii, 5, 7, 9-13, 15, 23, 26, 32, 53, 62, 73, 82, 117, 119-23, 125, 160, 171, 173-74, 177, 181
Primatology: effects of women researchers, 142
Privatization of women, 12, 50, 70-72, 122-23
Psychotherapy, 26, 29, 33
Reduction of gender bias, xvi, xx, 31-38, 111-12, 118, 126, 159
Research funding in science, 131
Ruling ideas, xvi, xix, 5, 7-9, 47-48, 67

Self-definition, self-reflection, 29, 125, 154, 157, 167
Sex: definition, xiv
Sexism, 1-4, 6, 18, 20, 22, 34-36, 45-46, 54, 69, 80, 91-93, 96, 117, 168-69
Socialization, xiv-xvi, xviii, 6, 16, 30, 43, 57, 67, 77-82, 98, 138-43, 158
Stereotyping, xiv, 25-27, 33, 41, 49, 51, 71, 79, 93, 96, 138
Subjective knowing, xvii-xviii, 106, 149

Unity of perspectives, xviii, 153, 159, 163, 183-84

Visual literacy, 99, 100; metaphor, 100

Women: as subjects, xvi, 2-3, 9-10, 34-38, 69, 85, 180, 183; as researchers, xiii, xvi, 10-11, 34-38, 69, 84-86, 132, 147, 153, 181-82; graduate students, 34, 137; postdoctoral fellows, 137; faculty, 101, 117, 137-38

NAME INDEX

Abel, Elizabeth, 51-52
Abu-Laban, Sharon, 4
Acker, Joan, 2, 65
Agustini, Delmira, 52
Andersen, Margaret, 16
Anderson, Nels, 3
Anyon, Jean, 83
Appiganesi, Lisa, 51
Apple, Michael, 67-68, 82
Ardener, Edwin, 8
Armour, Margaret-Ann, 139
Armstrong, Hugh, 7
Armstrong, Pat, 7
Arnot, Madeleine, 64-65, 68, 75-76, 81-83
Astin, H.S., 27, 65
Austen, Jane, 46, 48, 52
Ayim, Maryann, 66

Bakhtin, M.M., 52
Balakian, Anna, 56
Baltscheffsky, Margareta, 132-33, 137
Bardwick, Judith M. 26, 79
Bart, Pauline B., 4
Bayer, A.E., 65
Beauvoir, Simon de, 49
Beck, Evelyn T., 9, 170
Belsey, Catherine, 56-57
Bem, Sandra M., 27
Bennett, B., 105
Bennett, Jonathan, 156
Benston, Margaret, 83
Berg, B., 185
Berger, J., 105
Berger, Peter L., 2, 6, 8, 11, 14

Bergsson, Henri, 149
Bernard, Jessie, 1, 4-10, 16, 127
Bernstein, Basil, 67-68, 82-83
Berton, Pierre, 117
Bingen, Hildegard von, 162, 164
Black, Naomi, 119, 124
Blackstone, T., 68, 78
Bleier, Ruth, 87, 133-134, 141-142, 144, 181
Blishen, Bernard R., 3
Bloch, L., 103
Bonheur, Rosa, 107
Bourdieu, P., 67-68, 82
Bourque, Susan, 168, 170
Bowles, S., 81-82
Boxer, M., 64, 87
Bradley, Francis Herbert, 149, 163
Bridenthal, Renate, 123
Brodribb, Somer, 66
Brontë, Charlotte, 46
Brontë, Emily, 50
Broverman, D.M., 27
Broverman, I.K., 27
Browning, Elizabeth Barrett, 55
Brownmiller, Susan, 4, 177
Bunch, Charlotte, 66, 89
Burke, Carolyn, 55
Burnett, D., 108

Canaday, J., 103
Carlson, Rae, 4
Carrigan, Tim, 16
Carroll, Bernice, 123
Carroll, William K., 3
Cassatt, 103
Chadwick, W., 103
Chafe, William, 122
Chetwynd, J., 79
Chodorow, Nancy, 4, 122
Cixous, Hélène, 55
Clark, Shirley Merritt, 6

Name Index

Clarkson, F.E., 27
Clarricoates, K., 64, 66, 68, 76
Coleman, James S., 76
Colette [Sidonie Gabrielle], 46
Collins, G., 110
Collins, H.M., 13
Comte, Auguste, 81
Connell, Bob, 16
Conway, Anne, 162
Coquillant, Michelle, 49
Cornillon, Susan Koppelman, 45, 49, 51, 56
Coser, Lewis A., 6-7
Cott, Nancy, 85, 122
Courtivron, Isabelle de, 53
Crane, Diana, 6
Crean, 109
Cruz, Juana Inès de la, 48, 55-56
Culler, Jonathan, 54, 57

Daly, Mary, 83
Daniels, Arlene K., 2
Daniels, Pamela, 120
David, M., 65
Davies, Margaret Llewellyn, 127
Davis, Natalie Zemon, 120
Deaux, K., 30
Decore, Anne-Marie, 138
Deem, Rosemary, 65-66, 76
Degas, 103
Degler, Carl, 122
DeJean, Joan, 56
Derrida, Jacques, 57
Descartes, René, 50, 149
Dewey, John, 75
Diamond, Irene, 170
Di Blasio, M.K., 99-100
Dickens, Charles, 133
Diller, A., 66, 89
Dobash, R. Emerson, 4
Dobash, Russell, 4

Donovan, Josephine, 46, 48, 55, 57
Douglas, J., 82
Du Bois, B., 74-75, 85
Durham, Carolyn A., 47, 50
Durkheim, Emile, 81

Ehrenreich, Barbara, 8
Eichler, Margrit, xiii, 10, 12, 14, 16, 28, 65, 153
Eliot, George, 50
Eliot, T.S., 157, 161
Ellmann, Mary, 45, 56
Engels, Friedrich, 7
English, Diedre, 8
Epstein, Cynthia F., 2, 4, 9
Erikson, Erik H., 29, 67, 77
Evans, Mary Ann, 50

Faderman, Lillian, 127
Federbush, M., 78
Fee, E., 71
Feldman, E., 107, 110
Fenemma, E., 80
Ferguson, Janet, 66
Festinger, Leon, 13
Fetterley, Judith, 57
Finn, Geraldine, 83, 89
Fischer, Linda, 138
Flammang, J., 176
Fortin, Nina E., 8
Fox, B., 175
France, Marie de, 48
Frankenthaler, Helen, 102
Frazier, N., 65, 80
Freeman, Jo, 168
Freud, Sigmund, 29, 31, 77, 120
Friedenberg, Edgar, 66-68
Friesen, Gerald, 117
Frieze, Irene H., 25, 28, 35

Name Index

Gablick, S., 102, 106-107
Gagnon, Madaleine, 55
Galway, Kathleen, 6
Gardiner, Judith Kegan, 171
Garcia, Irma, 53
Gaskell, Jane, 65, 68, 76
Giddings, Paula, 123, 179
Gilbert, Sandra M., 52, 55
Gillett, Margaret, 71
Gilligan, Carol, 17, 28-29, 73, 80, 84, 86-87, 122
Gintis, H., 81-82
Giroux, Henri, 67-68, 82
Goode, William J., 180
Goodman, M., 37
Goosen, E.C., 102
Goot, Murray, 170
Gordon, Linda, 120, 185
Gordon, M., 71
Gornick, Vivian, 141
Gould, Meredith, 5, 14
Gould, Stephen Jay, 133, 181-182
Govier, K., 101, 107
Grady, K.E., 34
Grant, B.A., 34
Grant, Linda, 2-3, 5, 12, 17
Greenberg, C., 102
Greenfield-Sanders, T., 109
Greenglass, E., 27
Greer, G., 107
Griffin, Susan, 87
Grossholtz, Jean, 168, 170
Gubar, Susan, 52, 55

Hacker, Helen M., 16
Hall, C.P., 105
Halsey, A., 76, 81, 82
Hammersley, M., 82
Harding, Jan, 139
Harding, Sandra, 150, 153, 170, 176
Harnett, C., 79

Hartsock, N., 170, 175
Head, Tina, 117
Hébert, Anne, 52
Hegel, G.W.F., 50, 148-149, 159, 163
Heidegger, Martin, 148-149, 161, 163-164
Heilbrun, Carolyn, 172-173
Henshel, Anne-Marie, 16
Herrmann, Claudine, 56
Herzog, A., 3
Hickerson, Nathaniel, 67
Hintikka, Merrill B., 170, 176
Hitchman, Gladys S., 16
Hobbs, Jack A., 101, 106
Hochschild, Arlie R., 4
Holt, John, 66-67
Horner, Matina S., 26, 79
Houston, S., 65-66, 72, 89
Howe, Florence, 63, 75
Hubbards, R., 87
Hughes, Patricia, 74
Hull, G.T., 179
Hume, David, 149
Husserl, E., 149, 156, 163

Illich, Ivan, 66-67

Jagger, Alison, 75
James, Henry, 118-119, 122-123
James, William, 155
Janeway, Elizabeth, 65
Janson, H.W., 101, 104
Jean, Paula J., 13
Jefferson, Ann, 57
Jehlen, Myra, 49
Jelinek, Estelle C., 47, 55
Johnson, P., 25, 28, 35

Kahlo, Frida, 103
Kahn, Arnold S., 13
Kalin, R., 34

Name Index

Kant, Immanuel, 148-151, 154-157, 160, 163
Kanter, Rosabeth M., 1, 16
Kaplan, A.G., 29
Kaplan, Cora, 51, 56
Karabel, J., 76, 81-82
Kauffmann-McCall, D., 172
Kealey, Linda, 71
Keller, Evelyn Fox, 133-135, 185
Kelly, Jan, 122
Keohane, N., 75
Kierkegaard, S., 163
Kimball, Meredith, 25, 30, 35-38, 138
Koeske, Randi, 35
Kohlberg, Lawrence, 28, 73, 77
Kolodny, Annette, 45, 57
Komarovsky, Mirra, 16
Kristeva, Julia, 57
Kuhn, Thomas S., 84, 133

Labé, Louise, 52
Lafayette, Madame de (Pioche de la Vergne, Marie-Madaleine), 46
Laidlaw, T., 66, 68
Lamphere, Louise, 127
Lanser, Susan S., 9
Lapointe, Jean, xiii, 14, 28, 153
Lasch, Christopher, 122
Lasnier, Rina, 52
Laurin-Frenette, Nicole, 70
Lawrence, D.H., 49
Leclerc, Annie, 55
Lee, John, 16
Leibniz, Gottfried Wilhelm, 148
Lemons, J.S., 185
Lerner, Gerda, 123
Lewis, Jane, 123
Light, B., 71
Lindenberger, Herbert, 57
Lipking, Lawrence, 49, 53, 55
Lippard, L.R., 99, 106
Little, Judith, 56

Lofland, Lyn H., 3, 8
Lopata, Helena Z., 4
Lott, B., 30
Luckmann, Thomas 2, 8, 14
Luxton, Meg, 4

Maccoby, E., 78-79
MacDonald, M., 66, 68, 76, 82
McClelland, D.C., 27-28
McCormack, Thelma, 169, 178
McHugh, Maureen, 30, 35
Mackie, Marlene, 10, 14-16
MacKinnon, Catharine, 87, 170-71
McRoberts, Hugh A., 3
Malmo, Cheryl, 65, 84, 86
Marks, Elaine, 53, 56
Martin, Claire, 50
Marx, Karl, 7, 174-75
Mason, Alice Turnbull, 103
Masson, Jeffrey, 31
Matthews, Sarah H., 13
Mednick, Martha T.S., 25, 27, 34
Mednick, S, 79
Michel, A., 185
Mies, M., 74
Miles, Angela, 83, 87
Mill, John Stuart, 75
Miller, Jean Baker, 29
Millett, Kate, 49, 51
Millman, Marcia, 1, 4, 16
Mistral, Gabriela (Godoy Alcayaga, Lucila), 52
Moers, Ellen, 55
Moi, Toril, 46, 53, 56
Mora, Gabriela, 46
Moulton, Janice, 162
Mullins, Nicholas C., 6
Murray, Joan, 107

Name Index

Nagy-Jacklin, C., 78
Newton, Judith, 122
Nietzsche, Fredrich, 150-151, 160, 163

Oakley, Ann, 1-2, 4, 70, 87
O'Brien, Mary, 2, 65-66, 75-76, 81-82, 87
O'Keefe, Georgia, 105
Olsen, Tillie, 184
Owens, C., 104

Parker, R., 99, 102, 108-9
Parlee, M.B., 34
Parsons, J.E., 25, 28, 35
Parsons, Talcott, 81
Passeron, J., 67-68, 82
Paz, Octavio, 56
Peck, Jeffrey M., 55
Perun, P.J., 66
Phillips, J.C., 102
Piaget, Jean, 77, 102
Pierson, R., 65, 70, 84-86
Pisan, Christine de, 55
Plato, xiv, xv, 149
Pleck, Elizabeth, 85, 122
Pollack, S., 66
Pollock, G., 99, 102, 108-9
Pratt, Mary, 105
Prentice, Allison, 65, 70-72, 84-86
Prescott, S., 29-30
Pugh, David, 122
Pyke, Sandra W., 26, 32

Rapp, R., 175
Reid, Elizabeth, 170
Richardson, Laurel W., 4
Riecken, Henry W., 13
Riesman, David, 67-68
Rigolot, François, 52
Rilke, Rainer Maria, 152, 156
Ritzer, George, 3

Rivera, Diego, 103
Rizzo, D., 78
Roberts, H., 86-87
Roberts, J., 65, 84
Robey, David, 53
Robinson, W., 109
Rosaldo, Michele B., 127, 177
Rose, Phyllis, 120, 124-25
Rosenberg, Rosalind, 72
Rosenkrantz, P.S., 27
Rousseau, Jean Jacques, 163
Rowbotham, Sheila, 8-10, 175
Ruble, D.N., 25, 28, 35
Ruddick, Sara, 120
Rupp, L.J., 174
Russ, Joanna, 55
Ruthven, K.K., 179
Ryan, Mary, 122

Sadker, M., 65, 80
Sand, George, 46
Sandell, R., 110
Sapiro, Virginia, 168-70
Sappho, 48
Sarah, E., 80
Sario, T., 78
Sargre, J.P., 163
Sarup, Madan, 81
Sauter-Bailliet, T., 172
Scales, Ann C., 167
Schachter, Stanley, 13
Schopenhauer, Arthur, 163
Schwendinger, Herman, 9
Schwendinger, Julia, 9
Scott, Anne, 122
Scott, Joan, 136
Scott, P.B., 179
Scully, Diana, 4
Sévigné, Madame de (Rabutin-Chantal, Marie de), 50
Shack, Sybil, 66

Name Index

Sherif, C.W., 26, 34
Sherman, Julia A., 26, 78-79, 170
Sherwin, Susan, 148, 164
Showalter, Elaine, 45-46, 49-50, 55
Silberman, Charles, 67
Silverman, Eliane Leslau, 122, 127
Simon, Rita James, 6
Slatkin, W., 103
Smith, B., 179
Smith, Dorothy, E., 2, 5-11, 83-87, 173-75
Spender, Dale, 3-4, 6, 8-9, 14, 48, 56, 63-65, 68-69, 75-76, 83-84, 87, 170
Spinoza, B., 149
Stacey, Judith, 12-13
Stanley, Liz, 7, 73-74, 81, 87
Stark-Adamec, Cannie, 25, 30-32, 35-38, 40
Stein, Gertrude, 55
Stephenson, Marylee, 16
Stimpson, Catharine R., 9
Surrey, Janet L., 29
Sydie, Rosalind, 4

Tancred-Sherrif, Peta, 9, 12-14
Tangri, S., 79
Theodore, Athena, 6
Thibault, Gisele, 66, 68, 87
Thorne, Barrie, 12, 13, 176
Tittle, K.C., 78
Tuchman, Gaye, 4, 8

Unger, R.K., 34

Van Kirk, Sylvia, 117
Vaughter, Reesa M., 5
Vaughter, Rossa H., 27, 65, 80
Vickers, Jill McCalla, 6, 14, 34, 83-84
Vogel, S.R., 27

Walker, B., 81
Walker, L.E., 29, 31

Walker, S., 107
Walkowitz, Judith, 122
Wallston, B., 34
Wand, B., 32-33
Ward, Kathryn B., 2-3, 5, 12, 17
Weissman, H.J., 27
Weisstein, Naomi, 26, 74
Weitzman, L., 78-79
Welty, Eudora, 50-52
Westfall, Stephen, 103
Weyant, R.G., 34
Whitty, G., 67, 82
Wieland, Joyce, 108
Willinsky, John, 67
Willis, Paul, 82
Wine, Jerri, 79, 83-84, 86-87
Wise, Sue, 7, 73-74, 81, 87
Wittgenstein, Ludwig, 149, 163
Wollstonecraft, Mary, 55, 162
Wood, Caroline Sherif, 77-78
Woods, P., 82
Woolf, Virginia, 45, 48, 56, 86, 183-84

Yaeger, Patricia, 51-52, 57
Yalom, M., 176
Yeats, W.B., 167
Young, Michael F.D., 67-68, 82

Zellman, G., 25, 28, 35
Zuckerman, Harriet, 6

Also published by Wilfrid Laurier University Press
for The Calgary Institute for the Humanities

RELIGION AND ETHNICITY
Edited by Harold Coward and Leslie Kawamura

Essays by: Harold Barclay, Harold Coward, Frank Epp, David Goa, Yvonne Yazbeck Haddad, Gordon Hirabayashi, Roger Hutchinson, Leslie Kawamura, Grant Maxwell, Cyril Williams

1978 / pp. x + 181 / ISBN 0-88920-064-5

THE NEW LAND
Studies in a Literary Theme
Edited by Richard Chadbourne and Hallvard Dahlie

Essays by: Richard Chadbourne, Hallvard Dahlie, Naïm Kattan, Roger Motut, Peter Stevens, Ronald Sutherland, Richard Switzer, Clara Thomas, Jack Warwick, Rudy Wiebe

1978 / pp. viii + 160 / ISBN 0-88920-065-3

SCIENCE, PSEUDO-SCIENCE AND SOCIETY
Edited by Marsha P. Hanen, Margaret J. Osler, and Robert G. Weyant

Essays by: Paul Thagard, Adolf Grünbaum, Antony Flew, Robert G. Weyant, Marsha P. Hanen, Richard S. Westfall, Trevor H. Levere, A. B. McKillop, James R. Jacob, Roger Cooter, Margaret J. Osler, Marx W. Wartofsky

1980 / pp. x + 303 / ISBN 0-88920-100-5

CRIME AND CRIMINAL JUSTICE IN EUROPE AND CANADA
Edited by Louis A. Knafla

Essays by: J. H. Baker, Alfred Soman, Douglas Hay, T. C. Curtis and F. M. Hale, J. M. Beattie, Terry Chapman, André Lachance, Simon N. Verdun-Jones, T. Thorner and N. Watson, W. G. Morrow, Herman Diederiks, W. A. Calder, Pieter Spierenburg, Byron Henderson

1985, Revised Edition / pp. xxx + 344 / ISBN 0-88920-181-1

DOCTORS, PATIENTS, AND SOCIETY
Power and Authority in Medical Care
Edited by Martin S. Staum and Donald E. Larsen

Essays by: David J. Roy, John C. Moskop, Ellen Picard, Robert E. Hatfield, Harvey Mitchell, Toby Gelfand, Hazel Weidman, Anthony K. S. Lam, Carol Herbert, Josephine Flaherty, Benjamin Freedman, Lionel E. McLeod, Janice P. Dickin McGinnis, Anne Crichton, Malcolm C. Brown, Thomas McKeown, Cathy Charles

1981 / pp. xiv + 290 / ISBN 0-88920-111-0

IDEOLOGY, PHILOSOPHY AND POLITICS
Edited by Anthony Parel

Essays by: Frederick C. Copleston, Charles Taylor, John Plamenatz, Hugo Meynell, Barry Cooper, Willard A. Mullins, Kai Nielsen, Joseph Owens, Kenneth Minogue, Lynda Lange, Lyman Tower Sargent, Andre Liebich

1983 / pp. x + 246 / ISBN 0-88920-129-3

DRIVING HOME
A Dialogue Between Writers and Readers
Edited by Barbara Belyea and Estelle Dansereau

Essays by: E. D. Blodgett, Christopher Wiseman, D. G. Jones, Myrna Kostash, Richard Giguère, Aritha van Herk, Peter Stevens, Jacques Brault

1984 / pp. xiv + 98 / ISBN 0-88920-148-X

ANCIENT COINS OF THE GRAECO-ROMAN WORLD
The Nickle Numismatic Papers
Edited by Waldemar Heckel and Richard Sullivan

Essays by: C. M. Kraay, M. B. Wallace, Nancy Moore, Stanley M. Burstein, Frank Holt, Otto Mørkholm, Bluma Trell, Richard Sullivan, Duncan Fishwick, B. Levy, Richard Weigel, Frances Van Keuren, P. Visonà, Alexander G. McKay, Robert L. Hohlfelder.

1984 / pp. xii + 310 / ISBN 0-88920-130-7

FRANZ KAFKA (1883-1983)
His Craft and Thought
Edited by Roman Struc and J. C. Yardley

Essays by: Charles Bernheimer, James Rolleston, Patrick O'Neill, Egon Schwarz, Ernst Loeb, Mark Harman, Ruth Gross, W. G. Kudszus.

1986 / pp. viii + 160 / ISBN 0-88920-187-0

GENDER BIAS IN SCHOLARSHIP
The Pervasive Prejudice
Edited by Winnifred Tomm and Gordon Hamilton

Essays by: Marlene Mackie, Carolyn C. Larsen, Estelle Dansereau, Gisele Thibault, Alice Mansell, Eliane Leslau Silverman, Yvonne Lefebvre, Petra von Morstein, Naomi Black

1988 / pp. xx + 206 / ISBN 0-88920-963-4